Radical Media Ethics

Radical Media Ethics

A Global Approach

Stephen J. A. Ward

WILEY Blackwell

This edition first published 2015
© 2015 John Wiley & Sons, Inc.

Registered Office
John Wiley & Sons, Ltd, The Atrium, Southern Gate, Chichester, West Sussex,
PO19 8SQ, UK

Editorial Offices
350 Main Street, Malden, MA 02148-5020, USA
9600 Garsington Road, Oxford, OX4 2DQ, UK
The Atrium, Southern Gate, Chichester, West Sussex, PO19 8SQ, UK

For details of our global editorial offices, for customer services, and for information about how to apply for permission to reuse the copyright material in this book please see our website at www.wiley.com/wiley-blackwell.

The right of Stephen J. A. Ward to be identified as the author of this work has been asserted in accordance with the UK Copyright, Designs and Patents Act 1988.

All rights reserved. No part of this publication may be reproduced, stored in a retrieval system, or transmitted, in any form or by any means, electronic, mechanical, photocopying, recording or otherwise, except as permitted by the UK Copyright, Designs and Patents Act 1988, without the prior permission of the publisher.

Wiley also publishes its books in a variety of electronic formats. Some content that appears in print may not be available in electronic books.

Designations used by companies to distinguish their products are often claimed as trademarks. All brand names and product names used in this book are trade names, service marks, trademarks or registered trademarks of their respective owners. The publisher is not associated with any product or vendor mentioned in this book.

Limit of Liability/Disclaimer of Warranty: While the publisher and author have used their best efforts in preparing this book, they make no representations or warranties with respect to the accuracy or completeness of the contents of this book and specifically disclaim any implied warranties of merchantability or fitness for a particular purpose. It is sold on the understanding that the publisher is not engaged in rendering professional services and neither the publisher nor the author shall be liable for damages arising herefrom. If professional advice or other expert assistance is required, the services of a competent professional should be sought.

Library of Congress Cataloging-in-Publication Data

Ward, Stephen J. A. (Stephen John Anthony), 1951–
   Radical media ethics : a global approach / Stephen J. A. Ward.
      pages cm
   Summary: "Provides guiding principles and values for practising responsible global media ethics" – Provided by publisher.
   Includes bibliographical references and index.
      ISBN 978-1-118-47758-8 (hardback) – ISBN 978-1-118-47759-5 (paper)   1. Journalistic ethics.   2. Mass media–Moral and ethical aspects.   I. Title.
   PN4756.W375 2015
   174'.907–dc23
                                                                      2014048343

A catalogue record for this book is available from the British Library.

Set in 10/13 Palatino by SPi Publisher Services, Pondicherry, India
Printed and bound in Malaysia by Vivar Printing Sdn Bhd

1   2015

*To my friend Lynn Dupuis and my sister Ann Legere
for helping me cross to the brighter side of the road.*

Contents

Acknowledgments ix
Introduction x

Part I Theoretical Foundations — 1

1 Ontology of Ethics — 3
2 Ethics as Normative Interpretation — 33
3 Implications for Radical Ethics — 69

Part II The Shape of a Radical Integrated Ethics — 91

4 Radical Media Ethics — 93
5 Defining Journalism — 119
6 Theory of Meaning for Integrated Ethics — 143

Part III Principles of Global Integrated Ethics — 171

7 Political Values for Integrated Ethics — 173

Contents

8	Aims for Global Integrated Ethics	197
9	Realizing Global Integrated Ethics	215

Appendix: Ward Code for Global Integrated Ethics	223
Index	229

Acknowledgments

The development of my ideas on global media ethics has been stimulated by interaction with an extraordinary group of scholars. Together, we have planted the seed for a movement towards global media ethics in the years to come. We have written books and journals together. We have spoken at conferences. We have organized roundtables around the world and published the results. These discussions and writings have added to the scholarship of, and fledgling literature on, global media ethics. I have benefited greatly from my scholarly association with this august group of media ethics leaders. And, I might add, I have enjoyed the pleasure of their friendship and good company.

They are: Professors Clifford G. Christians of the University of Illinois (Urbana-Champaign), Lee Wilkins of Wayne State University-Detroit, Shakuntala Rao, State University of New York-Plattsburgh, and Herman Wasserman of the University of Cape Town, South Africa.

Introduction

This book responds to the impact of the current communication revolution on media ethics. Media ethics is in turmoil. Nothing less than a radical rethinking of its scope, methods, and principles will do. We need to engage in radical media ethics.

This is a book of ideas, a work in the philosophy of journalism. Why philosophize? As Lyotard said, to ask "Why philosophize?" is to ask a philosophical question. It is the fate of humans to philosophize because of the creatures they are – with consciousness, desire, language and a critical ability to question what *is* and to wonder what might be. Philosophy springs from the loss of childhood naivety followed by our adult experience of life as incomplete, fragmented, and lacking integration. Part of philosophy's philosophical mission is to recall humans back to their inherent capacity and need to philosophize, and to ask questions that "irritate everybody" (Lyotard 2013, 13). Philosophy calls on us to clarify and evaluate those ideas that define our worldview and justify our actions.

In writing this book, I have drawn deeply from philosophical, ethical, political, and communication theories. The book provides my conception of how media ethics should evolve. The conception provides a target at which our invention and construction can aim. I propose a radical media ethics that is global and integrated, applying across media formats and borders.

Transformations

Media technologies have transformed journalism and communication into a global, interactive enterprise practiced by an unusual cast of characters. Every day, networks of professionals, citizens, bloggers, politicians, activists, and others commit a million acts of journalism. Creators, sharers, and consumers of media are part of a global public sphere linked by a web of ever-new communication channels. Online networks offer information, analysis, and advocacy under conditions of social inequality, cultural difference, and imbalance in power. Formidable powers of communication can promote or damage prospects for peace, justice, and the good.

This new media ecology questions traditional ethical principles which were formulated a century ago for non-global newspapers long before the Internet. In question are principles such as objectivity in reporting and the rigorous verification of stories prior to publication or posting. A previous consensus on the principles of media ethics, created by professionals, has collapsed as professional and non-professional journalists, online and offline, quarrel. Media ethics is a fragmented domain where just about any notion, including the very idea of journalism, is debated. Media ethics, once a sleepy domain of mainstream media's codes of ethics, too often presumed to be invariant, is now a dynamic, chaotic space of contested values.

Therefore, the central question is: What are the aims and principles for responsible media practice and public communication in an era of global, digital media? The question is as crucial as it is difficult. Many journalists, editors, news outlets, media ethicists, and citizens are no longer sure what the answer might be. Or, they disagree on the answers. Some wonder whether there *are* answers.

We arrive at a crossroad. We have three options. First, we can be skeptics about media ethics. That is, we regard the idea of media ethics – commonly agreed upon norms for responsible practice – as an

Introduction

impossible goal for today's media world. Ethics, we may say, is irrelevant for a global, digital world. Or, second, we can be conservatives. That is, we call for a return to traditional media ethics and engage in a cautious reform of existing principles. Or, third, we can be radical. That is, we reconstruct the basic ideas of media ethics.

This book chooses the third option. Why? Because the other two options are unattractive.

Why Worry?

The first option is not acceptable, ethically. To reject media ethics holus bolus is irresponsible, given the impact of media as a practice and social institution. It is one thing to be skeptical about the relevance of traditional approaches or specific principles. It is quite another to think that a concern for ethics is not worth the bother.

Media ethics in any era is the responsible use of the freedom to publish, no matter who creates the content or who owns the means of publication. Journalism and all forms of public communication can do great good or great harm. Journalists can inform citizens or mislead them; they can investigate government wrong-doing or they can chase after celebrities; they can rigorously verify their stories or they can ruin reputations by trading in reckless rumors. Journalists can promote understanding among ethnic and racial groups, or they can spark tensions.

To reject ethics is to ignore a crucial link between media ethics and democracy. The health of our democratic public sphere depends, in large part, on a robust but responsible media system that encourages rational and informed analysis of crucial issues. Informed public discourse requires responsible media practitioners.

Citizens have an interest in the reliability, diversity, and ethical character of their media system in general. The ethics of media should be debated regularly by societies. A concern for media ethics does not belong to the owners of the press, to media associations, or to media professionals. It belongs, first and foremost, to citizens. In this debate, professional journalists will play an important part. Nevertheless, the primary question of media ethics is not: What are the rights and needs

Introduction

of journalists, or advertisers, or media owners? The primary question is: What sort of media system does our society (and world) need? What are the "media needs" of the public? Given these needs, we can define the duties and freedoms of news media.

The second option, of conservative resistance to major reform, is inadequate when we consider today's seismic shift in the nature of media and its relationship with the public. To call for a return to basics is a misleading nostalgia for a golden past that never existed. In Chapter 4, I will make a detailed case against conservatism in media ethics. For now, I simply state my view that reform must be radical in times of revolution. We *need* to engage in radical ethics if media ethics – clinging to traditional ideas – is not to sink into oblivion. The discipline of media ethics is ready for bold steps. It should show how the contradictions and tensions in journalism can be addressed by new concepts and approaches. To reject media ethics, or to fail to update its concepts, is to fail to rise to the challenges of a new era. Our media ethics must evolve with, and track, changes in the media system and in society. Also, to reject media ethics is to create an opening for irresponsible communication or erroneous editorial policies. If anything goes in journalism, than ethics can have little purchase on our conduct.

Integrated and Global

Articulating an integrated, global media ethics is a goal of this book.

By "integrated" I mean a coming together or agreement at the level of principle and aim which unifies media ethics as a whole. An integrated ethics must show how the many new forms of journalism today can find common ground in what I call ecumenical principles. These principles and aims provide a "unity in difference" – different practices sharing common values. These principles and aims, if endorsed by sufficient numbers of media practitioners, would constitute an integrated ethics, thereby reducing the fragmentation of media ethics today.

In media ethics, acknowledging a unity in difference among values and practices is not the same as acknowledging an irresolvable fragmentation among values and practices. The former recognizes local

xiii

Introduction

differences as an important source of values in media work. Yet the unity in difference approach also attempts to show how differing media values and practices can (and should) recognize common principles and overlapping aims.

Some believe media ethics is necessarily a fragmented domain and they are skeptical of the idea that there are commonalities across differences. They see the project of constructing unifying frameworks as based on a futile and unrealistic hope for commonality in a world of irresolvable difference. They believe that the ethical and value differences among individual practitioners, groups of practitioners, and cultures of media are so pronounced that unity in difference is impossible. There are only fragmented, conflicting, islands of values.

To the contrary, I will argue that there are conceptions of unity in difference that are not based on unrealistic expectations. Further, some form of unity in difference is crucial to the very idea of a media ethics. In what follows, I attempt to show how unity and difference can coexist as macro trends in today's global media. I oppose fragmentation in practice and in idea.

The book also provides a global foundation for this integrated media ethics. It proposes a number of global aims for journalism based on humanitarian values, human rights, and human flourishing. Once we adopt this global foundation, other parts of media ethics, such as the notion of who journalists serve, also receive a global reinterpretation.

Acts of Journalism

In this book, I will be concerned primarily with developing a new framework for thinking about ethical issues in journalism and news media. The reader may assume, incorrectly, that this means I can provide a clear, rigid, and unequivocal definition of "journalism" and "journalist." I cannot provide such rigorous definitions, especially in a time of rapid change. However, I do not regard this difficulty to be an insurmountable obstacle to ethical analysis. As I explain in Chapter 4, I do not believe such "rigorous" definitions in journalism and related social practices are possible or necessary. In fact, strict definitions cannot be given for many practices, yet those practices carry on, none

Introduction

the worse. However, in Chapter 4, I do provide a schema that amounts to a flexible definition of journalism. It begins with defining acts (and works) of journalism as an activity that, from the 17th to the 21st century, grew from an idiosyncratic concern of individual editors into a distinct social practice and institution. Public recognition of journalism as an institutional practice grounds journalism ethics since this recognition comes with public expectations that journalists fulfill certain roles and honor certain values. To anticipate, I define journalism as the timely and regular production of news and commentary for a public on publicly significant events and issues, the performance of which fulfills crucial institutional functions for democracy, such as informing a self-governing public.

For stylistic variation, I use the two pairs of terms, "media ethics" and "journalism ethics," and "media" and "journalism," interchangeably in the text. Media ethics is often used to refer to a wider group of media practitioners than what we find in newsrooms. It includes the ethics of media advertising, public relations, marketing, and so on. These are important topics but this book will not address them directly. For this book, media ethics is the ethics of news media, and the journalism of news media.

Nomenclature

Throughout this book I refer to the principles, norms, standards, maxims, and protocols of ethical systems and of media ethics.[1]

The term "principle" has a long history going back to ancient Greece, where it meant the origin, source, or fundamental cause of something, such as a primary element of nature. In physics, a principle, such as the principle of gravity, is a general law that explains the behavior of many things. In logic and mathematics, a principle is a premise of an argument or proof.

My meaning of principle is epistemic and is defined with ethics in mind. The term is defined in terms of its function in our ethical belief systems. A principle is a general and fundamental belief which helps to justify other less general beliefs and which applies, as a guide for conduct, to a range of specific practices and situations. The power of

Introduction

principles comes from their general nature – the fact that they apply to a large range of cases. For example, in journalism, the principle of avoiding (or minimizing) harm to others condemns the circulating of a salacious rumor while approving the practice of not identifying the victims of sexual assault. Psychologically, logically, and epistemically, principles are identifiable as "basic" beliefs, a term I will explain in Chapter 4. Psychologically, principles are basic because we regard them as the fundamental values of our ethical viewpoint, and so we tend to hold them with greater strength. For instance, I may admit that I was wrong to place a certain item on the list of human rights, e.g. the right to work, but I may still maintain, strongly, my belief in the principle of human rights.

Logically and epistemically, we use principles to judge the ethically right thing to do and to judge the value of norms and standards. Some principles, such as "maximize the happiness of the greatest number of people," are so general as to be considered a criterion of what is ethically good or right. What is good or right is whatever maximizes utility. General principles are not just formal or methodological, such as "any action that is not wrong is permissible" or "to test a rule ethically, universalize it to all people." Principles can also be substantive. They can promote actual goods, such as the ideal of human flourishing, to be explored in Chapter 8.

Norms have the same normative character as principles but they are of a less general nature. Their range of application is smaller and their justification depends on our accepting more general principles.[2] By norm, I do not mean what usually occurs, or what is accepted as normal conduct. I mean a belief that people ought to act in certain ways. There is the norm of treating my co-workers in a respectful manner. There is the norm of reporters identifying themselves and their purposes when seeking interviews. The norms of respectful treatment and self-identification are grounded in the principles of human dignity and not treating others as (only) a means.

Finally, there are maxims and protocols. I use these terms interchangeably to identify our most specific rules and procedures for recurring situations. There is the maxim in journalism to not base a story on anonymous sources *if at all possible*; and there is the protocol that, if journalists do use anonymous stories, they should follow certain procedures, such as informing their editor of the identity of their sources and using documents to cross-check the claims of these sources. In newsrooms, maxims and protocols can be found in editorial guidelines and in directions from the editor.

Principles, norms, and maxims (or protocols) are practical tools for the evaluation of conduct and practice. All of them give us reasons for acting or for refraining from action. As we will see, their justification is a complex, holistic affair involving all levels of our ethical scheme. These three ethical tools differ in terms of their scope and generality, their relative immunity from revision, and how basic they are to our ethical system.

Structure of the Book

The book's nine chapters and appendix describe the basic concepts of integrated, global ethics. I develop a radical theory of integrated, global media ethics by following a path that begins with the idea of radical ethics and radical media ethics, carries on to the idea of integrated media ethics, and ends with the idea of global integrated ethics.

In Part I, I provide the theoretical foundations. Chapter 1 examines the all-important ontology of ethics – what ethics *is*. I adopt a naturalistic ontology that sees ethics as part of a distinct social reality that depends on human intentionality and agreement. Chapter 2 explains ethics as normative interpretation of conduct and practice. Chapter 3 draws out the implications of Chapters 1 and 2 for my conception of radical ethics. I reject the presumed need for absolute and unchanging principles for the evaluation of human conduct. Instead, I view ethics as a constantly evolving interpretation of our values as we respond to ever new conditions.

In Part II, I construct the basic structure of radical media ethics. Chapter 4 explores the meaning of radical media ethics and the main features of media ethics today. Chapter 5 provides a schema for defining journalism. Chapter 6 outlines a tri-level theory of meaning for media ethics. The tri-level theory explains how an integrated ethics can consist of principles endorsed by many journalists, yet those principles can be applied and interpreted in different ways in specific contexts.

Introduction

In Part III, I lay down some basic principles and aims for radical media ethics. Chapter 7 puts forward one set of those principles – the political principles that hold for many forms of democratic journalism. Chapter 8 argues that the ultimate aims of integrated media ethics should be global, and cosmopolitan, promoting human flourishing around the world. Chapter 9 assesses the likelihood that a global media ethics will become a dominant normative interpretation of journalism. The appendix contains my own code for global integrated ethics. The code is a succinct statement of the principles explained at length in the book.

Notes

1. I regard principles as important to understanding moral reasoning and ethics. Therefore, I reject the position of "moral particularism" (Ridge and McKeever 2010) which denies that principles play a prominent role in morality.
2. I sometimes use the term "standard" which is an idea that extends beyond ethics. We establish certain things as exemplars or authorized units by which to judge objects. For example, we have standards of weight and measurement. In ethics, principles and norms act as standards to evaluate conduct. We judge how an action conforms to our standards of right or wrong. The idea of a standard is, etymologically, close to the idea of a norm. *Norma*, the root for "norm," is Latin for a carpenter's rule or square.

References

Ridge, Michael, and Sean McKeever. 2010. "Moral Particularism." In *The Routledge Companion to Ethics*, edited by John Skorupski, 629–639. New York: Routledge.

Lyotard, Jean-François. 2013. *Why Philosophize?* Trans. Corinne Enaudeau. Cambridge: Polity.

Part I
Theoretical Foundations

Chapter 1
Ontology of Ethics

Ethics today should be radical. In ethics proper, we need a radical global ethics of humanity. In media ethics, we need a radical global, integrated ethics of responsible practice.

But what is "radical"?

The first entry for "radical" in *The New Shorter Oxford English Dictionary* (1993) says the word means "going to the root or origin… affecting what is fundamental; far-reaching; thorough."

This is the sense of radical that informs this book. My radicalness is philosophical.

My radicalness seeks reform of fundamental ideas. Reform requires intellectual boldness and moral imagination: boldness to challenge outdated, yet cherished, ideas and imagination to invent new ideas. To be philosophically radical is to alter the structure of our thinking.

In media ethics, fundamental ideas such as responsible publishing and impartiality are like reinforcing rods that run through the structure, providing support for more specific values. Reform of fundamental ideas has a far-reaching impact.

Radical Media Ethics: A Global Approach, First Edition. Stephen J. A. Ward.
© 2015 John Wiley and Sons, Inc. Published 2015 by John Wiley and Sons, Inc.

I start, therefore, with meta-ethics. Why? Because meta-ethical beliefs color how we approach ethical questions. If I believe that ethics is God's absolute commandments for mankind, I may demand that society require all citizens to keep the commandments. Similarly, if I think ethics is a contemptuous attempt by the weak to restrain the strong, I feel justified in pursuing my interests at the expense of others. The need for meta-ethics is especially clear when we try to think in a new way about ethics. No radical media ethics is possible without radical meta-ethical thinking.

I proceed in this chapter as follows: In the first half of the chapter, I introduce my social ontology of ethics. That examines the mode of existence of ethics as a social activity for the regulation of conduct. I trace the origins of this activity to human nature, the intentional powers of the mind, and the evolution of human society and institutions. Ethics is not unique in this normative practice. Rather it is part of a distinctive human-dependent social reality whose objects, activities, and functions cannot be reduced to physical or biological properties.

In Chapter 2, I use this ontology to outline the psychology and epistemology of the practice of ethics – how it proceeds by way of holistic conceptual schemes and interpretations. In Chapter 3, I state the implications for ethics that flow from the two chapters. The result is a meta-ethical perspective on the nature of ethics as social, human-dependent, and interpretive.

Naturalist Ontology

What is ethics?

Ethics is the study and practice of what constitutes the best regulation of human conduct, individually and socially. Humans apply their notions of ethics by acting according to principles, norms, and aims. Ethics is the activity of constructing, critiquing, and enforcing norms, principles, and aims to guide individual and social conduct. The phrase "the best regulation" indicates a zone of critical and ever-evolving thought about the notions and norms of ethics. Existing norms may be inadequate, or even unethical.

Ethics takes all of life as its subject matter. Almost any form of conduct can fall under its critical gaze. Ethics applies to the conduct of individuals, groups, institutions, professions, and countries. Ethics asks how we, as persons and as a society (or species), ought to live. What are the primary goods that we should seek so people enjoy flourishing lives? How should we live together, so that our pursuit of those goods is just, dutiful, and respectful of others? How do we develop people of moral character who do what is right and serve the common good? The good, the right, and the virtuous: these are the three great, intertwined themes of ethics. Ethics, therefore, has three concerns: Appropriate ethical beliefs, correct application, and the disposition to act ethically. Ethics is about the most serious normative aspects of our existence: the most important goods in life, our basic rights and duties, our roles and how we carry out our responsibilities, and the pursuit of virtue. Ethics demands that we live in goodness and in right relation with each other. Ethics may require us to forgo personal benefits, to carry out duties, or to endure persecution.

Ethics is both individualistic and social. It is individualistic because individuals are asked to make certain norms and values part of their character. It is social because ethics is not about every person formulating their own rules of behavior. Correct conduct is honoring rules of fair social interaction – rules that apply to humans in general or to all members of a group. We experience ethics internally as the tug of conscience. We experience ethics externally as the demands placed upon us by codes of ethics, backed by social sanction. Psychologically, one learns ethics as a set of responses shaped by social enculturation and the ethical "climate" of society. My ethical capacities are nurtured and exercised within groups. Also, ethics requires that I adopt a social perspective that looks to the common good and transcends selfish individualism. Ethically speaking, "How ought I to live?" cannot be asked in isolation from the question, "How ought we to live?"

Ethics is practical. Ethics is an activity, a process, and a dynamic practice. It is something we do. We do ethics when we weigh values to make a decision. We do ethics when we modify practices in light of new technology. It may be convenient, but also potentially misleading, to talk about ethics as an object, the way we talk about our automobiles. Society and ethics is an evolving set of social interactions and processes,

Theoretical Foundations

not a "thing." Ethics is always situated in, yet transcendent of, a context. Reflection on ethics is carried out by fallible humans embedded in historical eras and in distinct cultures. Situated inquirers also scrutinize their beliefs. All societies, no matter how rigid or traditional, face the future. They cannot avoid struggling with new problems and new ethical questions. Both the cultures and their denizens are ever evolving, ever confronting new challenges. Ethics is not a static set of rules. Ethics is a natural and inescapable human activity. It is the attempt by individuals and societies to respond to quandaries created by changing conditions, unexpected issues, and new ways of thinking and acting.

Ethics at its best is reflective engagement with the urgent problems of the day, in light of where we have been and where we hope to be tomorrow. The questions are created by new technology and media, the progress of science, cultural and social trends, and the redefining of the planet's geo-political and environmental climate. In today's world there is no shortage of urgent normative questions. We live in a global world shaped by dramatic changes in technology and media, a world of vast inequalities in wealth and power, a world threatened by conflict and emerging technologies for war. Ethics is reflective engagement with questions that range from what developed nations ought to do to reduce global poverty to how media technology should be used to protect human rights. Engagement involves the reinterpretation of norms, the invention of principles, and the development of new and responsible practices.

Reflective engagement can occur in any area of society. For example, developments in genetic knowledge call for new ethical thinking in the sciences of life. Is it morally permissible to use genetic knowledge to "design" babies, or to force citizens to be tested for genes linked to debilitating diseases? In recent times, our concern about the impact of human activity on nature and on non-human forms of life has prompted the development of environmental ethics and the ethics of animal welfare.

Ethics starts from the lived experience of ethical doubt and plurality of values, and then seeks integration and theoretical understanding. Ethical theorizing can be divided into two types, meta-ethics (or philosophical ethics) and applied ethics (see Ward 2011, 7–51). Meta-ethics asks three big questions about the nature of ethics: What are we saying when we make an ethical claim? How do we know that what we say is justified? Why does ethics exist in the first place? There are plenty of ethical theories, from descriptivism and intuitionism to realism and relativism. Applied ethics, on the other hand, asks not what we mean by ethical concepts like good or right but what *is* good or right, and how to do what is good or right in certain situations. Examples of approaches to applied ethics are consequential theories of the good, deontological theories of the right, and theories of virtue.

In applied ethics, moral norms are often codified. Principles of ethics, such as "Help others in need" and "Live a life of non-violence and peace" are brought together to form moral systems, such as utilitarian ethics and Buddhist ethics. The Bible's Ten Commandments is one such code. In addition, there are codes of increasing specificity for doctors, lawyers, and journalists. As a set of principles, "ethics" can refer to something singular or multiple. We can understand "ethics" as the proper name for a single ethical system. One may believe that there is only one set of correct principles and that is what ethics is. Or, we can think of "ethics" as a general term that refers to many ethical systems. "Ethics" as a general term resembles "language," which refers to many language systems. I prefer to use "ethics" in this plural sense, reserving "ethic" for a single set of principles.

If ethics is a dynamic activity, ethics is not a set of rules to be followed blindly or defended dogmatically. In many cases, there will be legitimate debate as to whether and how rules should apply. Even principles we hold dear may have to be reinterpreted in light of new developments. For example, how should we apply the principle of respect for life to the issue of how long to keep a dying person alive through new technology? Moreover, the boundaries of ethics shift. In our time, ethics has come to include such issues as animal welfare, protecting the environment, and the rights of gay couples. Ethics is not just the disposition to adhere to rules but also the disposition to critique and improve our rules. The difference between living one's ethics and following mores is that the former rejects the sheer acceptance of rules and conventions. Ethics requires that we follow rules that we have examined critically.

Taken as a whole, ethics is the never-completed human project of inventing, applying, and critiquing the principles that guide interaction, define social roles, and justify institutional structures. Ethical deliberation

Theoretical Foundations

is *critical normative reason in social practice* – the construction of fair ethical frameworks for society.

Naturalism

A meta-ethics needs an ontology. Ontology is the study of what exists and how it exists. Is everything material? Do things exist external to my mind, and how do they exist? What types of things exist, e.g., do abstract entities like numbers exist? How does one part of reality, e.g., our thoughts, relate to other parts of reality, such as sub-atomic particles? Is the mind the brain?

Applied to ethics, ontology asks about the mode of existence of the ethical sphere of society – the activity of conduct regulation described above. How did the ethical domain arise in the evolution of society? Do values and norms actually exist in the world apart from our minds? What must exist in the world for an ethical judgment to be true or correct? How do our ethical conceptions fit with a scientific conception of the world?

A full ontology of ethics needs to explain three things – practice, language, and reference – and their place in our overall worldview.

Level of practice: First we locate ethics as normative conduct regulation, and assess, ontologically, this aspect of our social reality. How is this ethical sphere related to other normative domains, to society, and to the natural world?

Level of language and assertion: Given this view of practice, we assess the ontology of ethical language in terms of judgments, assertions, and claims. Is ethical language descriptive, potentially fact-stating, and true? Or, is it non-descriptive, and therefore a language that prescribes, not describes, what should be done, and is potentially correct or reasonable?

Level of reference: Do ethical terms and statements refer to objectively existing things in the world, e.g., moral facts? What must exist to account for ethical language?

Preferably, the direction of inquiry proceeds from (a) to (b) to (c). If we begin with level (c) and inquire into specific ethical terms, such as "right" or "duty," we fail to see how these terms work together, and we fail to place the use of such terms against the background of ethical practice in society. It is this social functioning that gives sense to the use

Ontology of Ethics

of individual ethical terms. An advantage of starting with (a) is that ethics as social provides us with a public and objective phenomenon to study – public conduct and public norms.

The question now is: What ontology best fits ethics as a social process? I believe the best ontology is naturalistic and evolutionary in approach.[1]

To construct an ontology of ethics we must presume, as background, some view about the world. Naturalism requires the ontology of ethics to be based on our leading and most plausible natural theories about the world – theories about nature, life, and society. The ontologies of such theories, e.g., what physics says exists in the world, should support and mesh with a naturalistic ontology of ethics. What are the leading and most plausible theories about the world?

They are a cluster of *large* understandings that define a naturalistic, scientific view of the world. I am not thinking about specific theories, such as the latest theory about the creation of stars. I am thinking about the overall view of the world as it arises from non-metaphysical, naturalistic inquiry. What are these understandings? First, that nature is physical. It is composed of non-purposeful, non-conscious forces and sub-atomic particles. In some manner, the universe evolved physically from a Big Bang (or some other originating moment) and, in time, the process created our planet, as one among many in an expanding universe. Second, that life and all biological species on Earth evolved through some form of Darwinian selective process, without the intervention of some transcendent deity or prior design. Third, that society arose from the evolution of the human species, a species that is biologically similar to other species, especially primates. Yet evolution also gave humans distinctive capacities such as consciousness, intentionality, rationality, and language, plus the ability to use such capacities to create distinct societies.

The natural and biological sciences (including neuroscience) provide the facts for a theory of the evolution of society and ethics. Like Russian dolls, the ontologies of these theories – natural science, biology, human society, and ethics – should fit inside each other.

Moreover, naturalistic explanations of ethics should be (a) historical, (b) contemporary, and (c) futuristic. By historical, I mean an account of how humans constructed society and then ethics as a normative

Theoretical Foundations

domain. By contemporary, I mean that it explains how ethics is practiced today, and how it relates to other normative domains. By futuristic, I mean that the account must be able to explain how ethics changes and is always future-orientated.

While these theory requirements are broad, they do constrain the construction of ethical ontology. One restraint is the rejection of an ontological dualism of mind and body, as found in Descartes. It also rejects the use of spiritual or metaphysical entities to construct explanations. We should avoid postulating different realities – mental, physical, social, and normative. As Searle insists (2010, 3–4), we need to explain how we move, live, talk, think, and ethically evaluate all in *one* world, a world that includes quarks and cocktail parties. Also, a naturalistic ontology has to find the "sources of normativity" – the compelling nature of duties and norms – in some naturalistic feature of human beings and society. It precludes, for instance, a religious theory of the authority of norms, as commandments from a deity.

The great question

The ontology of society and ethics is wrestling with profound questions about the place of humans in a natural world.

Since the emergence of modern times, and now in post-modern times, a deep question has haunted us, as a species. How is it possible for consciousness, social purposes, and normative ethics to exist in a physical universe that has no mental and normative properties – a universe explained by physics and chemistry? Searle (2010, ix) put the fundamental questions this way:

> How can we give an account of ourselves, with our peculiar human traits – as mindful, rational, speech-act performing, free-will having, social, political human beings – in a world that we know independently consists of mindless, meaningless, physical particles? How can we account for our social and mental existence in a realm of brute physical facts?[2]

Psalm 8 of the Bible wonders: What is man that thou art mindful of him?[3] Today, we ask a different question: What are humans that they are mindful of themselves in a mindless world? I concur with Searle

(2010, 3–4) that this question is the "fundamental question in contemporary philosophy," even if many philosophers fail to address it directly.

Some people believe that, in a post-modern world, it is implausible to find the source of normativity in God, who may not exist, or in nature, since nature lacks norms or purpose. As Larmore (2008, 223–224) has noted, this view has encouraged theories of ethics that see the source of norms, values, and purposes in the operations of the human mind. Norms are human creations and, as such, are inherently subjective phenomena; they are not literally part of an independently existing physical world.

Enabling Conditions

Given a naturalistic approach, what are the enabling conditions for the existence of ethics? The main conditions are: (1) existence of humans with an impulse to pursue what ought to be; (2) existence of human minds with collective intentionality; (3) existence of a distinctive social reality that combines social and institutional properties that do not reduce to physical properties, and are created through recognition and agreement; (4) existence of formal social systems for coordinating types of conduct, through the recognition of roles, powers, and functions; (5) existence, as part of (4), of normative domains created to articulate and monitor the honoring of certain types of norms, such as the domains of law and ethics.

Let's examine each of these conditions in turn.

Existential sources

The source of all ethics is neither critical philosophical reason nor social traditions. It is the human condition; the conditions of our existence.

The human condition is the intersection of human nature, the state of the world, and the social context in which we live. Human nature contributes the fundamental capacities that are essential (and common) to life and within the range of all humans.[4] It includes the basic physical, biological, and mental features of the human species, including essential needs. Human nature is distinctive in never being a settled fact. Humans have a yet-to-be-completed nature that is always seeking development both organically, mentally, and ethically. The distinctive forms of human consciousness, language and society, create normative impulses about what ought to be, impulses which are foreign to other species. That is one reason we can talk about a human condition, apart from the "given" condition of tigers or ants.

The motivation for doing ethics arises from the peculiarities of our existence as conscious, social, language-wielding creatures. Ethics is an inescapable expression of being human. No amount of skepticism about the objectivity of ethical rules, or cynicism about morality, will eradicate the ethical impulse.

What is that impulse?[5]

I begin with an assertion that sounds paradoxical: We are factual creatures but we don't live in a world of facts. To be a factual creature is to exist as a material, biological entity. We exist. We eat, digest, desire, feel, think, talk, move about, cooperate with others, and sleep. Your existence is a fact; you are an item in the physical world. You can be a datum in statistical surveys of the population; your body can be studied scientifically like any other physical object. As a matter of fact, we have a body that is the result of centuries of evolution of nature and species. As a matter of fact, we occupy a certain location in a certain culture.

This is the factual substratum for all we do.

However, humans are more than facts. Usually, people think that "more" refers to human consciousness and the life of the mind. That is part of what "more" means, but there are other considerations. Principally, we live in a *hybrid world* of facts and values, a social world where fact and value are intertwined. Only later do we separate fact and value, and wonder about their relationship; only later do we call values "subjective."

How is this possible? It has to do with the nature of our consciousness and our agency.

We are aware of the world's existence and how things usually go, but we are also aware of how things might go, or go better. The human world is shot through with strivings and yearnings that go beyond what is; with criticisms, disappointments, and dissatisfactions with what is; with goals and reform of what is; with utopian dreams beyond what might ever be.

Also, we are practical agents who must act, individually and in groups. We have interests to pursue. For every fact and earthly condition we encounter, we feel compelled to change it, to transform what exists, to create artifacts and technology, to develop non-natural environments. To act means we choose ends and means. This prompts us to judge, compare, assess, affirm, and evaluate what is. We propose how what is could be better. The essential category of the human condition is not thought but action. Action is a doing that incorporates a sense of who one is and how things stand with oneself and the world. Humans are called into action and into valued ways of living by a self-reflective agency. We ask "What am I doing?" which is intimately linked to the "anthropological" question which Augustine was apparently one of the first to ask explicitly. He asks, "Who am I?" and distinguishes it from "What am I?"[6]

Therefore, we wonder, at least at times, what to make of this existence, if anything. We wonder what sort of person we should be, what desires we should have, what type of character and virtues we should develop. From a factual life in a factual world, humans envisage the normative counterfactual – what might be, what ought to be for myself and others. All of these activities are future-orientated because we are a species for whom, as Heidegger said (1962, 1, 68) our existence is a "possibility" and time is the "horizon" for any understanding of being.

Harry Frankfurt provides a description of how ethics grew from this development of a consciousness that could assess current conditions and desires. Evolution created a space between reaction and action by developing in humans the ability to think, to interpret, to intend, to reason, to engage in symbolic thinking, and to evaluate our emotions and desires. These capacities allowed humans to take themselves seriously by not responding unreflectively to desires and by not simply following existing norms. Evolution has given our species the ability to question and restrain the onslaught of restless desires and to sort out conflicts among values. Ethics is possible because we can reflect on desires and values and seek to integrate them into a good life, dominated by a conception of who we should be. With regard to living, Frankfurt (2006, 45) says, we want to "get it right." How is it possible for us to take ourselves seriously? It is "our peculiar knack of separating from the immediate content and flow of our consciousness and introducing a sort of division within our minds." In addition to the level of immediate content, we have an "inward-directed monitoring oversight" which enables us to focus on ourselves. This self-objectification allows us to form higher-order responses to our experiencing. We may like the person we are, or want to change it. We come to value things; care about things.

Ethics is a way of saying what we should make of ourselves, and how we should live. Ethics is needed because there is always a gap between what is and what we think ought to be.

Metaphysical fools

Human life would be difficult enough if our ethical task was to develop a consistent set of goals and values for ourselves, as individuals. If this were so, we could imagine society as consisting of individuals on separate normative trajectories. They would be individuals free to pursue their values in splendid isolation. But life is more complex than that, and so is our encounter with what might be. Our personal values and goals conflict. As complex creatures, humans are torn between their different desires and attachments. We occupy many roles and incur many duties. Inevitably, conflict arises as I try to follow a coherent plan of life. How do my duties as a parent line up with my career ambitions? How do I balance my desire to help the poor with a desire to retire to my garret to paint my masterpiece? To make matters worse, we feel the inadequacy of our current beliefs, such as when our norms lead to troubling consequences. For instance, we question the value of patriotism when it leads to extreme nationalism. Also, the impulse to be better conflicts with our desire for sex, power, and domination, among our many passions. Moreover, the schemes for evaluating actions and values are plural. We balance moral, aesthetic, and legal views.

The same conflict is writ large on the level of society – in our relationships with family, friends, colleagues, and citizens. Not only does my trajectory come into tension with your trajectory but also a host of moral systems contend for the status of "most consistent and reasonable" view of how society should greet the future. We disagree about the rules of conduct and the ends they pursue.

Torn by conflict, we feel a lack in our existence, a losing of control, an insufficient degree of unity in life. What to make of our factual existence is never a simple question. Consequently, the impulse to rise above factual existence is weakened by the fragmentation of our judging and valuing. The fragmentation cannot be ignored because it affects practical judgments about what to do.

What is, is never enough.

Life rarely fulfills all of our desires or wishes; and it is rare when we feel completely at rest with ourselves ethically, admiring oneself as a fully virtuous person. We know that "what is, is never enough" is true, existentially, even if we have given up on hopes to improve ourselves or the world. We know it is true even if we have become cynics of life, or just tired of life's pain, unfairness, drudgery, and death. One response to fragmentation is integration. We attempt to integrate this unruly crew of demanding values, even if integration only amounts to ruling out some values and finding a partial ranking of remaining values.

However, at this point we need to ask tough questions: Are we assuming that all people *want* to pursue high values and goals? That all seek integration? What if some humans say "nay" to the pursuit of perfection or even simple improvement, ethically? This question points to a primordial fact about moral psychology: humans must choose between affirming or denying the value of life and its ethical development.[7] Humans, subconsciously or consciously, affirm or deny that they care about making something out of their factual existence. Do we affirm life, in all of its dimensions, or do we say "nay" to it? Humans express a verdict on this choice through their actions, even if they never explicitly think about the choice in this manner.

Denial can take many forms. Instead of affirming life, we could remain neutral to the passing show. We live as others live. Severely depressed or lacking resources, one may simply go along with life day to day. We try to exist as a matter of fact, avoiding entanglement with strivings and ideals which disturb one's calmness.

One may seek distraction from reminders of what one ought to be by burying oneself in office work or by living a life of transitory pleasures, as well described by Kierkegaard (1959). Some people silence the normative voices inside with drugs. The need for silencing only points to the power of normative impulses that come with being conscious, rational, and social. Consciousness can be a burden, as it eats away at our cunning and our places of refuge.

Although the need to affirm life lies below the surface of our daily lives, it can come to the fore when people suffer a traumatic experience, such as the death of a spouse. The event robs them of the ability to care deeply about their life, their future. Yet, even if we have become lost souls, lacking a home and a meaning, there usually remains a small speck in us that longs for meaning, for something better than what is.

Some modern philosophers have urged humans to continue to seek meaning in a world where God may not exist. Albert Camus, in *The Myth of Sisyphus*, says that in a world where God may not exist, we are "condemned" to death. We feel the tension between the human need for meaning and "the unreasonable silence of the world." Nonetheless, we must seek meaning, passionately, in an "absurd" world where humans are aliens. We aim to live and to create, in the very midst of the desert (2000, xxi). Camus wants affirmation without metaphysical guarantees.

Others portray this affirmation more positively as a matter of becoming more human. This view owes much to Plato's idea that humans exist as a "becoming" somewhere between being full real and being unreal. Jean Vanier's book, *Becoming Human*, describes a process of becoming, a liberation of the human heart from the "tentacles of chaos and loneliness" resulting in an openness to others and a discovery of our "common humanity" (1998, 6–7).

Humans are metaphysical fools. They keep hoping, against evidence and the odds, that the world can, and should, become better.

Collective intentionality

The human impulse to live in a hybrid world usually occurs in society. But ethics does not exist in all types of society, e.g., a society of ants. The second enabling condition is that humans have a mind of a special kind. It is obvious that ethics cannot exist without minds. Mentality is necessary because ethics is about the conscious choice of actions guided by beliefs. But not just any kind of mind will do. Ethics needs a mind that is self-conscious and has intentionality – the ability to direct its attention to the world through beliefs, desires, and perceptions.

Moreover, ethics (and society) needs minds that are capable of "collective intentionality" (Searle, 2010, 42). Collective intentionality is the ability for minds to share attitudes and goals, and to agree that people and things have certain social roles and functions.[8] Collective intentionality makes possible intentional, collaborative action – the type of actions that define society.

Examples of conduct based on collective intentionality include rowing a boat together, pushing a car to a gas station, or playing trumpet in a jazz band. What is crucial is a sense of collectivity, a sense of doing something together. You and I play on the same hockey team. I am the goaltender, and you play on defense. As a player from another team approaches *our* goal, you intend to challenge the player to force him to settle for a weak shot on goal; I intend to move out to the limits of my crease to reduce the angle and prepare to stop the shot. We engage in a collective intentionality for the purpose of preventing a goal and, ultimately, winning the game.

Ontologically, collective behavior must emerge from the individual minds of people. There are no free-floating "intentions to associate" apart from what intentions exist in individual minds. Yet we also need more than each human's mind having its own intentionality. We need each mind to be capable of sharing a collective intentionality that exists in other minds. We need to be capable of acting according to shared aims, desires, and beliefs. Later we will see that this collective intentionality also makes possible something crucial to ethics – a collective recognition of certain roles and functions.

Distinctive social reality

Collective intentionality makes possible a distinctive social reality among humans. This social reality provides the structures needed for ethics to emerge as a domain of norm-governed conduct.

But what is society? For my purposes, I need only a simple conception of society. Sociologists can provide more elaborate conceptions.

Society is a group of individuals who interact and come into relation to achieve common needs and goals. They share resources and create political, educational, and legal systems to meet goals and to govern the interactions of members. This coexistence makes possible goods and services that would not exist if everyone was an isolated individual. Bees work together to maintain a hive. Families of elephants take care of each other.

Robinson Crusoe on his island is *not* a social world. Nor are random and temporary collections of people in the same space, even if each is pursuing a similar end. Airplane travelers and casino gamblers are not societies even if each person in the group shares the goal of getting to one's destination or hitting the jackpot. They lack the right internal relations among themselves. The members of society enter into relations that are collective and cooperative. They share common goals, whose achievement requires their cooperation. This cooperation for mutual benefit *creates* a social reality, as opposed to a physical reality or a biological reality.

Societies also display an internal complexity, whereby people and activities are organized into social structures. The structures include simple, informal, and often local social activities such as cocktail parties, football games, academic conferences, playing bingo at the Legion, dancing at the Ritz, and forming a movie club in your condo association. All of these activities have rules and etiquette for appropriate conduct.

An important social structure is formal and society-wide institutions and practices based on explicit and rigid norms, laws, and authorized processes. Institutions and public offices are established and recognized by the state or government, e.g., the education system, the tax system, the office of the public prosecutor. Societies of any complexity orchestrate, coordinate, and regulate the conduct of their members by establishing these mediating systems for fair and legal collaboration, from legislatures and the courts to the institutions of marriage, private property, and the limited liability corporation. Also, the institutions and practices may be private, e.g., news media and the profession of medicine.

These institutions shape social interactions; they normatively define correct conduct and require appropriate and necessary procedures. They recognize and authorize what counts as a valid transaction, such as applying for a passport. These institutions are constructed around hierarchies of officials overseeing multi-stage processes. Officials are assigned certain roles and powers that are justified by the functions served by the institution, as endorsed by citizens.

In many cases, social activities and institutional structures go together to make possible what appear to be simple social events. Take, for example, Searle's description (1995, 3) of the "invisible" ontology of a routine social event – ordering food at a cafe in Paris. The waiter comes and I utter a fragment of a French sentence. I say, "Un demi, Munich, s'il vous plait." The waiter brings the beer and I drink it. I leave money on the table and leave.

Note that the activity depends on the prior recognition of social roles, such as "waiter" and "customer." Each role has a certain social status and function, and having that role implies certain rights, permissions, obligations. The roles also define appropriate conduct. I, as a customer, have a right to be served but I also have an obligation to pay for the service. Who is a legitimate customer is a matter of social recognition and regulation. For example, the waiter chases away street people who want to sit in his cafe without buying anything. Moreover, the "simple" serving of beer is made possible by institutions, such as ownership of a business, in this case ownership of a cafe. Ownership implies the existence of the institution of private property in France. The production of the beer I selected is regulated by quality laws and, by law, all cafes must list all of their beers. I only have to pay the listed price. The money I left on the table presumes the institution of money – the recognition of certain things as counting as French money, and a monetary system of financial transactions, not a system of barter. Finally, I am able to sit and order beer only because, in the first place, I am a citizen of Canada with a valid passport and have entered France legally.

A similar analysis could be provided for countless "simple" social activities, from attending a rock concert to participating in graduation ceremonies at a university.

From an ontological (and ethical) perspective, the interesting questions are *how* do such social roles, functions, and institutions come to exist, and what is the source of their normativity? How can such social properties as "x is a waiter" and "this paper counts as money for beer" come into existence to form social reality?

The answer is collective intentionality. We collectively recognize that people and objects can occupy certain roles to perform various functions. We collectively agree, implicitly or explicitly, that certain things can have certain social properties, e.g., something counts as money given the observance of certain rules governed by social structures. Humans literally create social reality and impose meanings, functions, and norms on things. We create social reality by agreement, recognition, and imposition, rather than by discovering pre-existing social properties and structures in nature. Collective intentionality is the key to the invention of social reality and its normative dimension.

Searle (2010, 7) calls this human capacity to create social properties the assignment of "status functions" to people, processes, and things. It is "the distinctive feature of human social reality." We assign status functions to certain people or things, e.g., x is Prime Minister of Canada. The form of attribution is always: "X counts as Y in context C," as in "John counts as a police officer in Canada," or "saying 'I do' counts as agreeing to be married in the context of a duly authorized agent," or "placing a marked ballot into a box counts as voting in an election." The assignment of status carries with it functions and norms, rights and responsibilities. The assignment of status functions goes beyond the familiar attribution of functions to objects based on their physical features, e.g., this is a screwdriver, or this log would be a good place to sit during our beach party. When we impose status functions we impose functions on objects that the objects cannot perform solely in virtue of their physical structure.

Let's consider a few more examples of social invention. We create the institution of policing when we collectively recognize that some people have the status of police officer for the purpose of carrying out certain social functions such as keeping the peace. The assignment of the status function of police officer has three normative components: (a) it provides a means for evaluating how anyone is fulfilling the role or function; (b) its gives powers to the role. Police officers have the power to determine how people ought to act in situations, according to the norms of law; (c) it implies that the role exists because it serves some recognized and valued public function, such as maintaining security.

Why are status functions important for society and ethics? We have already indicated the answer. Status functions carry with them rights, duties, obligations, permissions, authorizations, and entitlements. They act as a sort of normative glue that keeps our society together. Status functions give us reasons for acting that are independent of our inclinations and desires. If I recognize objects as your private property – that is, I recognize the institution of private property – then I am under an obligation not to steal them. I can steal from you and still recognize your right not to have your possessions stolen.

The attribution of a status function is part of a web of status functions and institutions. Ontologically, it is an elaborate creation and reiteration of human intentionality and agreement. Any one status function will rub up against other status functions. The police officer interacts with judges, prosecutors, court officials, and citizens.

Examples of status functions could be multiplied at will. Consider symbolic acts and recognitions. Imagine a tribe that recognizes a simple line of stones as marking the border of another tribe, even though there is nothing physical about the stones that amounts to a wall or barrier.[9] The stones have the social property of being a border because of mutual agreement. Or, consider the formal opening of a new session of the Canadian Parliament. It features the role (and status) of a Sergeant-in-Arms who knocks on the door of the Commons to ask permission to allow members of the Senate into the Commons to hear the Speaker of the Commons read the Speech from the Throne. The pomp and circumstance of the occasion, and the roles and functions played by the Sergeant, the Speaker, and the politicians, is a creation of the human mind in a social setting.

How humans are capable of such abstract (non-physical) attributions of role and function is a long story to be told by evolutionary and social psychology, by studies in symbolic thought and mental representation, and by other disciplines. What is important for an ontology of ethics is that the capacity *exists* and leads to norm-governed social conduct. Humans create another level of existence in the world – a social reality with its own ways of being, which are irreducible to the properties or laws of the natural sciences. From a purely physical evolution come the evolution of minds and then the evolution of society as a distinct layer of reality.

Normative domains

Every society must regulate the conduct of its members. Good behavior, reciprocity, altruism, and non-criminal conduct cannot be assumed of every citizen. The only question is how much regulation is necessary, what the norms are, and who exercises the powers of regulation.

Theoretical Foundations

We can think of society as having a normative sphere – the sum total of areas where behavior falls under norms, rules, and standards. Many values and norms are not ethical, such as the value of a good beer or norms for greeting someone in the street. There are norms of fashion, aesthetics, architecture, and law. Norm enforcement is diffuse and overlapping. One and the same person may receive ethical advice from their pastor, teacher, parents, and peers.

Most social systems and institutions, such as schools, have rules and other normative components because the systems exist to guide conduct and to validate, officially, that certain activities have been appropriately carried out. They determine whether people deserve a social status, e.g., are a graduate from college or have passed a driver's license test.

However, in addition to institutions that enforce norms of conduct, there are also institutions whose primary focus is monitoring whether people are following certain types of norms. These institutions oversee "normative domains." Etiquette is one normative domain, enforced by social conventions and social pressure. Ethics and law are two other notable domains. Etiquette consists of a plethora of rules for what is appropriate and inappropriate conduct in social settings, from playing host to visiting dignitaries and inviting someone to your marriage to observing certain niceties of eating when at a common table. Etiquette usually does not deal with rules as serious as law and ethics. Yet it has a function. It coordinates actions, letting people know what to do. Many violations of etiquette, such as using the wrong glass for wine at a formal dinner, are neither illegal nor unethical. However, extreme violations of etiquette, such as boorishness to a foreign visitor, can violate the ethical principle of respect for others.

The domains of law and ethics deal with the most important areas of conduct, i.e., actions that have serious implications for individuals and groups. The contents of ethics and law overlap. Murder is illegal and unethical. However, it not easy to clearly differentiate the domains. We can think of law as stipulating the bare minimum of what is required in a situation, backed by the state's coercive powers. For instance, the dentist must obtain, legally, your informed consent. Therefore, people talk of ethics as going beyond what the law requires. For example, it may be legally "safe" to publish an inaccurate, sensational portrait of a politician. Libel action is not a significant threat. But we can go "beyond law" and ask if the publication would be an ethical act. Sometimes ethics is contrasted with, or put in opposition to, law. For instance, people say that laws can be unethical, such as the apartheid laws that once existed in South Africa.

Structurally, the norm governance of law is more concrete, formal, and harshly punitive since it is an expression of the state's coercive power over citizens. Law's normative domain consists of written laws and courts with the power to restrain, imprison, or fine. The domain of ethics is less structured.[10] It is taught in schools, preached from pulpits, advanced by professional associations, monitored within institutions by ethics committees, and informally enforced among citizens by the practices of praising and shaming.

In other works (Ward 2010, 2011), I have argued that there is no hard line between ethics and law, yet ethics has distinguishing features. In terms of content, its subject is, as noted above, foundational rights, duties, good, and virtues, which we reason about from an impartial perspective that is fair to all interested parties. Ethical reasoning goes beyond the selfish and prudential forms of reasoning. It considers the overall good. Also, I contend that ethical principles and notions are the most basic principles of society's normative sphere. Even the law, including constitutions, is grounded normatively in some ethical vision of the good society.

These criteria fail to establish a hard line between ethics and other normative domains. The distinctions are matters of degree, such as ethics being more fundamental than law. We should not expect hard and fast boundaries. Etiquette, prudence, law, and ethics all deal with regulating behavior. All speak of what ought to be done, in contrast to what is done. Consequently, there is overlap in language and among the rules. Human society only gradually distinguished these normative domains. Originally, to violate the commands of a tribal chief was socially repugnant, an ethical breach, and against the gods – all at the same time. Law only became a distinct area when societies built legal systems with their own rules, practices, and institutions.

The ontological basis for these normative domains is the same as the basis for the social structures previously examined. The norms of ethics and law are human inventions based on collective intentionality, status function, and the social mechanism of agreement and recognition. These normative domains are part of a distinctive human social reality.

In summary, the enabling conditions for the existence of ethics are: the existence of an ethical impulse, collective intentionality, a distinct social reality based on status functions and agreement, formal social systems with normative components, and normative domains. Once all of this is in place, ethics as social phenomenon, and as we know it, exists.

But *what* sort of existence? We need to identify the ontological presumptions of the enabling conditions.

Ontological Features

Here, as a summary, are the central features of my ontology of ethics.

Ontological naturalism

Ethics is a natural and necessary human activity that governs conduct according to a society's notions of the good, the right, and the virtuous. It is an activity that constantly evolves. The manner of existence of ethics is the same as, and is no more mysterious than, the existence of humans, their minds, and their social activity. Ethics is a natural part of a natural world, even though its evolution may be distinctive and surprising. Ethics does not require a religious, spiritual, or metaphysical explanation.

Creation and invention

Ethics is a human creation. It is a response to normative problems and questions. Intentionality and collective intentionality play a large part in our ability to recognize and propose aims, values, and norms for the regulation of conduct.

Properties by agreement

The intentional nature of our minds and the collective nature of society allow humans to create social and ethical properties, as a distinct layer of reality, rather than discover social and ethical properties existing independently in nature, apart from minds. Social contract theory (Ward 2005, 23–24) has long imagined how humans may have constructed a government so as to escape a state of nature, where no social order exists. However, here, we are not imagining the creation of government. We are imaging the creation of ethics. We apply the notions of recognition and agreement, previously political notions for setting up a state, to the ontology of society and ethics.

Non-reducible properties

Human society is a distinct layer of reality because types of social and ethical properties are not reducible to types of physical, chemical, or biological properties. The language of physics, chemistry, and biology cannot adequately capture the features of simple social events, such as buying beer in a Parisian cafe. There is no adequate physico-chemical description for the property of being a restaurant, a waiter, a sentence in French, money, or a screwdriver, even though all instances of restaurants, waiters, sentences in French, money, and screwdrivers are physical phenomena. In addition, social and ethical functions, like all functions, are properties that can be realized in indefinitely many physical ways. Mousetraps have many physical forms and realizations, as do social functions such as "was elected to office" and ethical functions such as "promotes human flourishing."

Being a judge, a waiter, or a piece of money is not due to the fact that judges, waiters, or pieces of money have some common physical or chemical feature. Someone counts as a legitimate customer, a waiter, a judge, a head of state, or certain things count as money, payment of a bill, and signaling that a goal has been scored, *only because* humans decide that it is so.

Ethical properties such as "is a duty" or "is good" are social properties similar to "is opening Parliament," "is money," and "is correctly driving." They are not reducible to physical properties. There is no adequate physico-chemical property that captures the feature "is a good police office" or "is a duty to perform."

Theoretical Foundations

Observer-relative features

Social and moral features are not intrinsic features. They are observer-relative features (Searle 1995, 9). Intrinsic features exist in nature independently of any minds, attitudes, opinions, or agreements. The (traditional) realist thinks we discover that objects have ethical properties the way we discover that natural objects have certain intrinsic, objectively existing, properties based directly on their physical natures, e.g., mass, shape, and material composition. As realists, we don't think that physical facts, such as the fact that hydrogen atoms have one electron, are imposed by humans. We don't think the physical mass of an object is determined by agreement. Natural objects have intrinsic, not observer-relative, properties. The facts about hydrogen and mass are "brute facts" (Searle 1995, 34–35). They are the facts upon which social and ethical facts are built.

Observer-relative features are features that exist because they are features for an observer, and their existence depends on human minds, attitudes, and agreements. Functions, such as being a screwdriver, or protecting the security of a community, are observer-relative properties since they only exist as functions *for* some human interest or purpose. This $20 bill in my wallet could not count as money if there was no institution for money and financial transactions. My sketch of the beach near my home could not count as a symbolic representation of the beach unless human consciousness existed, along with human practices for symbolic representation. Take away the human element and it is just a physical object, a brute fact. Similarly, things we find ethically valuable – aims, goals, functions, guiding principles – are only valuable for some human or human group. Ethics is not about using our theoretical reason to describe mind-independent objects, properties, or facts. It is about the use of our practical reason to make wise choices concerning which observer-relative values promote our social and ethical goals – goals which are also observer-relative.

Humans, in ascribing social and ethical properties, transcend the "realist" format for ascribing properties to objects.

Acts of valuing

In my view, all values are ontologically dependent on human acts of valuing. Values do not exist independently of human acts of valuing. There is no external and independently existing order of ethical values in nature. Values are experienced by humans, in and through purpose-driven activity. Values come into existence through acts of valuing and affirmation. Values, including ethical values, are an expression and recognition of valued objects, experiences, and projects. A world without human sentience would be a world without value.

Encounter, value, propose

We articulate and support certain values through a threefold process. We seek to make something of ourselves and our society. We encounter certain things, social roles, goals, and ways of acting to be of value to us and our normative counter-factual impulses. Some of these things will be naturally occurring things such as the goodness of food, or certain biological desires. Or, we will find value in aspects of human nature, such as our capacity to think and imagine. Other values will be social properties such as responsible media reporting, or judges acting impartially. Some of these valued things will be experienced as so basic and fundamental that we will call it a "basic value," such as the avoidance of violence and pain. We then propose these values to others, seeking collective recognition for the governance of conduct.

The fact that the thing being valued exists in nature or human nature does not mean that ethical properties are values existing in nature, independently of mind. Properties of things do not become ethical properties until they are recognized and affirmed by humans for some purpose.

"Ethics as proposal" holds even for bedrock moral intuitions, such as the value of human dignity, or for universals such as truth-telling. A universal value is not universal because it is an objective, independently existing value in nature. It is a universal because some person or group proposes it as a universal for their moral scheme. They claim the value is so fundamental that it should be accepted by everyone as a principle for governing conduct. To say that x is a universal normative principle is a covert way of saying it should be a universal. It is to say that x is justified or normatively worthy of being affirmed as a universal principle in the conceptual scheme of group y, according to our best normative arguments.

Ontologically subjective facts

Is ethics objective or subjective? The question is too simple. We need to distinguish between two senses (Searle 1995, 7–9) of the objective-subjective distinction – the epistemic and the ontological.[11] The epistemic distinction has to do with the objectivity (or subjectivity) of types of claims and statements – how such statements are known to be true. Statements are epistemically subjective if their truth cannot be settled objectively by facts because their truth depends on human attitudes, emotions, or viewpoints, e.g., x is the most beautiful picture in the world. Statements are objective if they can be determined to be true or false by the facts of the world. They are true or false independently of anyone's attitudes or feelings. Corresponding to objectively true judgments are objective facts. The ontological sense applies the objective-subjective distinction to entities, and their modes of existence. Pains and colors are subjective because their existence depends on them being felt or seen by sentient creatures. Mountains and planets are ontologically objective because they exist independent of any observer or mental state.

The two senses of the distinction cover a range of statements. For example, we can make an epistemically subjective claim about an ontologically objective entity, e.g., Mount Everest is more beautiful than Mount Whitney." Or, we can make an epistemically objective claim about an ontologically subjective entity, e.g., "I now have a pain in my lower back." The claim reports an epistemically objective fact because it is made true by the existence of an actual fact that is not dependent on the opinions of observers. But pain itself has a subjective mode of existence.

Turning to ethics and society, observer-relative features do not add new material objects to the world but they add what Searle (1995, 10) calls "epistemically objective features" to reality where the features exist relative to observers and users. We can state facts about these objects such as the fact that x is a screwdriver. It isn't just my opinion that x is a screwdriver; it is an "objectively ascertainable fact" (Searle 1995, 10). So ethics is ontologically subjective in origin but that does not mean that it is arbitrary or exists only in my mind.

We can talk about facts and objective claims *within* the ontologically subjective domain of ethics once the phenomena have been come into existence through human intentionality. The fact that an object has observer-relative features does not make it impossible to talk factually and objectively about such features. In the same way, we can talk about facts regarding passports and hockey once such ontologically subjective entities have come into existence through human agency.

Human-based realism

My ontology of value entails that my ethical naturalism is not a robust, traditional realism that regards the referents of ethical terms to be intrinsic properties of the universe. But I am not an anti-realist in the sense that I see ethical language as only a subjective expression of emotion or lacking any "cognitive meaning." I am a stolid traditional realist in general. I believe there exists a world that is independent of any human mind, and that truth is a matter of getting our beliefs to reflect how things exist in that world. But I embrace what might be called a "human-based realism" in the area of ethics. Here, we deal with objects and properties that exist because of humans, yet are as real as anything else in our social world. My realism in ethics wears a human face.

Ethical statements are avowals or affirmations of values that we project onto the world and organize into rational frameworks. Ethical claims are not descriptions of fact but practical proposals about how best to act. Ethical judgment is an action-guiding choice based on reasoning that is reasonable or correct, rather than true or false. Ethical thinking does not seek a true description of an external, moral reality. It seeks reasonable judgments and standards for action.

We can think of ethical rules and principles as fallible hypotheses: principles are fallible, experience-based general "hypotheses" that form part of our experiments in living well. They evolve through imagination, dialogue, and social change. For example, principles of justice are hypotheses about how to construct fair systems of justice. The utility principle, the greatest happiness for the greatest number, is not a factual truth about society. It is a hypothesis about how to make social decisions. This process of affirmation and judgment-making is rational. That is, it is under rational restraint. Principles and frameworks are open to rational assessment by a holistic set of norms, which we will examine later in this book. The purpose of ethical affirmation is not simply to project my values onto objects. The primary purpose of avowal is to persuade myself and others of what norms should coordinate our conduct.

Conclusion

In summary, here are my answers to the three questions asked of any ontology.

- *Ontology of practice*: Ethics is a natural human activity that has evolved from the natural history of life and the universe. Ethics belongs to a special social layer of reality that it is part of the history of the universe. An account of ethics does not need non-natural elements. Our naturalistic ontologies are congruent.
- *Ontology of language*: Ethical language is not descriptive in the realist sense of describing intrinsic properties. Ethical language is a language of practical proposals for action that are correct or reasonable relative to some normative context and conceptual scheme.
- *Reference*: What must exist to account for ethical language are humans coming together with collective intentionality, an ethical impulse, a capacity to find value, and an ability to propose and recognize social and moral properties for governing our lives and society. Ethics, as a normative domain, gets its authority from its successful coordination and governance of conduct, in light of the society's most fundamental goals and functions.

Notes

1. I use the term "naturalism" with some trepidation, given the misunderstandings that surround the term. Naturalism, for me, is not reductionism. It is *not* the attempt to reduce all sciences and knowledge to one class of laws, e.g., the laws of physics. Naturalism is the ontological view that human life is the product of only natural processes and entities, and there is no appeal to non-natural or metaphysical entities. See Ward 2010.
2. Daniel Dennett (2003) attempts to answer the same questions from a naturalistic perspective.
3. I recall, when I was studying at Harvard University, that my wife, Glenda, and I walked up to the building that housed the university's famous philosophy department. I looked up to the frieze on the front of the building and saw the above-mentioned biblical passage carved into the stone. It struck me then that I had been asking that question since I began studying philosophy as a young man. I am still asking versions of that question.
4. For a conception of the human condition, see Arendt (1998), especially the prologue and chapter 1.
5. I call it an impulse not to suggest it is a fleeting, non-rational mental state such as a sudden impulse to eat chocolate ice cream. By "impulse" I mean a fundamental need rooted in our being human. It gives us motivation to reflect and cannot be easily silenced, at the cost of our very humanness. I suggest an analogy: Plato's notion of "eros" or love as a fundamental erotic impulse that ranges from sexual desire to love of wisdom.
6. Cited in Arendt (1998, 10n2).
7. Philosophers will recall that much of Nietzsche's philosophy was an attempt, however misguided, to say "yay" to life. His affirmation was a response to Schopenhauer's pessimistic "nay" to life. I see the decision to affirm as crucial but I do not endorse Nietzsche's interpretation of that affirmation as will to power. Also, I think the decision to affirm does not depend on people reading Nietzsche or Schopenhauer. Ordinary people make such decisions, consciously or unconsciously, in living their lives.
8. For Searle (1995, 24), collective intentionality is a "biologically primitive phenomenon."
9. This is from Searle (1995, 39).

Theoretical Foundations

10. I am speaking here of society's general enforcement of what Gert (2004) calls the "common morality" such as principles of avoiding harm, keeping promises, telling the truth, and so on. Ethics enforcement in specific areas of society may be more formal and specific, such as the ethics of scientific research institutions.
11. I independently developed a similar analysis of objectivity in my first book, Ward 2005.

References

Arendt, Hannah. 1998. *The Human Condition*. Chicago: University of Chicago Press.
Camus, Albert. 2000. *The Myth of Sisyphus*. Trans. Justin O'Brien. London: Penguin.
Dennett, Daniel C. 2003. *Freedom Evolves*. New York: Viking.
Frankfurt, Harry G. 2006. *Taking Ourselves Seriously & Getting It Right*. Stanford, CA: Stanford University Press.
Gert, Bernard. 2004. *Common Morality*. Oxford: Oxford University Press.
Heidegger, Martin. 1962. *Being and Time*. Trans. John Macquarrie and Edward Robinson. New York: Harper & Row.
Kierkegaard, Søren. 1959. "Equilibrium between the Aesthetical and the Ethical in the Composition of Personality." In *Either/Or*, Vol. 2, 161–338. Garden City, NY: Anchor Books.
Larmore, Charles. 2008. *The Autonomy of Morality*. Cambridge: Cambridge University Press.
Searle, John. 1995. *The Construction of Social Reality*. New York: The Free Press.
Searle, John. 2010. *Making the Social World: The Structure of Human Civilization*. Oxford: Oxford University Press.
The New Shorter Oxford English Dictionary. 1993. Vol. 2: N–Z, edited by Leslie Brown. Oxford: Clarendon Press.
Vanier, Jean. 1998. *Becoming Human*. Toronto: Anansi Press.
Ward, Stephen J. A. 2005. *The Invention of Journalism Ethics: The Path to Objectivity and Beyond*. Montreal: McGill-Queen's University Press.
Ward, Stephen J. A. 2010. *Global Journalism Ethics*. Montreal: McGill-Queen's University Press.
Ward, Stephen J. A. 2011. *Ethics and the Media: An Introduction*. Cambridge: Cambridge University Press.

Chapter 2
Ethics as Normative Interpretation

In Chapter 1, I approached ethics as part of a distinctive social realm that was made possible by the natural evolution of humans. I argued that the existence of ethics required the evolution of human consciousness, language, and collective intentionality.

I stressed ethics' role as an important social *practice* – the practice of articulating certain norms of conduct that promote cooperation, fair institutions, and right relations among individuals and groups. The norms are based on a broad interpretation of what constitutes the good and the right in society. The norms can be seen as proposals for how to evaluate and regulate conduct. As proposals, they depend upon recognition and support from citizens.

This was my reply to the ontological question of what ethics *is*. In this chapter, the topic changes from the ontology of ethics to the psychology and epistemology of ethics. I consider how we develop interpretations of what is good and right with regard to social conduct and practices. I distinguish ethical interpretation as a form of intentional understanding of objects – an understanding that attributes purposes, intentions, and other mental traits to objects. Ethical interpretation focuses on the intentions and purposes that social groups and practices should have, or honor. It seeks to see forms of conduct and types of practice in their best light, from an ethical and public perspective. These normative interpretations employ complex conceptual schemes consisting of "non-rigid" concepts.

Why do I emphasize interpretation in a book on ethics? The reason stems from the discussion in Chapter 1. Ethics is not a neutral, facts-only description of a practice nor is it a description of pre-given moral facts existing independently in the world. Ethics should not be conceived of as unchanging "content" – a static code of principles, or a system of absolute truths apart from human interests or history. Instead, ethics refers to a view of what rules people should follow to govern their conduct; a set of proposals on what norms our social practices should follow. When we do ethics, we do not describe uniquely existing moral facts, we propose and prescribe. We *interpret* the normative purposes of practices, and we propose conduct-regulating rules for action. Other interpretations are always possible, and we can never say in advance which proposals will gain the recognition and support of society. By stressing the interpretive nature of ethics, we direct our attention to the all-too-human, practical, non-absolute, and social nature of ethics.

Ethics, as we will see, is a meta-practice – the practice of proposing, altering, and debating the norms of other practices. Ethics is one of many interpretive practices (or enterprises), such as law, and disciplines in the humanities and social sciences. By calling ethics a "normative interpretation" I point to a distinct and far-reaching view of ethics. I mean more by that phrase then the plain fact that interpreting occurs in ethics, e.g., we interpret principles. I argue that the *entire* enterprise, from top to bottom, and across time, is interpretive, in a special and important sense. Radical implications follow from adopting this view of ethics.

Meta-ethics, then, needs a clear theory of interpretation, and of the interpretation of social practices. However, a clear philosophy of interpretation is a challenging intellectual project. It must discuss complex concepts such as truth, evidence, facts, human understanding, and intentionality. Philosophy is necessary because common sense is not a good guide for clarifying what we mean by interpretation. Because everyday life is redolent with interpretation, we mistakenly think that interpretation is easy to do – everyone does it every day. Interpretations occur to me without effort. The ubiquity of interpretation prompts people to be skeptics of the activity. They dismiss all interpretations as equal – all are equally subjective. People say, "this is just an (or, just *your*) interpretation," or "one interpretation is as good as any other," or "in science we deal with facts, in ethics it is just interpretations."

This skepticism is itself an interpretation, an interpretation of interpretation. It is not without its own problems. The skeptics are, like all humans, up to their ears every day in interpreting their experience – and defending their interpretations. Why do they bother to justify their interpretations if every interpretation is as good as every other interpretation?

I take it that this extremely skeptical view of interpretation is at least contestable. We need a more nuanced understanding of interpretation. I cannot review the enormous literature on interpretation. I refer to that literature to the extent necessary for readers to understand my position. My exposition begins with the type of conceptual schemes used in ethics, and follows with an analysis of types of intentional interpretation. The second half of the chapter uses these ideas to delve into the nature of normative interpretation in ethics.

This chapter's philosophical discussion of conceptual schemes and interpretation will clear the ground for what follows in the rest of the book. For example, Chapter 3 will develop the implications of Chapters 1 and 2 for our idea of ethics, while the discussion of "non-rigid" concepts and holistic conceptual schemes will be used to develop the key notion of integrated media ethics in Chapter 6.

Conceptual Schemes

Concepts

Interpretations, like all intellectual tools, are creatures of concepts. More precisely, they are creatures of networks of concepts, or conceptual schemes. My interpretation of Boccherini's Cello Concerto in G Major depends on a network of concepts on the meaning and intent of many

Theoretical Foundations

passages. My interpretation of a group of stars as the Great Dipper is based on a network of ideas about our galaxy and ideas about how we perceive stars from Earth. The way ideas link together has been a fascination for philosophers from at least the association psychology of the 17th-century empiricists (see Locke 1959 [1689]). Therefore, I prepare us for a discussion of interpretation by discussing concepts and conceptual schemes.

A good way to look at something as abstract as a concept is think about its mental function. Concepts help the mind organize and categorize the objects of our experience (Anglin 1977, 1). We group things into categories and label them with a term, such as "dog" or "laptop." Categorization helps us to anticipate what is to come by noting how types of things are likely to behave. Without concepts, we would encounter a confusing barrage of ever-new stimuli. To know the concept of a tree is to be able to pick out trees, expect trees to have certain properties, and to make assertions about trees. To grasp a concept is to know how to apply it correctly in various contexts; and to apply it correctly shows that one grasps the concept. We speak, in an almost tangible sense, of "grasping" and "wielding" a concept the way we would grasp or wield a hammer. We "wrestle" with concepts and struggle to make them clear. These are metaphors to describe our engagement with ideas.

There are many theories about concepts. Locke seemed to regard ideas as images in the mind, viewed by introspection. Kant saw the mind as containing innate categories for organizing our intuitions of things in space and time. In psychology, the traditional approach is to think of concepts as clear and rigid – the concepts support terms that apply unequivocally to a clearly defined set of instances, and have clearly defined meanings (Anglin 1977, 6–7). But there are other views. The reply to the traditional approach (Neisser 1967; Fodor 1972) is that most natural concepts of trees or persons are "fuzzy" and somewhat ill-defined. One alternative to the idea of concepts as rigid is prototype or schema theory (Posner 1973). Instances are compared to a prototype of "best examples." When a person is presented with instances of a concept, she creates an internal representation of the central tendencies of the instances which guides the classifying of new instances. Some theories think a concept must have, in addition to prototypes, a "core" meaning. The core of "odd number" is defined mathematically in terms of indivisibility, although we may use prototypes of odd numbers to quickly identify instances.

Other psychologists, from Piaget (1962) to Nelson (1974) have stressed the importance of function in learning concepts. For a child, the term "ball" is learned functionally as something one can roll, throw, kick, and use to play games. Minsky (1975) defined concepts as "frames" or symbolic structures that specify, for a concept, various slots and default values. For instance, the frame representing the concept "whale" would have the slot "size" and the value "large." Default values do not define concepts rigidly into necessary and sufficient conditions. They express typical expectations. Meanwhile, connectionist approaches in computational psychology think of concepts in terms of brain patterns – patterns of activation distributed over neuron-like units in a highly structured network. A concept is not stored in the brain (Rumelhart et al. 1986) the way data is stored in a digital computer. The concept "emerges when needed from the interaction of large numbers of connected nodes" (Thagard 1992, 25). We will see, later, that the idea of "fuzzy" or non-rigid concepts is crucial to understanding how ethical concepts can have multiple meanings that evolve over time and come to apply to new objects.

The moral of these approaches is that concepts are part of complex, dynamic structures.

These mental structures contain several types of linkages and connections among concepts. For example, Thagard (1992, 29–30) explains that concepts contain: (a) kind-hierarchies and part-hierarchies. Our concept of animal is linked by kind-hierarchies to the concept of bird, mammal, and reptile, and the concept of bird is related to the concept of a part, e.g., a beak. Moreover, the concept of bird is related to kinds of birds such as the canary and the blue jay. These kinds are linked to examples. The concept of canary includes the instance "Tweety" and we know, through our conceptual scheme, that Tweety is an animal. Our concepts are also related by property relations, e.g., our concept of canary is linked to the property of being yellow. Concepts also contain: (b) a core of criteria or properties that define the category; (c) prototypes or paradigmatic examples of the concept, e.g., Socrates as the prototype of a philosopher; (d) inferences to other ideas. For instance, if we see the head of a large whale appear above water, we infer it has a tail under the water; (e) causal knowledge and beliefs about the object. We judge

Theoretical Foundations

a man who jumps into a swimming pool at a party as drunk because it causally explains the behavior; and (f) synonyms and antonyms. If we accept this view of concepts then it is difficult to separate the understanding of a concept from the understanding of a cluster of related concepts, or a conceptual system. And it is difficult to separate the meaning of concepts from beliefs about the object in question.

These connections foreshadow our discussion in the next chapter that the best metaphor for a conceptual system, including a conceptual system in ethics, is that of a web of concepts.

Concepts undergird our use of language. What concepts are to mentality, meanings are to language. Concepts give meaning to terms, phrases, sentences, and sets of sentences. The meaning of general terms such as "whale" or "quanta" is given by our concepts of whales and quanta. Without concepts, language would have no meaning. Historically, theories of linguistic meaning explained the "meaning of meaning" as a combination of extension and intension. A term's referential meaning consists of the objects that fall under the term as examples. The extension of "dog" is the dogs that run about the world. The term's intensional meaning is the term's concept, which says something about what dogs are, and therefore guides us in calling something a dog or not. Intension, through concepts, determines extension.[1] The intensional meaning of a term may vary although its extension remains the same. A Hindu and myself may agree on the extension of "cow" but have different concepts of a cow. Extensions don't fix meanings. Meanings, via concepts, fix extensions.

Concepts perform the same meaning-giving function for sentences (or propositions) as they do for terms. To grasp a concept entails not only being able to use it to apply a term but also being able to use it when asserting propositions and sentences. Propositions are composed of concepts that we express in language and in thought, the way "men," "bachelor," and "married" help to form the proposition, "All bachelors are unmarried men." The intensional meaning of a declarative sentence is the proposition it expresses; its extension is the fact in the world that it describes. The intensional meaning of a sentence determines its truth conditions – the conditions that must exist for the sentence to be true. The intensional meaning of a sentence fixes its extension. The meaning of "snow is white" determines that it is true if snow is actually white.

Finally, concepts and their schemes explain what we mean by a "viewpoint" or "perspective." Talk of how individuals have their own ways of "seeing" the world, and their own narratives about what they experience, is ubiquitous. Here, having different views of one and the same world is compared to being able to perceive one and the same object from different perspectives. The mechanism behind plural viewpoints is the conceptual scheme (see Case 1997; Lynch 1998). To adopt a different scheme is to "see" the world differently.

Models of conceptual schemes

Three models of conceptual schemes have been influential – the models of Kant, Quine, and Wittgenstein. The idea of a conceptual scheme is implicit in their writings even if they do not use the term. Kant argued that the mind's faculty of "understanding" shapes all of our sensory experience. The mind makes sense of our experience by organizing it according to such supremely general categories, such as the categories of space, time, and causality. We don't learn these categories. They are innate to all minds. We are born with the capacity to see experience as occurring in space and following in time, and to see objects related as cause to effect. The categories are not categories of specific objects. Rather the categories make possible *any* experience at all. Quine, focusing on language and science, was not interested in Kantian innate concepts that make experience possible. He was interested in how terms and sentences combine into linguistic structures (or conceptual schemes), such as scientific theories, laws, and hypotheses. He saw our knowledge of the world as webs of terms and sentences (or beliefs), not in terms of individual terms and sentences. Therefore, he thought the linguistic structures – hypothesis, theory, or crucial principle – were confirmed by agreeing with experience, existing beliefs, and other factors. The scheme as a whole faces the "tribunal" of experience and logic in a holistic manner. He went so far as to claim that the totality of what we know in science is a man-made "fabric" or web of sentences we regard as true. It "impinges on experience at the edges" (1953, 42) and no parts are immune from revision.

Wittgenstein's view on schemes of concepts, as found in his *Philosophical Investigations*, was not a view of how experience is possible

Theoretical Foundations

or how scientific theories are confirmed. He wanted to know how people actually use concepts in everyday life, and as expressions of a "form of life."[2] For our purposes, two parts of his investigations are important – his idea of non-rigid concepts, to be explored later, and his view of how conceptual schemes are organized into basic and less basic concepts and beliefs. A basic belief is one that is more general than other beliefs and is used to support other more specific beliefs. In physics, our basic beliefs concern the laws of interaction between matter and energy. Darwin's theory of natural selection grounds many other beliefs and theories in evolutionary biology. In ethics, our basic beliefs are principles of the common good and justice. For example, my belief in the moral equality of all people supports my belief in human rights, and the latter supports my specific beliefs about what laws and policies are immoral or violations of human dignity.

In his interest in basic beliefs, Wittgenstein was similar to Quine. The latter argued that no beliefs in any conceptual scheme are absolute and totally immune from revision, or falsification. Future experience can always show our most central beliefs to be inadequate or out of date. What Quine had in mind when he talked about basic beliefs were general principles of science and logic. Even long-held and supremely important scientific laws were not granted an absolute status by Quine. Instead he regarded basic beliefs as those parts of our conceptual scheme that are more remote from direct empirical confirmation or disconfirmation. And they are beliefs we are less willing to change and alter, given that changing such a belief entails large-scale revisions to other beliefs. Imagine that our understanding of gravity or of sub-atomic forces were shown to need revision, or replacement. Or that Darwin's principle of natural selection was shown to be false. In such cases, the entire fields of physics and evolutionary biology would have to be recast. None the less, Quine believed that immunity from revision and what is basic is a matter of degree, and relative to our current conceptual schemes.

Wittgenstein's treatment of basic beliefs also presumed that "basic" did not mean absolute or unchangeable. Wittgenstein used a powerful metaphor to explain how worldviews are organized. He compared a worldview to a river bed where certain "hardened propositions" function as the bed of the river, giving a form that contains and guides the less basic and ever-changing beliefs which "flow" over them. Even

Ethics as Normative Interpretation

the river bed may shift – nothing is immune to revision. Yet we can still structurally distinguish at any given time between the movement of the water on the river bed and a shift in the bed itself (1969, 15e). There is no hard and fast distinction between the elements of a conceptual scheme. The river bed affects the water flow yet the changing course of the water can alter the river bed. Similarly, our basic and non-basic beliefs, as they change, will influence each other; and as our beliefs alter, so do our concepts.

The idea of conceptual schemes in this book borrows from Quine and Wittgenstein. From Quine, I take the notion of webs of belief (and sentences) that confront experience as a whole. From Wittgenstein, I take the metaphor of a river bed to explain my notion of basic ethical principles. The metaphor explains my assertion in Chapter 1 that beliefs about ethical universals are basic not because of the nature of universals. They are basic because they perform a crucial role in ethical conceptual schemes – they function as basic beliefs. Beliefs in universals form the river bed for less basic ethical beliefs.

Interpretation and Purpose

Given this overview of conceptual schemes, we can take up the topic of interpretation. An interpretation is a way of conceiving an object or process – some part of the world. An interpretation employs concepts as mental tools. The concepts are part of conceptual schemes organized on the basis of logical hierarchies, causal links, and which beliefs are basic, as explained above. But what is distinctive about interpretations as conceptual schemes, especially interpretations of practice? Let's begin with the idea of how we understand anything.

Understanding and interpreting

Two types of understanding   At the heart of all inquiry, thinking, and interpreting is the desire to understand something. All forms of human understanding are of two types: non-intentional and intentional. Non-intentional understanding seeks knowledge of objects, events, natural forces, and processes that are thought to lack intention and purpose.

Theoretical Foundations

Intentional understanding seeks knowledge of objects, events, and processes that are thought to have intentions, purposes, and goals. Gravity is a non-intentional phenomenon; human action is intentional. Let me elaborate on this distinction:

Non-intentional understandings: These understandings use descriptions and causal explanations that do not posit purposes or intentions in the object of inquiry. Take, for instance, explanations of mechanical objects. My watch keeps time through the interactions of physical parts according to physical laws. I do not posit mental agents to keep the hands of the watch moving, the way that medieval thinkers posited spirits to keep the planets rotating. The designer of the watch intended it to keep time, but I don't think the watch intends to keep time. Similarly, rivers flow to the sea through a natural, non-intentional process. Despite what poets say, the river is not "trying" to reach the sea. If my car breaks down as I drive to the airport, I do not treat it as an intentional agent. I don't berate the car for intentionally breaking down, perhaps to test my patience. Rather, I seek a non-intentional causal explanation in the malfunctioning of mechanical parts. Every day, we use a non-intentional "folk physics" to understand the objects about us.

Intentional understandings: These understandings comprehend intentional objects and processes, from the actions of animals to works of art. These understandings use explanations that posit intentions, meanings, purposes, and goals. In ordinary life, we use an intentional approach to comprehend the conversation of my friend, or the actions of a stranger. What did she intend by saying *x*? What is the stranger trying to do? In the humanities and the social sciences, we use intentional terms and methods to explain the practices of foreign cultures, the meaning of historical events, and the intent of a novelist.

The distinction between the two understandings has been discussed for centuries. The success of natural science prompted writers to exalt non-intentional inquiry over all else. In response, writers defended the intentional approach of the social sciences and philosophy by claiming that these enterprises achieved a special "understanding" or *verstehen* (Henrik Von Wright 1971, 5).

Despite these disputes, I use the distinction for several reasons. First, whatever philosophers and scientists say about the distinction, most people understand their world using these two types of understanding, often switching from one to the other, or combining the approaches. When I remark on the odd behavior of my friend, whose wife has recently died, I may interpret his conduct as due to mental stress. I explain his impatience with and avoidance of people in intentional terms, as a deliberate strategy based on his anger at the world, or perhaps it is based on his need for solitude. I say he suffers from grief or trauma. He should seek psychological counseling. Then, a minute later, I may switch to non-intentional discourse, talking about the physiological basis for my friend's grief and how drugs might help. I combine intentional and non-intentional elements in a discourse about my friend.

Some time ago, Dennett (1978, 3–22) analyzed how we adopt different interpretive "stances" toward objects. He noted that we can move between three types of explanation – an intentional stance that treats the object as intentional; a design stance that explains the object by its internal design; and a physical stance that focuses on the materials that make up the object. The stances are useful in interpreting everything from human action to a computer's program. For example, we could explain my friend's grief-stricken conduct by focusing on his mental states, or his psychological design (subconscious psychological functions or patterns of brain activity), or physical processes in his nervous system. Interestingly, we often continue to use intentional language to explain non-intentional processes, such as what my laptop is "trying to do" when I click on a program link. We apply intentional concepts because such language is familiar and less technical than the "real" explanation in computer language.

To anticipate misunderstandings, let me add some caveats. I do not assume that the application of "intentional" and "non-intentional" is always clear. The development of robots and computers creates grey areas where we are not sure whether to say the computer thinks or has intentions. Moreover, I am not saying that these forms of understanding cannot (or should not) work together to explain phenomena. My naturalism holds that they can and should cooperate. For instance, the scientific tracking of brain patterns can shed light on our mental and emotional life, and therefore our intentional understanding of ourselves (Davidson 2013).

Theoretical Foundations

What is interpretation?

To interpret anything is to understand it in a certain way through the use of concepts, e.g., noise on the tracks signals an approaching train. "Interpretation," as I use the term in this chapter, is not a vague, implicit, or pre-linguistic understanding of something. I have a tacit, bodily understanding of how to ride a bicycle but it is not an interpretation. To have an interpretation of x is to arrive at some definite, explicit understanding of the object, and to be able to express it in concepts and language. Interpretations are conscious understandings, usually in the form of a judgment, hypothesis, or theory. This approach does not deny that interpretation at the conscious level may use and rework unconscious or intuitive materials.[3] We arrive at some of our interpretations quickly, as when we interpret the meaning of a sentence or the trustworthiness of a stranger. We arrive at other interpretations carefully, by analyzing our judgments and data.

In its simplest form, an interpretation is an act of categorization. We understand x as an instance of F. We perceive x as a lion in the dark, we interpret x as a mocking gesture, we think y is dangerous. Or, interpretation is a more complex act of understanding such as developing a scientific theory. For instance, we interpret light as quanta of energy, but this is based on a complex physics of energy. We theorize that Johnny's inability to learn is due to an attention deficit disorder. In ethics, we interpret an action as a duty according to Kantian ethics. We understand an action as violating the principle of not stealing. More abstractly, we interpret the concepts that constitute our interpretations. We debate interpretations of duty or attention deficit disorder.

Interpreting involves a *choice* of concepts, even though in some cases we may feel there is only one way to interpret something, e.g., to interpret certain stimuli as an approaching dog. Yet, even for simple perceptions, there is an unspoken background of possible choices. To understand something before me as a sparrow, and to utter the observation sentence, "This is a sparrow," is to place the stimuli under one specific concept, and *not* to place them under the concept of a robin, or under the idea of an unidentified flying object. There are plenty of possible interpretations of objects, given our conceptual creativity. Drawings that are no more than a series of dots can be seen as a duck or as a rabbit (Wittgenstein 1958, 194). My backyard digging can be interpreted by neighbors as the burying of a body, preparing the ground for flowers, or the search for a leaking pipe. We can interpret mental problems as a sign of personal weakness, as God's punishment on us, or as a chemical imbalance in the brain. A firm statement by a political leader at the United Nations on the dangers of global warming can be interpreted as empty words to deflect criticism, or as preparing the public for a tough new environmental law.

We interpret effortlessly and almost without notice. We interpret a few black streaks on the sea's horizon as smoke from a ship. We quickly interpret a friend's sharp remark as sarcastic – recognizing that the remark's meaning is the opposite of what he literally says. We interpret images on the television screen as a news report. Interpretation plays a major role in the humanities and the social sciences. As Dworkin (2011, 123) reminds us, historians interpret events, psychoanalysts interpret dreams, sociologists and anthropologists interpret societies and cultures, lawyers interpret documents, critics interpret poems, plays, and pictures, priests interpret sacred texts, and philosophers interpret "contested concepts."

In *The Invention of Journalism Ethics* (2005), I developed a theory of interpretation from within my neo-pragmatist view of inquiry. I called it "holistic interpretation." My first premise was that we are *always* interpreting. Interpretation is ubiquitous for two reasons: First, interpreting is all but synonymous with conceptualization and cognition. Second: we have no direct, cognitive contact with reality. We make cognitive contact with the world but it is never unmediated. Contact occurs through the mental representation and interpretation of embodied agents pursuing purposes in concrete contexts. Our behavior consists of responses to a world, responses that are mediated by our interpretations of stimuli and many other things. Some of this mediation is hard-wired, and seems unmediated. Stimuli must be quickly understood as threatening or pleasurable. I duck bullets without logic. Yet even our seemingly direct perceptions of objects are the result of the processing of stimuli by our perceptual system.

Interpretation is a complex and holistic activity. It is misunderstood if interpretation is thought to be the imposing of concepts (or mental schemes) upon uninterpreted "raw" material, the way a cookie-cutter gives form to dough. On this view, the non-interpreted material is stimuli picked up by our senses. Interpretations are cookie-cutters giving different forms to one and the same sensory material. On this view, interpretation is a separate, independent, and subjective act of the mind, a mental activity that works in regular ways upon hard data provided by observation. Interpretation is located within a two-tiered theory of mind. The mind directly perceives objects (the dough) and then sends these sensuous materials to the interpretive part of the mind (the cookie-cutter).

Psychologically, this is an over-simplification of how the mind works. We have little knowledge of what the senses provide except as data that is already conceptualized, at least to some extent. The color red is perceived not as a red datum but the red color of my car. We experience a fusion of perceptual stimuli and concept. The materials of interpretation are themselves the products of information processing, and conceptualization. Moreover, many interpretations do much more than form concepts from stimuli. They bring together a variety of materials – stimuli, values, beliefs, and other interpretations. Also, the interpretive scheme may change over time. The metaphor of a cookie-cutter does not do justice to interpretation.

Cognitively, we never get outside the circle of interpretation. But this doesn't mean we do not interpret a world external to us. We are not solipsists, living within our minds. We are embodied agents who live in this world. But the materials we have for understanding it are mediated materials – beliefs, theories, views, and perceptions.

The ubiquity of interpretation leads me to blur the distinction between understanding and interpreting. Rather than say we approach the world through intentional and non-intentional understandings, we can just as easily say we approach the world through intentional and non-intentional interpretations. On my view, all understandings are interpretations, whether they are scientific theories or political views. My view differs from that of Dworkin, who divides human understanding into non-intentional scientific explanation on one side and interpretation on the other. Interpretation is limited to the intentional sphere. Dworkin (2011, 123) treats interpretation "as one of the two great domains of intellectual activity," a "full partner with science to create an "embracing dualism of understanding." On my view, there is no dualism. Non-intentional scientific explanation is a distinct and powerful form of interpretation. Intentional historical explanation is also a distinct and powerful form of interpretation.

Types of intentional interpretation

To understand ethics we need to distinguish the types of intentional interpretation. The most important difference is the difference between interpreting what individuals do, and interpreting what individuals do as part of groups and traditions.[4]

Interpreting what individuals do

Linguistic interpretation: The primary example of linguistic interpretation is the interpretation of everyday communication. We interpret what people say to us in face-to-face conversation and in other forms of communication. We figure out the meaning that the speaker intends to communicate. We don't treat a person's conversation as meaningless sounds or as physiological responses. Here we try to read the speaker's mind – the meanings that are part of his intentions and mental life.

Creative interpretation: This interpretation seeks to understand the meaning of the symbolic creations of individuals. The creations include books, poems, plays, and symphonies. Interpreting these works differs from interpreting what another person says to me. The object of interpretation is more objective and complex. Instead of interpreting sounds coming from someone's mouth, creative works exist independently from the authors and artists that produced them. The paintings hang on museum walls; the plays are acted out on stage; the symphonies are written down on paper and are played by orchestras before audiences. The products are complex and heavy with a plurality of possible meanings. As a result, the works are able to be interpreted by many people over many years. Traditions of interpretation spring up and often conflict.

In creative interpretation, we are not interpreting something internal to the author, e.g., the meaning in her mind when she created the work. Instead, we interpret a product that is external and available to examination by others. It is public. This externality implies that the symbolic work can be interpreted in ways that go beyond (or are different from) what the author supposedly intended. Its meaning is, to a large degree, independent of (or not reducible to) what was in the author's mind at the moment of creation. The author's intentions in creating the work are important but not unquestionable, and they are not the only source of interpretation. For example, what Raphael intended to say by his High Renaissance frescos in the Vatican is interesting and informative. But many influences may have been unconscious to the author. Also, his work can be viewed, and reinterpreted through, the ever-evolving lens of social, cultural, artistic, and political theories of this period of time. Creative interpretation is not just the reading of the author's mind, even if it were possible to do so. Interpretations may depart from the author's stated intentions.

Interpretation of individual actions: We interpret the bodily movements of people (and other intentional beings) as meaningful by adopting Dennett's intentional stance. John's fist in my face means he is angry with me. A student slouching in his desk during math class expresses an indifference to or boredom with the subject matter. These interpretations assume that the behavior is not coerced or accidental. They are actions with intent and purpose. There is a world of difference between someone accidentally tripping into me at a party and causing my drink to spill over several people, and my intentionally spilling a drink over the same people.

Interpreting what groups do

Interpreting societies: We interpret societies and cultures, including smaller groups that make up society. We examine their common goals, intentions, and understandings of the world. We interpret their social activities. Anthropology is redolent with attempts to explain cultures. Governments hire analysts to interpret other nations and their leaders.

Interpreting practices: Interpreting what groups do includes interpreting an important part of any society – the practices of professional (and other) groups. Interpretations of practice can be empirical or normative.

a. Empirically, sociologists, historians, and others describe and explain the genesis, current state, and future of certain important practices found in the professions, scientific inquiry, religious communities, civic groups, and institutions.

It is important to note that social activities are not practices (or enterprises). Attending a concert or going to a friend's party is a social activity but it is not a practice. However, representing individuals in court is part of the practice of law. Social conduct becomes a practice when members of a group join in a common effort to reach certain objectives and to promote distinct and valued ways of acting. Usually, practices apply special methods and knowledge which require a range of people with expertise and skills. Practices often occur within institutions and enterprises, e.g., within the justice system, or within corporations. Being the CEO of McDonald's restaurants is to practice certain skills within a business enterprise. Acting as the anchor of NBC Nightly News constitutes practicing journalism within a media enterprise. The Pope leads a world-wide religious enterprise with many component practices. Given these roles and practices, empirical interpretation sets out to describe what the practices achieve or are trying to achieve, the factors that influence the practice, the laws that limit the practice, and the history (and future) of the practice.

b. Normative interpretation builds upon empirical interpretation. It begins with established practices. It asks: What is the value or purpose of such practices? What are some paradigmatic examples of good practice and who are the practice's best practitioners?

For most practices, normative interpretation has already taken place, and continues to occur. Practitioners are aware they should conform to certain norms that are expressed often in codes of ethics. The code expresses a general interpretation of the purpose of the practice. A practice is normative in this sense if it explicitly articulates and follows a set of norms, which are generally considered to be ethical and of value. Normative interpretation also occurs when the practitioners reflect on existing norms, improve upon them, and promote them. These practitioners do not take existing norms for granted. Therefore, a practice is normative in this second sense when it studies norms and how they apply in various situations.

One and the same practice can follow, study, and promote norms. It depends on the practitioners' current focus and aim. When practitioners follow norms, their aim is not the promotion of norms (or normative behavior) per se. The aim is to achieve whatever goals the practice happens to have. Accountants want to achieve accurate accounting results, journalists want to report important stories, emergency ward doctors want to save lives. Norms are part of the methods by which these practices responsibly achieve their goals. When practitioners (and others) study the practice, the norms become the focus of attention. However, when we promote parts of society's normative sphere, we do more than follow or study norms. We promote and enforce. A professor of law who studies the norms of her country's legal system is not acting normatively in the third sense. However, if the professor of law becomes a judge in a courtroom, she joins a norm-enforcement practice in the third sense. In fact, the courtroom judge participates in all three senses of the normative practice of law. She follows certain legal norms in hearing cases; she studies laws and rulings pertinent to the cases; and, in judging and sentencing, she participates in law enforcement.

Similarly, good journalists follow the norms of media practice and, from time to time, stop to study and question their norms. Journalists may attend conventions where normative issues are studied, or they may attend media ethics courses, or they may study and promote norms as part of a newsroom committee established to create new set editorial guidelines. Journalists may also participate in professional journalism associations such as the Society of Professional Journalists in the United States or the Press Council of India. These associations differ from newsrooms that follow norms in producing journalism. These associations study and promote norms.

From this analysis, we can now begin to see how ethics and interpretation fit together. Ethics is the normative interpretation of group practices. It interprets practices normatively in all senses: part of ethics is following norms, part of it is studying norms, and part of it promoting certain norms which are part of society's normative sphere. Essential to all three activities is an underlying interpretation of the nature and value of the normative practice in question. Hence, interpretation will be central to these activities.

Some readers may presume that my categorization of interpretation draws a clear line between practices, on the one hand, and our attempts to interpret them, on the other. Not so. To the contrary, practices, even if not particularly reflective in spirit, or not interested in the study of its norms, have interpretations embedded in them. Practices do not exist independently of interpretation and interpreters. In many cases, the interpreters are themselves practitioners, following the very norms they interpret, such as journalists or doctors.

Explicit interpretation – the conscious articulation and study of a practice – is *itself* a practice. Over time, these ways of interpreting practices become traditions or schools of interpretation, such as a Freudian interpretation of Greek myths, or a "social responsibility" interpretation of journalism's ethical duties, or, outside ethics, the New Orleans tradition of interpreting the blues. Interpretation of normative practices is social, not individualistic; worldly, not solipsistic. Even the medieval monk, writing commentaries on St. Augustine alone in his monastery, was connected to a history of biblical interpretation.

There is no interpretation in general or in the abstract. There are traditions for different types of interpretation for different kinds of intentional objects. We join existing traditions of interpretation and practices. We learn to interpret *Hamlet* because we join an interpretive practice already underway, complete with different views about what such interpretations are for. We learn their language, their ways of interpreting.

I now explain, in more detail, the elements of normative interpretation.

Normative Interpretations of Practice

Elements

Normative interpretations of practice are similar to interpretations of creative works because both interpret external things available to many people. They interpret worldly objects and practices that can be observed by many people.

The elements of normative interpretation are:

1. *Shared practice*: Interpretation starts with shared practice, as explained above.
2. *Shared understandings*: There is a shared understanding about the practice, often implicit and operating as a set of background

Theoretical Foundations

    presumptions. The shared understanding includes agreement on who its practitioners are and paradigmatic examples of the practice.

3. *Purpose of the practice at its best*: Interpretation of practice is anchored in some idea of the point of the practice. The point of the practice is its social and moral value, not its economic value or how it serves my self-interest. Moreover, the point of the practice is the purpose served by the practice at its best, and when properly conducted by practitioners.

An interpretation says what the practice should be, ideally. The purpose we assign to the practice influences what norms we embrace, and how we resolve issues. Dworkin (1986, 52) states: "A participant interpreting a social practice … proposes a value for the practice by describing some scheme of interests or goals or principles the practice can be taken to serve or express or exemplify."

4. *Explicitness of shared understandings*: For some practices, agreement on the practice and its purpose will be implicit, underdeveloped, or pre-theoretical. For other practices, practitioners can provide explicit and elaborate interpretations of their practice.
5. *Degree of consensus*: Interpretation of practice starts from shared ideas and ways of acting, but it does not require universal consensus. Nor does it presume that an interpretation can never be challenged or changed. Sometimes, a practice carries on despite significant disagreements in interpretation of the practice. For example, in journalism today, the practice persists despite substantial disagreement on almost all of the interpretive basics, from the point of the practice to who its practitioners are. The nature and degree of disagreement differ across disciplines, and across space and time.

Examples of normative interpretation

Practice of courtesy Dworkin provides many examples of normative interpretations in the course of developing his philosophy of law and ethics. His example of the practice of courtesy among members of an imaginary society is a good place to start (1986, 47).

Dworkin imagines a community that emphasizes courteous, deferential behavior. Citizens remove their hats in the presence of nobility and exhibit other displays of deference to community leaders. They engage in normative practice that seeks to respect people of a certain kinds. Let's call these people the assenters. They assent to the practice of courtesy as embodied in their culture.

For many years, the community does not question these norm-guided practices. The community, therefore, doesn't develop an explicit or elaborate interpretation of the practice. But gradually, some community members begin to question the practice. Let's call them the dissenters. They make three points: (1) Rules of courtesy don't just exist. They need a justification. It should be clear how the rules advance some good for the community. Simply following norms, or unstudied deference, is an unacceptable attitude. (2) Traditional acceptance of rules fails to see that certain rules, even if justified, can be misunderstood and misapplied. (3) Courtesy should be understood in a non-deferential manner, consisting of egalitarian displays of respect to all people.

What are the dissenters doing when they assert (1)–(3)? They put forward a different *interpretation* of the practice of courtesy, which affects their definition of the acceptable rules and practices they would accept. The dissenters interpret courtesy not as deference to authority but as an egalitarian sign of respect. They adopt a critical interpretive stance toward a common social practice, and its previously accepted norms. This impulse to reinterpret presumes that practices are human constructions. Purpose is something that humans give to practices. Hence, humans can interpret practices in different ways. Change is possible.

The difference between the dissenters and the assenters is not the difference between having and not having an interpretation of courtesy. It's a difference between two interpretations, one that is implicit and one that is explicit. The dissenters take time to examine the interpretation of courtesy as practiced and bring its assumptions to light. They also articulate, explicitly, a new interpretation. The assenters have a view about courtesy but it has been underdeveloped – until the dissenters question their assumptions. It is not hard to imagine the reasons for showing deference. Perhaps they believe courtesy expresses and helps to maintain a "natural" social order of nobility and deferential commoners.

Theoretical Foundations

The assenters and dissenters engage in normative interpretation, and they construct different interpretations. All the elements are there. They start from shared practice and shared understandings. The interpretations are views of the practice at its best. There are differences in the explicitness of the rival understandings and, in the end, less consensus. As Dworkin states (1986, 47): The dissenters "now try to impose meaning on the institution – to see it in its best light –and then to restructure it in light of that meaning." The dissenters not only want to show why courtesy exists, and how the rules are part of this social practice. They also ask what, properly understood, the practice requires, given its valued purposes. Dworkin adds (1986, 48): "Value and content have become entangled." Interpretations start to conflict and evolve. Perhaps other interpretations of courtesy will come forward over time. Some people may say that courtesy is not a crucial social value. It is a relic of the past, the "manners" of a previous era. Each step in the reform of a shared practice is interpretive not only of the practice but also of what the last phase of interpretation achieved. Traditions of interpretation evolve.

The dissenters show how interpretation can be a normative affair. The dissenters do not ask for an empirical description of what people do under existing rules of courtesy. They want to know how people *ought* to act. Yet their new interpretation is not an entirely new construction that rejects all aspects of the practice. Instead, it is normative re-construction, re-ordering, and re-understanding of what exists. They want to rationally construct the best ethical justification for the practice and use it as a guide. It is as if they tell themselves: "We have this practice. It is a fact, but parts of it seem unclear or questionable. And there is some dispute about its overall purpose. So we will re-construct how the practice *should* be understood and practiced. We will keep the best parts of it, but we can't guarantee that all rules will survive our normative analysis."

What is law? The practice of law is another example of the importance of normative interpretation. Here we have a shared practice that is centuries old and central to sound government. Although there are established laws and ways of practicing law, there is substantial tension between varying interpretations of the practice. Participants – judges, lawyers, professors, journalists, and citizens – debate the soundest interpretation of the purpose of law, and what it requires. Rival interpretations about the purpose of law become part of legal cases and judicial practice.

Take the question of whether (and how) judges should observe, in their judgments, "fidelity" to existing law. This depends on your view of the nature and purpose of law. Do judges discover the law they announce? Or, do they invent it? If they invent it, is invention a tyranny of the courts, a wrongful activism? For example, if someone says American judges in the 1960s discovered the illegality of school segregation along racial lines, this person appears to mean that segregation was illegal before any such ruling in a court. If a person believes that judges invent law (at least in some cases), then this person seems to hold that school segregation was not illegal before judges changed the law.

In the philosophy of law, rival theories interpret the purposes of law. As Dworkin notes (1986, 94–98), one view in Western societies is the "rule of law" conception. Legal practice exists to guide a government's use of its coercive powers in a society that takes seriously individual rights and liberties. New laws and judicial judgments should be consistent with laws and judgments in the past. This constitutes the rule of law, not the rule of individual leaders or power brokers. This consistency with past law is given a sharp interpretation in the "plain fact" view, for which fidelity to existing law is all. Follow the law. Don't try to improve on it. Opposed to the plain fact view is a host of other interpretations of the shared practice of law. They note that the plain view's dictum to follow existing law fails to address situations where a law is obviously bad, or where new developments in society demand new laws. A good judge prefers justice to law and extends law to apply to unexpected cases and issues. So what is the point of requiring legal decisions to honor past legal decisions?

One answer is the interpretation of law called conventionalism. It accepts the "rule of law" view. It sees the point of consistency with past decisions in the predictability of law and the procedural fairness that follows from many cases interpreted consistently. Conventionalism is not a "plain fact" view. It holds that where issues are new and not covered by past decisions, then judges are free to create new conventions.

Another view is legal pragmatism, which is skeptical that the common good is served by judges following past decisions in a strict manner. It proposes that judges should make whatever decisions are needed to advance the good of their community today and in the future. There is no reason to privilege past decisions. A third view, one that Dworkin advances (1986, 96), is "law as integrity." Law as integrity accepts the rule of law and consistency. However, it goes beyond conventionalism. Consistency with the past is not only good instrumentally – because it provides consistency and predictability and procedural fairness. It also makes a community "more genuine and improves its moral justification" for its exercise of political power.

These examples show that "What is law?" is answered by normative interpretations. The interpretations influence judicial decisions and practice. The debate is over what law *should* be. What seems like a factual question is actually a normative and interpretive question. Like the more concrete disputes about courtesy, disputes about law are also disputes among interpretations, all of which seek to describe legal practice in its best light. All theories start from agreed-upon examples of the practice and then seek "to achieve equilibrium between legal practice as they find it and the best justification of that practice" (Dworkin 1986, 90).

MacIntyre (2006, 58) has examined the relationship of normative analysis and practice. He says that schemes of evaluation are "devised and only fully intelligible" as parts of human activities and practices. Evaluative schemas are "practices of rational justification" embedded within larger practices aiming at truth or correct conduct. Practices develop through time in directions dictated by the conceptions of achievement internal to each, the achievement both of the goods specific to each particular type of practice and of excellence in pursuit of those goods" (MacIntyre 2006, 46).

Interpreting creative works   Elements of normative interpretation can be found outside of society's normative sphere and professional practices. Authors, painters, and musicians work within traditions of interpretation. The creative artists – and their critics – interpret what they are doing according to some view of what their practice is at its best, or what the practice requires. Political and social views influence the process. For example, Marxists may look more favorably than non-Marxists on the value of early Communist propagandist art, such as the street posters created in Russia before and during the revolution. Lovers of pop culture may revel in Warhol's depiction of everyday objects and celebrity, since they see the depiction of pop culture to be as valid a topic as the depiction of saints.

Normative interpretation can be found in popular cultures. Consider the idea of "seriousness" in art and music. It is a normative call on artists to create works that are not superficial but deep and serious. We find such a call in unlikely places. In the 1950s, rock and roll became as a dominant form of popular music, combining elements of country music and the blues. The music of Elvis Presley and Jerry Lee Lewis, and the early work of the Beatles and the Beach Boys, was not deep or serious. Its purpose was to entertain and to provide dance music. It was an accessible form of music with a great beat. Topics of songs were everyday experiences such as falling in and out of love, surfing at the beach, and driving fast cars.

But in the late 1960s, social problems prompted rock artists to "get serious" – to use their songs to challenge war, to criticize the "Establishment," to call for racial equality, and to promote a free-wheeling lifestyle of sex and drugs that rebelled against the stricter lifestyle of their parents. At the Woodstock rock festival in the state of New York in the late 1960s, it was expected that the performing musicians would be critical of the ongoing Vietnam War. Rock lost its roll. The music was reinterpreted as having a serious social purpose. The words of Bob Dylan and the Beatles were studied in university classrooms.

As rock artists were profiled by news media, the role of interpretive traditions was stressed. Interviewers of rock stars in alternative press venues such as *Rolling Stone* invariably asked the musicians about their roots – their musical influences. Typically, white guitarists such as Eric Clapton talked about how they learned to play by listening to the tradition of blues guitarists that stretched back to early black American musicians.

Anyone who doubts the influence of interpretive traditions in popular music need only participate in a blues jam in an American bar. The musicians share a tacit understanding of playing the blues correctly.

There are the familiar chord structures, the appropriate growling style of singing (an operatic voice is out of place), the lyrics about pain and suffering, and the practice of allowing each musician to "speak" through alternating solos. These are the shared ideas and values that make up an interpretation of what good blues is all about.

Interpretation, with its norms and ideals, lives *in* practice, shaping its expression.

How is ethics a practice?

How should we apply the normative interpretation of practice to ethics? First, is ethics a practice?

It is. The shared practices of ethics are our agreed-upon ways of following, studying, and promoting ethical norms. Ethics is the practice of acting ethically, across society or in smaller groups and professions. The practice is one of honoring rules and ways of acting.

In ethical practice, groups agree to a significant extent on what it means to act rightly, justly, virtuously, and fairly. Groups share practices that show respect for other people's rights and fulfill our duties to others. For instance, I show respect to other people's rights by not infringing on their privacy. As an employer, I show respect by allowing an employee a fair chance to answer allegations of corruption before dismissal. The origins and purpose of ethics are intimately bound up with this role of articulating shared norms and participating in practices that coordinate conduct within groups. We grow up in cultures where people share such practices, even if we do not agree with every practice, or with current definitions of what is just or right.

The centuries of ethical systems and theories are interpretations of ethics – to state its value and purpose, and to draw out the implications of that purpose for conduct.

It is possible, if difficult, to not participate in the ethics practice of a group. I may attempt to remain aloof from ethics discourse and its demands. I may say that I follow Nietzsche in being "beyond good and evil" and have only contempt for conventional moral practices. Yet nihilism in ethics is difficult to maintain. Even revolts against morality promote alternate values. Revolts may signal not nihilism but a questioning and redefining of a practice, as we saw with the dissenters.

Moreover, the necessity for norms in society makes it difficult for individuals to escape entirely the ethical expectations of others.

Ethics practice includes contestation and pluralism. All societies have mechanisms and practices by which certain values and ethical norms are taught and enforced. But, also, all societies have sub-groups, such as specific religious and ethnic groups, who practice their own specific ethics practices. The sub-groups challenge dominant ethical practices. Hence, perhaps we should speak in the plural about the ethical practices of society.

Interpretation in ethics

Now that we have examined examples of normative interpretation, we can proceed to apply it to ethics. Ethics interprets our shared ethics practices and shared ethical understandings in terms of the point of the practice. The purpose guides us as to what the practice requires in terms of rules, norms, and goods. This purpose-guided analysis happens on multiple levels.

On the first level, the interpretation of ethics in its best light dominates meta-ethics. Consider the aforementioned division of ethics into theories of the good, the right, and the virtuous. Is the purpose of ethics to realize goods, defend rights, or develop character? I have argued (2010) that the tripartite division of ethical theories fragments the unity of ethics. The purpose of ethics is to establish congruence among the good, the right, and the virtuous.

Normative interpretation also occurs when we are seeking the meaning of core ethical concepts. For example, David Johnston (2011) provides a historical analysis of competing interpretations of justice. His book as a whole is a work of normative interpretation. Johnston complains that the tendency to divide theories of justice into either (a) teleological or utilitarian theories of what promotes the good or (b) deontological theories of duties to others ignores other possible interpretations. The teleological-deontological division, he argues, has only been present since the eighteenth century. It ignores or is "neglectful" of the preceding 4,000 years of thinking about justice. Gathering insights from history, Johnston (2011, 1–5) advances a different interpretation of the criteria of justice – what promotes reciprocity in relations among persons.

Theoretical Foundations

Johnston explains how the meaning and importance of justice have changed. In pre-classical Athens, justice and fairness among citizens was less important than the excellence of a warrior because a society with little central government valued men willing to protect people. Justice was considered a secondary value, a matter of retribution and fairness in distributing benefits. Justice was a matter of how hierarchies of society treat each other. However, when Athens started to become a commercial power and experimented with democratic institutions, the popularity of warrior values declined. Less hierarchical notions of fair cooperation among many types of people became popular. Justice was redefined as a framework for cooperation among people with different interests, such as tradesmen, professionals, and so on. Plato's idea of justice in *The Republic* was a rejection of this less hierarchical notion of fair dealing. He conceived of a highly hierarchical society where people of certain natures occupied certain social positions for which they were "naturally" suited. The unequal relationships between the ruling philosophers, the military auxiliaries, and the ordinary people were relationships of command and obedience based on human nature.

Johnston's book traces the path of normative interpretation with regard to a central concept. Each new theory of justice is a new and major act of normative interpretation.

Purpose-driven interpretation also affects applied ethics – the application of ethical systems to policy and conduct. Applied interpretations include "consequential" theories such as utilitarianism. Utilitarian positions on issues, from distributive justice to prison reform, are anchored in an interpretation of what ethics should be. In the 17th and 18th centuries, Bentham, and the utilitarians who followed him, wanted to change how society thought about ethics. They wanted to change a prevailing normative interpretation. Rather than base ethics on religious or metaphysical knowledge, classic utilitarianism wanted to ground ethical decisions on a more scientific and impartial basis. Utilitarians appeal to utilities which they presume are naturally occurring things that can be counted and aggregated, such as pleasure or preferences. What the utilitarian in Bentham's time was doing was normative re-construction. In effect, utilitarians said: let's interpret ethics in this way: ethics is at its best when it promotes utility.

Application to journalism

Media ethics is a form of reflective engagement with the world (Ward 2010, 53–102). We begin by approaching journalism as a social practice with a collective responsibility, not as an activity of separate individuals following their own values (see Borden 2007). Journalism ethics is not so much about the norms that live inside each journalist's mind. It is about the public norms of a social practice. Any interpretation of journalism must start with shared values and understandings about the point of the practice. The interpretation follows the pattern for normative interpretation described above.

Ontologically, journalism's manner of existence is no different from other practices. It is a non-reducible part of a humanly constructed society based on collective intentionality and agreement. Journalists fall under society's attempt to regulate their conduct, legally and ethically, and to ascribe status functions and institutional responsibilities to journalists. The same applies to the broader notion of media ethics – the various social practices of advertising, marketing, and public relations. Media ethics is the name for the normative interpretation of these practices. The content of ethics – it principles – are proposals for conduct regulation.

Journalism is shot through with interpretation. Practitioners interpret events and publish reports. Journalists also interpret, implicitly or explicitly, what they are doing and the point of their work. Different interpretations of the point of journalism can be found among modern journalists, from Walter Lippmann and Edward R. Murrow to Hunter Thompson and current citizen journalists. The practitioners' self-identity is influenced by the culture of journalism. As discussed, to join in the activity of journalism is similar to joining a blues jam, where interpretation about competent and good practice lives *in* the practice. Meanwhile, interpretations are developed into meta-ethical theories about journalism and journalism ethics.

Journalism ethics, then, is doubly interpretive: it is the interpretation of an interpretive practice. In journalism ethics, almost every code begins with an inspirational preamble that states the social purposes of the practice. For instance, the preamble to the influential code of the US-based Society of Professional Journalists (SPJ) once stated:

> Members of the Society of Professional Journalists believe that public enlightenment is the forerunner of justice and the foundation of democracy. The duty of the journalist is to further those ends by seeking truth and providing a fair and comprehensive account of events and issues. Conscientious journalists from all media and specialties strive to serve the public with thoroughness and honesty. Professional integrity is the cornerstone of a journalist's credibility. Members of the Society share a dedication to ethical behavior and adopt this code to declare the Society's principles and standards of practice.

This preamble, which was revised in 2014, is a classic example of a normative interpretation of the aims of journalistic practice, of seeing journalism in its best light. However, the SPJ interpretation is only one of many interpretations of journalism within and without the United States.

Our new mindset should also stress the idea of ethics as emergent, contested, and engaged. Media ethics is a zone of contestation. Emergent media ethics is moving toward a mixed media ethics with a global mindset. Even when media ethics enters a stable period of consensus, its ethical values should always be up for challenge at any time. Media ethics is naturally and rightly contested.

Press theories It is important to see how my notion of normative interpretation is related to the more familiar notion of "press theories." Our understanding of journalism has been influenced by press theories, such as the theory of a free and democratic press. How do these press theories fit into my notion of normative interpretation of journalism? "Normative interpretation" and "press theory" are similar in meaning but they are not synonymous.

One of the most influential books on press theory is *Four Theories of the Press*, published by the University of Illinois Press (Siebert, Peterson, and Schramm 1956). Although the book is outdated, its categorization of media inadequate, and its methods criticized, it is still regularly referenced by media studies and used in media courses.

Four Theories defines "press" as all media of mass communication, but the book emphasizes professional journalism and the printed press. The four theories are Libertarian, Social Responsibility, Authoritarian, and Soviet Communist. However, the book revolves around the difference between (a) a libertarian view of a free press that informs the public and acts as a watchdog on government, and (b) an authoritarian view of the press as a regulated institution that serves the government and its policies. The Soviet Communist and Social Responsibility theories are treated as developments of authoritarian and libertarian theory, respectively.

How did *Four Theories* conceive of its task? *Four Theories* (1956, 1–2) sets out to describe and explain, factually, why the press is "as it is." Why does the press serve different purposes and take on different forms in different countries? The authors stress one factor: a country's social and political structure, and the philosophies that justify that structure. They pay attention to "certain basic beliefs and assumptions which the society holds" especially "the nature of man, the nature of the society and the state, the relation of man to the state, and the nature of knowledge and truth."

Differences in press systems are explained, ultimately, by differences between philosophies. For instance, a libertarian theory of society leads to a libertarian theory of the press. *Four Theories* is intellectualist in approach. It stresses the importance of ideas, reason, and intellectuals in forming, justifying, and sustaining social structures.

It seems uncharitable to point out the limitations of a book written about media some sixty years ago (Nerone 1995). Yet it is necessary because of the continuing influence of *Four Theories*. Here are some problematic features: its confusion of libertarianism with liberalism; its exclusion of many press theories around the world; its focus on professional print media; its strong intellectualist leanings – ignoring the non-philosophical causes of media development and the accidents of history. The book is a long normative argument for a free and responsible press in the Western tradition. Press theories such as Soviet Communist play the role of a "bogeyman" to be avoided (Nerone 1995, 181). Appearing in the middle of the Cold War, the book could not avoid becoming part of the political debate between West and East.

Theoretical Foundations

Let's consider a recent attempt to develop a better system of categories for press theory. *Normative Theories of the Media* (Christians et al. 2009) sees its role as going beyond liberal press theory, advancing a more nuanced system of categories than found in *Four Theories*, and creating "cognitive maps" for critiquing media practice.

Normative Theories of the Media, unlike *Four Theories*, begins with a normative approach to media systems. What is the role of journalism in a democratic society? A normative perspective moves from "factual landscapes toward values and objectives (2009, vii). The book's main contribution is to show how the four-category scheme of *Four Theories* should be replaced by a more complex scheme. The book argues that theorists need to refer to three levels of analysis when thinking about theories of the media.

The first level is "philosophical" because it identifies philosophies of life and society that are used to justify norms of communication. This is the level at which *Four Theories* does its work. But *Normative Theories* uses more and different philosophies – corporatist, libertarian, social responsibility, and citizen participation. These are "normative traditions" which are complex sets of values on how to carry out public communication in democracies. A corporatist view rests on a cosmic view of harmony in the universe, and harmony in society. It contains a communitarian view of media as cooperative partners in sustaining a harmonic society as a whole, and is "open" to democratic forms of communication. The libertarian view makes liberty primary, including freedom of expression. Social responsibility stresses the right of the public to expect their media to fulfill a range of public duties. The citizen participation model argues that media belong to the people and have "an emancipatory, expressive and critical purpose" (2009, 25).

On the second level are four models of democracy. There is pluralist democracy which, like libertarianism, stresses individual freedom, market economics, a maximally free press, and a limited state. Administrative democracy thinks democracies need to be led by experts, professionals, and other elites, upon whose activities the media report. Civic democracy thinks a healthy democracy needs citizens to be directly involved through media in public discussion and decision-making. Direct democracy favors government by plebiscites and referenda – a populism that is promoted by grassroots media voices, opinionated bloggers, and so on.

On the third level are the roles of journalism in democracy. The roles are: the monitorial role (the vigilant informer), the facilitative role (providing services to society), the radical role (critical of government), and the collaborative role (e.g., working with agencies to fight terrorism) (2009, 30–31). With these three levels of analysis, we have an approach to normative media analysis that is suitably complex for the real world of democratic communication.

So how does my concept of normative interpretation compare with the idea of press (or media) theory found in these two major works?

There are two similarities between the idea of press theory in *Four Theories* and my idea of normative interpretation. Both refer to philosophies of humans and society even if they operate only as background premises. Both are normative in using purposes and norms to distinguish theories. However, the differences are several. I do not put forward an intellectualist history of ideas to explain normative interpretations. What is right about the intellectualist approach is that it takes ideas seriously. But *Four Theories* places too much emphasis on the role of ideas, ignoring non-philosophical factors. Further, a normative interpretation contains more elements than a press theory in *Four Theories*. In *Four Theories*, a "theory" is a description of a handful of general features, such as a belief in negative freedom or the marketplace of ideas. A normative interpretation contains principles at various levels, specific norms, and other content.

The concept of normative interpretation is similar to the idea of media theory in *Normative Theories of the Media*. Both my normative interpretations and their normative theories aim at stating how the media should act. Both believe an adequate theory or interpretation is part of a normative tradition. Both believe any adequate view will be complex and contain many elements and levels. Finally, both approaches limit their inquiries to journalism in democracies.

A major difference is the practical intent of normative interpretations – their hope to guide actual practice and how it emerges from shared practice. Normative interpretations of journalism include codes of ethics or editorial guidelines. The promoter of an interpretation shows her favored interpretation would address ethical disputes. A normative interpretation is a practical, multi-use tool. Also, my holism leads to me regard the support for an interpretation to come from above (principles,

Theoretical Foundations

philosophy), below (success in guiding practice in actual situations), and in the middle (useful standards for forms of journalism). In *Four Theories* and *Normative Theories*, the main aim is theoretical and justification is top-down, originating in high-level principles. There is not much talk of support from below or in the middle.

Conclusion

This chapter has examined ethics as a form of normative interpretation – a normative interpretation of conduct and practice. In particular, it looked at ethics as the normative practice of social groups and professions, including journalism. The first part of the chapter showed how interpretations consist of intentional understandings that use conceptual schemes. The second part showed how conceptual schemes become normative interpretations. It listed the main elements of normative interpretation and discussed examples of normative interpretations. The third part showed how ethics is a form of normative interpretation where practices are viewed in their best light, and how such interpretation occurs in media ethics.

Now that we have the basic ideas of ethics and normative practice before us, we can examine the implications of adopting such notions. In Chapter 3, I note how looking at ethics as normative interpretation of practice changes our meta-ethics in general, and the meta-ethics of journalism.

Notes

1. However, for a famous discussion – and criticism – of the extension-intension tradition and its view that meanings are "in the head," see Putnam 1987.
2. Responding to an imagined interlocutor, Wittgenstein writes: "'So you are saying that human agreement decides what is true and what is false?' – It is what human beings *say* that is true and false; and they agree in the *language* they use. That is not agreement in opinions but in form of life" (Wittgenstein 1958, para. 24, p. 88e).

3. Kahneman (2013) stresses how humans, using System 1 thinking, can arrive quickly and without conscious effort, at specific intuitions or judgments. These intuitions are materials for further ethical reflection by System 2, which requires conscious mental effort. In this chapter, I am most interested in the conscious interpretations of System 2.
4. This scheme adapts Dworkin's categorization in *Law's Empire* (1986) and his more recent *Justice for Hedgehogs* (2010).

References

Anglin, Jeremy M. 1977. *Word, Object, and Conceptual Development*. New York: Norton.
Borden, Sandra. 2007. *Journalism as Practice: MacIntyre, Virtue Ethics and the Press*. New York: Routledge.
Case, Jennifer. 1997. "On the Right Idea of a Conceptual Scheme." *Southern Journal of Philosophy*, 35(1): 18.
Christians, Clifford G., Theodore L. Glasser, Denis McQuail, Kaarle Nordenstreng, and Robert A. White. 2009. *Normative Theories of the Media: Journalism in Democratic Societies*. Urbana: University of Illinois Press.
Davidson, Richard J. 2013. *The Emotional Life of Your Brain*. New York: Penguin.
Dennett, Daniel. 1978. *Brainstorms*. Montgomery, VT: Bradford Books.
Dworkin, Ronald. 1986. *Law's Empire*. Cambridge, MA: Harvard University Press.
Dworkin, Ronald. 2011. *Justice for Hedgehogs*. Cambridge, MA: Harvard University Press.
Fodor, Jerry. 1972. "Some Reflections on L. S. Vygotsky's *Thought and Language*." *Cognition*, 1(1): 83–95.
Henrik Von Wright, Georg. 1971. *Explanation and Understanding*. Ithaca, NY: Cornell University Press.
Johnston, David. 2011. *A Brief History of Justice*. Oxford: Wiley-Blackwell.
Kahneman, Daniel. 2013. *Thinking, Fast and Slow*. New York: Farrar, Straus, & Giroux.
Locke, John. 1959 (1689). *An Essay Concerning Human Understanding*. New York: Dover.
Lynch, Michael P. 1998. *Truth in Context: An Essay on Pluralism and Objectivity*. Cambridge, MA: MIT Press.
MacIntyre, Alasdair. 2006. *The Tasks of Philosophy*. Vol. 1 of *Selected Essays*. Cambridge: Cambridge University Press.

Minsky, Marvin. 1975. "A Framework for Representing Knowledge." In *The Psychology of Computer Vision*, edited by P. H. Winston, 211–277. New York: McGraw-Hill.

Neisser, Ulric. 1967. *Cognitive Psychology*. New York: Appleton-Century-Crofts.

Nelson, Katherine. 1974. "Concept, Word and Sentence: Interrelations in Acquisition and Development." *Psychological Review*, 8(1): 267–285.

Nerone, John, ed. 1995. *Last Rights: Revisiting Four Theories of the Press*. Urbana: University of Illinois Press.

Piaget, Jean. 1962. *The Origins of Intelligence in Children*. New York: Norton.

Posner, Michael. 1973. *Cognition: An Introduction*. Glenview, IL: Scott, Foresman.

Putnam, Hilary. 1987. "The 'Meaning' of Meaning." In *Mind, Language and Reality*, Vol. 2, *Philosophical Papers*, 215–271. Cambridge: Cambridge University Press.

Quine, Willard V. O. 1953. *From a Logical Point of View*. Cambridge, MA: Harvard University Press.

Rumelhart David, James McClelland, and the PDP Research Group. 1986. *Parallel Distributed Processing*. 2 vols. Cambridge, MA: MIT Press.

Siebert, Fred S., Theodore Peterson, and William Schramm. 1956. *Four Theories of the Press*. Urbana: University of Illinois Press.

Thagard, Paul. 1992. *Conceptual Revolutions*. Princeton, NJ: Princeton University Press.

Ward, Stephen J. A. 2005. *The Invention of Journalism Ethics: The Path to Objectivity and Beyond*. Montreal: McGill-Queen's University Press.

Ward, Stephen J. A. 2010. *Global Journalism Ethics*. Montreal: McGill-Queen's University Press.

Wittgenstein, Ludwig. 1958. *Philosophical Investigations*. Trans. G. E. M. Anscombe. New York: MacMillan.

Wittgenstein, Ludwig. 1969. *On Certainty*. Oxford: Basil Blackwell.

Chapter 3
Implications for Radical Ethics

It is time to take stock of how far we have come. What are the implications for ethics of adopting the notions put forward in Chapters 1 and 2? The implications, as a whole, amount to a fundamental reorientation of how we think and do ethics.

As I will explain below, this radical ethics contains the following ideas. Ethics is a normative interpretive practice that is: (1) holistic, non-foundational, and independent; (2) emergent and inventive; (3) naturally contested; and (4) a form of activism. I believe this constellation of ideas corrects for flaws in other views of ethics and provides the right mindset for constructing a new ethics for global interactive media.

Implication 1: Respect for Ethical Thinking

The view that ethics is normative interpretation encourages respect for thoughtful ethical discourse. For too long, many people have regarded ethics as a subjective domain of value judgments that are not much more than individual (or cultural) biases. They have no more objective

---

Radical Media Ethics: A Global Approach, First Edition. Stephen J. A. Ward.
© 2015 John Wiley and Sons, Inc. Published 2015 by John Wiley and Sons, Inc.

Theoretical Foundations

basis than personal likes or preferences. Ethics is portrayed as a domain where serious thinking, using evidence and logic, cannot occur.

The negative impact of this view is incalculable. Citizens enter public discourse with the view that ethics amounts to simply *stating* one's values, while ignoring or rejecting the views of others. This attitude does not encourage deliberation. Public discussion is caught in an awkward inconsistency. Reformers, politicians, policy experts, and citizens portray their views as an informed, rational, and objective approach to public issues. These views respond to ethical questions. Are the current laws on gay marriage correct or fair? Is the tax system just? Does the state have an obligation to assist unemployed workers? How much foreign aid should our country provide? Policies are praised or condemned as fair, cruel, generous, or disrespectful of minorities. However, if ethics is inherently subjective, what is the basis for such views? We cannot consistently hold that ethics is subjective yet maintain that our policies are justified from an objective perspective.

Ethics as an important interpretive social practice works against this skepticism.

Using what was said in Chapter 1, ethics as a practice is said to be ontologically subjective and observer-relative because its existence depends on human minds. Yet, once human society exists, the practice of ethics also exists, as much as any other social practice. Ethics, as I have said, is part of the practices that make up society's normative sphere. The practice of ascribing values is concrete and observable.

Ethics should be given the same respect as any other normative domain, such as law. We start from a social, external perspective, not a personal, subjective perspective. We start with the evident need for people in society to agree on ethical standards for cooperation.

Moreover, for any mode of conduct or social practice, ethics provides normative interpretations for discussion and application. Given certain agreed-upon ethical goals and norms, we have a rational basis for informed reflection on (a) the value of the goals of the practice, (b) the suitability of the principles of the practice, and (c) current applications of the principles to issues. Within this field of reflective engagement, there is, admittedly, no one absolute answer and no one answer that can garner universal consensus. But if we drop our demand for absoluteness and uniqueness, we can regard ethics as a discussion that is rational, non-arbitrary, and not simply subjective. Our claims that actions are correct or reasonable can be epistemically objective, at least to a significant degree. Such claims are not just my opinion.

If we emphasize the public logic of ethics, an extreme relativism or subjectivism loses its bite and appears irrelevant to the whole point of ethics. Extreme relativism and nihilism share the view that there are no objectively valid values or standards and, therefore, that no one view is better than another. Even if these views were true, society would still need to "do" ethics. We would still need to decide how conduct should be governed and how individuals and groups should cooperate. Whatever the meta-ethical status of our beliefs, we need normative reasoning in the public sphere about rules, norms, and values. We must find a way to make such discourse as insightful and reasonable as possible, not avoid the issues by saying that everyone has their own ethics, and that is the end of the matter.

In the end, as Dworkin (2011, 155–156) says, extreme relativism or nihilism is not the greatest problem for applied ethics. Relativism and nihilism may "color our metaphysical moments" but such doubt is the natural product of deep theoretical musings, from the stance of an observer. In practical life, an agent needs to act, and citing the mantras of nihilists or relativists is of little help. The question, "What is the best thing to do?" remains a constant and unavoidable query even if everything is relative.

Ethics deserves respect because it deals with what is central to so much of our life – how we relate to others, and whether how we relate contributes to human flourishing. Ethics is central to all of those important human areas where, knowing the facts, we still need good judgment, wise decisions, and an ability to weigh values. Ethics pressures us to view life in the round, and to carefully estimate the impact (and correctness) of public policies. To those who say ethics is suspect because it goes beyond facts, one can only reply: the greatest wisdom is to know the worth of facts, the worth of things, and the worth of life.

Implication 2: Egalitarian Pluralism

The second implication is that ethics as normative interpretation provides an attractive epistemology. My approach incorporates into moral reasoning the role of emotion, procedures for weighing values, insights from moral psychology, and the facts behind ethical issues. This epistemology fits what actually occurs in serious interpretive work in ethics.

Two epistemic themes are central in my approach: ethics, at its best, is egalitarian pluralism and holistic interpretation.

Pluralism is a way of understanding things. Pluralism emphasizes "the many," as opposed to stressing "the one" (or what unites the many). A simple pluralism asserts that some phenomenon consists of many parts or objects. I have several stones in my pocket. They are a simple plurality. Nothing much follows. Interesting forms of pluralism say more about the many. They claim that these parts are irreducible, significant, and must play a central role in our thinking about the phenomenon. Pluralists insist that, when we explain things, the fact of plurality cannot be denied as an illusion or considered insignificant; it cannot be reduced to an underlying unity. In addition, pluralists may provide a theory on how the many are related, e.g., as members of a web.

Non-pluralism is an opposing way of understanding things. It stresses the one (or "the few") or what unites many things of one kind. In physics, the unifying entity may be an underlying substrate that makes up all objects, such as some form of matter or energy. In ethics, the unifying entity may be a universal moral principle. Monism is the opposite of pluralism. It asserts that pluralities are best understood by a unifying principle or element. The existence of unifying entities, such as a universal ethical principle, is not an illusion. Monists do not have to deny that many things exist, or that we have many different conceptions in ethics. They only have to claim that what unites the objects or conceptions exists and is of fundamental importance. It explains and justifies the plurality by noting what the many parts have in common.

The tension between pluralism and monism is as old as the philosophical problem of the one and the many. In metaphysics, for example, pluralism is the belief that reality consists of many different kinds of things, as opposed to the view that there is one type of thing, such as matter or spirit. Culturally, pluralism holds that a society should politically and culturally have structures that recognize its many types of ethnic groups, religious traditions, languages, and conceptions of the good life. In contrast, some forms of monism favor structures that promote one religion or ethnicity, or one set of values.

How you react to these debates indicates how you see yourself and the world. Do you tend to see similarities among things, or do you see differences? Do you think that all cultures share one set of values or do you think there many conflicting systems of values? Do you see the world optimistically, as open, pluralistically, to many possible futures – futures that can be shaped by humans? Or do you think, monistically, that everything is preordained by one fate, one God, or one iron law of history?

Pluralists can use a descriptive approach which describes the members of the plurality, e.g., a description of the many languages and customs in a region of the world. Or they can use a normative approach that asserts that a plurality of customs or ethical norms is a good thing and should be encouraged. For instance, proponents of democratic pluralism do not stop at noting, descriptively, that many democracies are pluralistic in composition – many sub-cultures, many traditions, and many values. They also argue, normatively, that this is a good thing and that political institutions *ought* to represent and respect this pluralism. Similarly, supporters of multiculturalism are normative pluralists of this type. They promote the differences among cultures as culturally enriching.

In ethics, the monism-pluralism debate is over whether there exist unifying universal principles and whether we should regard our many ethical beliefs as deducible from a few unifying and basic beliefs. Monism organizes the many values according to a hierarchy of significance and justification. This hierarchy is top-down. In its strongest form, monism identifies one ethical principle as the most basic, unifying belief. Other beliefs are deduced from this supreme principle. For instance, J. S. Mill's utilitarianism is a hierarchical monism. Mills argued that the many goods that we cherish share a feature – they all contribute to utility. Utility is both the criterion of good and evil and the supreme moral principle. In Mill's formulation, the principle of utility is the greatest happiness of the greatest number. In a weaker form, monism identifies several principles as basic, unifying values, such as the Ten Commandments. Philips (1994, 89) calls these core principles a "supercode."

Monists believe there is a unique and correct ranking among ethical values. Kekes (1993, 8) describes monism as "the view that there is one and only one reasonable set of values. This system is the same for all human beings, always, everywhere." Monism regards differences in moral belief as either variations on a common morality or the result of mistakes in moral belief. This view of ranking appears in many areas of life, far beyond ethics. For example, monistic forms of hierarchy can be seen in the structure of organizations, such as the army or the Vatican. Metaphorically, a monistic hierarchy is a house built on foundations, or a Christmas tree where a central pole supports everything else.

Egalitarian pluralism avoids hierarchies, especially of the monistic kind. Instead of the top-down dominance of one or a few principles, it stresses a holistic, more horizontal structure which emphasizes the relative equality (in significance) of the parts. Also, elements on all levels influence elements on other levels. No one part or supreme principle always trumps other parts or principles. How the parts are related may be called "egalitarian," taking a term from political theory. A metaphor for such orderings is a web where support is shared among nodes running in multiple directions. Another apt metaphor is a stone arch over a walkway. It is an egalitarian structure. The integrity of the arch as a whole depends on mutually supporting relations between all of the stones. An arch has no one foundation or central pole.

To see how the choice of structure affects ethical thinking, consider views of the good life. Monists hold that human lives are good to the extent they conform to one system of objective general values, organized around a central principle. Egalitarian pluralism disagrees. There is no one uniquely correct moral system for all humans and all situations. Instead, there are contending values that humans need to prioritize in general and in specific situations. The central belief of pluralism is that "good lives require the realization of radically different types of values, both moral and non-moral, and that many of those values are conflicting and cannot be realized together" (Kekes 1993, 11). There are diverse sources of ethical value such as the good, duty, personal ideals, love, loyalty, justice, and human rights. Humans are motivated by non-moral values such as pursuing a career, creativity, playfulness, adventure, and style. As noted in Chapter 1, humans experience conflict not only within their moral schemes but also between their moral life and politics, law, art, and self-interest. Values come into conflict, and we must choose among them. To make things complicated, there may be several ways to rank these values.

Ethical reasoning in a pluralistic approach, then, is weighing conflicting values and ways of evaluation. As noted in Chapter 1, to achieve a good life, humans seek a coherent ordering of their many, interacting values. The ordering is *not* a monistic hierarchy.

I embrace egalitarian pluralism for many reasons. One reason is that it opens us up to the future, to new experiments in living, and new values, which is central to my pragmatic view of life and social reform. Also, an egalitarian approach supports my emphasis on conceptual systems and webs of meaning.

Implication 3: Holistic Interpretation

Egalitarian pluralism is a view about the structure of our ethical schemes and interpretations. But how do we construct pluralistic schemes in the first place, and how do we support and justify both the scheme and its parts? My view, implicit in what I have said so far, is holism. Our normative interpretations are holistic structures and justified through the holistic method of reflective equilibrium. But what is holism?

Holism is the belief that, when interpreting anything, we need to understand the whole of which it is a part. Holism focuses on structures, schemes, and contexts where parts have *important and defining relationships* with other parts and with the structure as a whole. The parts are not isolated and independent atoms.

Methodologically, holism is usually opposed to individualism. A strong individualism in social science seeks to show how the actions of individuals account for the actions of a whole society. For example, the consumer decisions of individuals explain trends in the economy. A strong holism holds the opposite. What happens on the individual level does not explain what happens at the level of society. It is the reverse. For example, social psychology might explain individual conduct as conformity with group conduct.

Of course, there is plenty of theoretical room between these two positions. I hold a modest holism, metaphysically and methodologically. I am a pluralist and a holist. I recognize the reality of many parts and of their whole, and the importance of their interactions. My modest holism claims that understanding individual elements is crucial but that also we are required to understand their logical, causal, or epistemic relations to the whole of which they are a part.

What sorts of things call for modest holistic understanding? Hockey teams, computer networks, the engine of your car, your bicycle, the human body, the workings of group psychology, and the logical evaluation of complex arguments. Perception is also holistic. We recognize an individual object against a larger, background gestalt. Change the gestalt and you may see a different object. Words have meaning depending on the role they play relative to other words. The word "can" is either a verb or a noun depending on how it operates in a sentence, relative to a context.

Concepts are holistic structures, as explained in Chapter 2. In Ward 2005, I defined objectivity as a holistic concept. It contains a plurality of criteria. Objectivity is multi-dimensional. Objectivity cannot be defined, monistically, by one concept, e.g., reporting "just the facts." As I will explain later, to test a report for objectivity is to ask to what extent a report satisfies a range of related criteria, such as empirical sufficiency and coherence with existing knowledge.

Normative interpretation in ethics is holistic on three levels. (1) The meaning of many ethical concepts, especially general concepts such as goodness or duty, is multi-dimensional like objectivity. (2) The interpretation, as a whole, brings together many types of things, from norms and knowledge of existing practices to facts about the world and beliefs outside of ethics proper, e.g., social and political beliefs. An interpretation seeks a reflective equilibrium among the nodes in our ethical scheme. As we saw, the interpretation of courtesy is holistic. The dissenters' interpretation did not simply place certain types of actions under the concept of "courtesy." It did not deduce courtesy from one supreme principle. Instead, it appealed to a web of related notions such as respect, egalitarian social order, and citizen equality. (3) Ethical thinking is holistic in seeking to integrate a plurality of values into a moral way of life.

Therefore, an interpretation usually can't be disproved "atomistically" by noting how it conflicts with a fact. We need to show how the interpretation is inadequate across a wide range of measures – facts, logic, practical consequences, and so on. Moreover, a major change of interpretation is holistic in nature. It requires a shift in a large part of the conceptual scheme, including the basic propositions that make up Wittgenstein's "river bed."

Dworkin thinks the difference between disagreements in normative domains and disagreements in other domains is due to differences in the type of concept under discussion. Some discussions use "criterial" concepts (Dworkin 2011, 6). We agree about what criteria to use in identifying examples. We agree, except for borderline cases, on examples of the concept. For example, "book" is a criterial concept. We agree on how many books are on the table because we agree on the criteria for what counts as a book. There are cases, such as a large pamphlet, where we might disagree on whether it is a book. Even if, as mentioned in Chapter 2, our normal concepts are "fuzzy," disagreements on many cases, such as book or chair, are rare and they don't undermine our confidence in the concept or our ability to identify and agree upon examples of books and chairs.

However, there is a range of concepts that don't act like criterial concepts, such as concepts of law, justice, equality, and rights. Dworkin (2011, 6) calls them "interpretive concepts." Examples are the basic concepts discussed in Chapter 2. When we disagree about basic concepts, we disagree on the criteria for applying these terms. Therefore, we also disagree on the application of the concepts in many cases.

Dworkin (2011, 73) notes that we often do not follow shared linguistic criteria for deciding which facts make a situation just or unjust. Our most intense disputes about justice, such as about the fairness of an income tax system or affirmative action programs, are about "the right tests for justice" not whether the facts satisfy some agreed-upon test in some particular case. A libertarian thinks income taxes are unjust because they take property from its owner, without proper consent. It doesn't matter if the taxes increase the general happiness because they violate more important principles – the principles of individual liberty and private property. For the libertarian, the criterion of "is just" is whether it supports or is consistent with individual liberty, ownership, and personal merit. However, a utilitarian may regard income taxes as just if they increase the general happiness, and she may claim that general happiness trumps personal merit or liberty. For this utilitarian, the criterion of "is just" is different from that of the libertarian. The libertarian and utilitarian differ on their conceptions of justice. These

Theoretical Foundations

interpretive disagreements are genuine, important, and difficult to resolve because the disagreements involve basic concepts.

But now a question arises. How can the libertarian and the utilitarian even discuss issues of justice if they deploy quite different concepts of justice? Why do we not say, instead, that they are talking about different topics or subjects? The "different topics" view, however, is not plausible because both the libertarian and utilitarian themselves believe they are talking about the same thing, that is, justice and what it means. Yet, how do they carry on? What do they hold in common to make the discussion possible? Dworkin's answer, which I support, is that we can discuss such topics because we share social practices and experiences in which these concepts figure, such as being treated unjustly or arguing publicly that some policy is just. The libertarian and utilitarian share a history of practices regarding justice. We disagree because we *interpret* differently the practices we share. The result: different criteria for basic concepts. Philosophy can play a role in such disputes. Further philosophical reflection may show libertarianism to be an unattractive interpretation of justice at large, or unacceptable in some part, such as its view on income taxes. Or reflection may indicate that utilitarianism or libertarianism have difficulty stating why our shared, paradigm examples of injustice – punishing innocent people, slavery, and the rich stealing from the poor –are unjust.

This shows how such debate is possible. Yet how do we engage in critiquing and justifying interpretive concepts? My reply is: If our interpretations are holistic structures, attempts to justify our interpretations and their principles are also holistic (see Fodor and Lepore 1992).

John Rawls's method of reflective equilibrium is an example of holistic justification. Rawls thought that one of the best ways to formulate and justify principles of justice is to find a balance among beliefs about what is just at various levels, from general principles to specific maxims. In constructing a theory of justice, we seek reasonable principles that "match our considered judgments duly pruned and adjusted" and "at all levels of generality" (Rawls 1992 [1972], 19). We ask whether the principles "match our considered convictions of justice or extend them in an acceptable way." Under reflective equilibrium, "no one level, say of abstract principle or that of particular judgments in particular cases, is viewed as foundational. They all may have an initial credibility" (Rawls 1993, 8n8).

As Nussbaum says (2006, 299–300), Rawls's ideas of justification are "holistic" and "internal." Reflective equilibrium presumes that we are "starting in the middle" of an imperfect conceptual scheme with inevitable tensions between levels and with problems in the application of principles. The scheme provides "provisional fixed points," such as rejecting racial intolerance, for the start of reflection. There are judgments, concepts, and principles that we feel are basic and sound *at this point of time*. However, such convictions are fallible, and we would be prepared to change them if confronted with a strong counter-argument. This reflects the view of Quine, who said that, in a holistic scheme, nothing is immune from revision. New cases may shake our confidence in a principle, or in our theory as a whole. The challenge is to re-establish reflective equilibrium. We cannot say in advance what the result will be.

Dworkin endorses a similar holistic approach. He says that when we interpret what ethics is, or when we interpret what we mean by justice, we link together concrete moral opinions and abstract principles. We seek "an integration of background values and concrete interpretive insights" (Dworkin 2011, 134).

In summary, the last two sections support the conclusion that an egalitarian pluralism and moderate holism are the right approach for understanding normative interpretation in ethics.

Implication 4: Expect Slack

A holistic approach to normative interpretation assumes that there will be some slack between our interpretation and the facts which provide support. Facts underdetermine our interpretations. Several interpretations may find support from the same set of facts, and may be equally supported by the facts.

After all I have said, slack should come as no surprise. If we do not have direct contact with reality, a variety of interpretations for the facts are always possible. Also, as Quine noted (1953), we don't verify interpretations by verifying each sentence (or belief) in isolation. The interpretation as a whole faces the tribunal of facts and experience, so it is always possible to overcome a conflict with a fact (or some facts) by altering some portion of the interpretation. Finally, the justification of interpretations includes more than facts. Therefore, the fit between interpretation and fact is not tight and unequivocal.

For those who think this slack proves that ethical interpretation is subjective or arbitrary, I have bad news. The same slack exists in science and other areas commonly thought to be rigorously empirical. Facts by themselves don't indicate, decisively, where a theory may be inadequate or wrong, or what needs to be changed. Even worse, several scientific theories may be consistent with existing facts. In these cases, we fall back on a web of non-factual criteria of evaluation such as simplicity of theory and coherence with other theories.

If Quine is correct, scientific theorizing is a form of holistic interpretation amid empirical slack. It may be that the natural sciences have strict methods to empirically test theories, but my point remains: slack, by itself, is not sufficient to question the enterprise of normative interpretation.

Implication 5: Independence of Ethics

Throughout the history of ethics, philosophers have sought ways to "ground" ethical beliefs. Grounding meant that the meaning and justification of ethical beliefs was to be found in non-ethical beliefs, such as facts about human emotions, reason, or society.

Hume and Kant undertook scientific inquiries into the basis for ethical beliefs, finding the ground in sympathy and a self-legislating practical reason, respectively. In this way, ethics could be shown to be a rational enterprise as opposed to cultural indoctrination. Assent to ethical principles is objective if assent is based on some natural fact. Thinkers such as Kant found the source of normativity in the operations of the human mind. Others, such as J. S. Mill, defined the "greatest good" in naturalistic terms, as the happiness of the greatest number. Happiness, in turn, reduced to pleasures and pains of varying quantity and quality. Why is this a persuasive definition of the good? Mill said (2006, 90) the reason is that people actually desire utility, as pleasure or happiness. It is a fact about humans.

These approaches assume that ethics is an area of belief and reasoning that is dependent in some fundamental way for its validity and normative

Implications for Radical Ethics

power – its very claim to be reasonable – on something outside of ethics proper. It is dependent on something outside of normative thought entirely: facts, natural processes, emotions, or prudential reasoning. The sort of dependence in question is not causal, or psychological, but epistemic. For example, facts about society are often used not just to explain why humans invented ethics, but also to justify ethical principles. The fact that human society needs cooperation can be used to justify the ethical principle of reciprocity. Or, if someone discovered that all human brains have innate centers for kindness, they might argue that this justifies its importance in morality. Valued forms of conduct are explained and justified by facts from empirical domains.

As a naturalist, I do not discount the importance of naturalistic inquiries into how people learn values, or the neurological basis for ethical emotions. What I deny is that such studies, no matter how impressive as causal explanations of conduct, can "save" ethics from skeptics by providing an external, scientific justification. I have several reasons for the denial. My previous exposition of ethical claims as practical proposals means that they are not descriptions of facts, or directly reducible to facts. There are normative proposals that include but transcend facts. A different form of reasoning must occur – practical, holistic arguments for what is good for society. Also, as we saw in Chapter 1, ethical properties, similar to other social properties, are non-reducible to physical properties, which precludes a definition of the good as pleasure or other natural property. Moreover, a naturalistic treatment of ethics never bridges the is-ought gap. Let us presume that we find a brain structure responsible for feelings of kindness toward others. This fact no more entails that we ought to be kind than discovering that the brain has a center for cruel behavior entails that people ought to be cruel. In moral reasoning, some of the premises must be normative premises, which are not reducible to factual premises. Ultimately, for any fact about ourselves that seems relevant to ethics, we still have to argue that the fact or natural process is worthy to be affirmed and should guide our actions. We still need a moral argument for accepting the fact in question as a value to guide conduct.

Between a "naturalistic grounding" and ethical skepticism there is a middle ground: the practical and social independence of ethics. Ethics is independent socially as I described it in Chapter 1 – as a humanly

Theoretical Foundations

created normative dimension that gets it authority from agreement and proposal.[1] Ethics is also independent in reasoning and justification. As Dworkin states (2011, 131), morality is moral "all the way down." The phrase "all the way down" means the justification for ethics is not to be found on some firmer, factual ground somewhere outside the ethical sphere of normative argument. The basis for a moral statement is another moral statement. When we justify our ethical principles, our reasons contain principles that are themselves moral principles. The best argument for the moral principle of respecting privacy is privacy's role in promoting human flourishing and self-development. Flourishing and self-development are moral principles. And if we try to go deeper and justify our belief in flourishing we will not escape an appeal to other moral values like growth, dignity, and happiness. It is a mistake to seek an objective basis for ethics that stands outside of ethical reasoning.

One motivation to seek external justification for ethics is the misconception that we need to start ethical reasoning from firm, perhaps absolute, principles. But then we find that there is no escaping the circle of normative concepts. There is no magical place where we can engage in non-presuppositional thought, apart from any larger context of ideas and situations. What we *do* have are ethical systems and social practices that already exist. A better, holistic approach is to start by accepting a good deal of our ethical beliefs as correct or reasonable, yet acknowledge that some beliefs are questionable. Using reflective equilibrium, we question, repair, or replace specific beliefs. We argue for ethical beliefs by appealing to other ethical beliefs. We lean on our ongoing ethical system and "river bed" beliefs as we change parts of our ethical conceptual system. We don't seek to step outside all of our beliefs and seek absolute, external foundations. Rather, we reform as we go along, pragmatically.

Philosophers have provided metaphors that convey this idea of evaluation within evolving conceptual schemes. Otto Neurath compared the inquirer to a sailor who repairs his boat while he sails along. Quine (1960, 3) added that scientific inquirers are sailors whose boat they "must rebuild plank by plank while staying afloat in it." Epistemically, this means that inquirers should not imitate Descartes. They should not attempt to start from scratch by searching for absolute principles while,

Implications for Radical Ethics

in the meantime, placing their beliefs in abeyance until philosophical reflection can find the presumed absolute principles which then justify the rest of our beliefs.

Rather, a better approach is to employ a limited skepticism that questions specific beliefs from within their evolving conceptual scheme. We stand on planks to repair the other planks of our ethical system, already under sail.

Implication 6: Between Absolute and Arbitrary

So far, my theses of pluralism, holism, and independence of ethics point to a form of thinking and justification that exists between the arbitrary and the absolute. My aim is to avoid absolutism and its penchant for confusing truth with certainty (Lynch 2006, 28–30). Absolutism tends to collapse from within. We realize that absolute truth cannot be found in a domain such as ethics, so we turn skeptic about *any* claims made in that domain. Humans have a psychological propensity to shuttle between absolutism and skepticism. In either case, we underestimate and undervalue the less than certain, but important, forms of reasoning that we find in many disciplines and walks of life.

I believe we should practice a moderate form of relativism that sees claims as relative to broad conceptual schemes but rejects the view that every belief is as good as any other. We acknowledge that between the arbitrary and the absolute there is much space to defend rationally and objectively our beliefs and to identify better beliefs. In practice, the set of viable ethical interpretations is never infinite. We rarely face a situation where all and any views are considered equal in value. Instead, the restraints usually reduce our options to a small number of plausible and reasonable positions. Ethics is a form of understanding where there are better and worse interpretations, even if the results are always open to contestation.

In ethics, we work within conceptual schemes, as described in Chapter 2. But – and this is the crucial point – our beliefs are not "merely" relative in the strong sense of being unable to provide reasons, unable to critique positions, or unable to reform views. Notions of correct, reasonable, and well-evidenced belief can exist in the middle ground. Moreover, it is not the case that these systems are hermetically sealed systems. Part of the power of ethical thinking is its ability to critique systems and build new schemes.

Non-absolute practical thinking is what happens when we interpret a practice. Non-arbitrary in this context means that one's views are restrained by objective factors (see Ward 2010). As we have seen, interpreters are not free to make up any type of interpretation about an established practice. Not if they want their interpretation to be taken seriously. They need to account for paradigmatic examples of the practice, be consistent with the history of the practice, start from shared understandings, and advance arguments that are plausible to practitioners. In short, they work between the absolute and the arbitrary; they work with imperfect but not arbitrary ways of thinking that deal with vital areas of human association. In the middle ground, no one expects an absolute set of rules.

The idea of reaching considered judgments by holistic interpretation and reflective equilibrium extends beyond ethics to wherever we seek considered judgments. Elgin (1997, 198) sees the process of reflective equilibrium as a way of being rational amid uncertainty and complexity:

> A system of considered judgments in reflective equilibrium is neither absolute nor arbitrary: not absolute, for it is fallible, revisable, revocable; not arbitrary, for it is tethered to antecedent commitments. Such a system neither is nor purports to be a distortion-free reflection of a mind-independent reality. Nor is it merely an expression of our beliefs. It is rather a tool for the advancement of our understanding.

The view that ethics needs certain foundations is an unhelpful meta-ethics in a world of constant change and plural conceptions of life. Rather than look for absolute foundations amid the winds of change, we should work from within our ethical frameworks but always be ready to revise, improve, and adapt our thinking to the world. We need to view ethics in general as ever-evolving normative responses to practical problems caused by changing social conditions. Accordingly, media ethics consists of ever-evolving interpretations of ever-changing media practice. This is the naturalistic and experimental approach to ethics found in the works of pragmatists such as William James (1974) and John Dewey (2004 [1920]) If the world is pluralistic and open to the future, then the main task of ethics is not to preserve and protect, but to reflectively engage the future with new ideas, new tools. We should use experimental and experiential reasoning to identify and adapt norms for a rapidly changing world.

This "imperfectionist" approach to thinking and ethics (Ward, 2005, 34–35) means that we must deal directly with uncertainty, contestation, and plural values. There is no perfect state of knowledge which is safe from the winds of change or the skeptic's gaze. But is this so bad, especially in ethics and in democratic society? Would we prefer to live in a society where robust ethical debate is restricted or non-existent because all is known and settled, or no one bothers to truly deliberate with others because all is subjective?

Implication 7: Emergent and Contested

When a new ethics system is being constructed, or when old and new values clash, we can refer to ethics in these areas as emergent. In such cases, we see a tension between new and old ethical thinking. New ethical interpretations and values begin to be articulated. They enter into an uneasy tension with older interpretations and values. Emergent ethics seeks to establish a beachhead on the terrain of ethics, currently dominated by other perspectives. Invention in ethics often occurs in this dialectic between the established and the emergent. Not all of ethics is emergent. Some practices remain stable for long periods of time. Some ethical systems don't change quickly. The ethics of a religion can remain unchanged in essentials for centuries.

How and why ethics becomes emergent is a topic far beyond this chapter but we can say several things about it. The emergence of a new ethics is usually prompted not by ethicists or philosophers constructing new systems apart from practical problems and changing social contexts. The motivation to discuss a new ethics comes from important social changes, such as when a practice undergoes dramatic change in its technological or economic conditions. The development of bioethics and the ethics of technology with military applications are examples of emergent ethics. In these areas, the almost overwhelming swiftness of the pace of technological development swamps the ability of current principles to provide adequate guidelines. Hence, many people begin to construct new principles and processes for decision-making. Ethics becomes emergent.

A powerful example of emergent ethics comes from humankind's experience with two world wars in the previous century. The Holocaust prompted emergent legal ethics in terms of new forms of international law and new tribunals to judge acts against humanity. It also prompted emergent ethics in terms of the human rights movements which began to articulate non-parochial standards for all humans, for all leaders of all states. Beitz (2009, 13) defines human rights as a practice that is emergent, from which we take our concepts of human rights.

In recent decades, another macro-trend has caused more invention in this area of emergent international ethics. This is the much-discussed process of "globalization" which is bringing fundamental change to politics, economics, finance, culture, and communication. In response to such sweeping changes, some people have begun to develop an emergent global media ethics since nation-based ethical views are thought to provide inadequate guidance for global issues. A cosmopolitan ethic has begun to emerge, building upon the human rights movements and coexisting in an uneasy tension with ethical views based on nationalism and national interests (see Ward 2010, 2013). As we will see in the next chapter, an emergent ethics is also at work in newsrooms as journalism practice adapts to new forms of media and media practitioners. The emergent ethics appears to be moving toward a "mixed" media ethics with a global mindset.

The meta-ethical view that ethics needs unchanging foundations is closely associated with a negative view of disagreement in ethics. Therefore it sees emergent ethics as a sort of threat to the moral life, because it challenges the foundations of our house of ethics. Disagreement and change are threats to the "authority" of ethics. On my view, the social, interpretive enterprise of ethics is not grounded in unmovable, absolute pillars. Ethics is imperfect and never finished. Ethics is essentially – and rightly so – always contestable. Invention, disagreement, and change should be seen as inherent to ethics, not as regrettable aberrations to be repressed or eliminated.

My notion of normative interpretation implies that our interpretations will be emergent in times of fundamental change. Therefore, in this chapter, the notions put forward to define normative interpretation – pluralism and holism, among others – are well placed to help people understand and develop the process of emergent ethics. This capacity to deal with changing, emergent ethics will be valuable when we deal with media ethics today, as we will see.

Implication 8: Ethics as Activism

The final consequence of adopting radical media ethics is that ethics is seen as a form of activism. It is a broad activism for a better world, based on a pragmatic meliorism that believes humans can shape their own destiny. The essence of ethics is not to preserve what exists but to improve what exists. The essence of ethics is not following norms under social pressure and the force of tradition. Ethics is not about making descriptive claims about moral facts existing in the world. It is about articulating proposals for action and reform. It is about realizing a better world out of the promise and potential inherent in today's concrete situations. As a form of activism, ethics can never be static and conventional. It must be open to change and invention, to the emergence of better and more appropriate ways of guiding human association. Later, I will explain how ethics as activism is a new form of reforming media.

Conclusion

Over three chapters, I have argued that what the world needs is not a comforting, familiar ethics. We need radical reform. We need a radical ethics. I explained what I mean by ethics and the normative interpretation of practice. In this chapter, I examined eight implications that follow from adopting these notions.

I now move on to Part II, where I apply this meta-ethics to our understanding of media ethics. I begin by exploring more fully my idea of radical media ethics.

Note

1. Larmore (2008, 1–2) argues that the principles of ethics can only be autonomous and capable of our rational assent if we see them as "binding on us from without." Autonomy and proper assent cannot be derived from the autonomy and internal functioning of our minds. We have to see "reality as embodying a normative dimension" if we are to be able to talk about objective reasons for ethical principles. But Larmore is not clear how reality has this "external" normative dimension. It seems to be a mysterious property that is reached by a Kantian-like transcendental reduction. We must presume that such principles have an external validity. If we do not, there is no authority in ethics. I do not think any mystery is necessary. The normative dimension is created through human agency and society, as described in Chapter 1. The source of autonomy and independence of morality is naturalistic and human.

References

Beitz, Charles. 2009. *The Idea of Human Rights*. Oxford: Oxford University Press.
Dewey, John. 2004 (1920). *Reconstruction in Philosophy*. Mineola, NY: Dover Publications.
Dworkin, Ronald. 2011. *Justice for Hedgehogs*. Cambridge, MA: Harvard University Press.
Elgin, Catherine Z. 1997. *Between the Absolute and the Arbitrary*. Ithaca, NY: Cornell University Press.
Fodor, Jerry, and Ernest Lepore. 1992. *Holism: A Shopper's Guide*. Oxford: Basil Blackwell.
James, William. 1974. *Pragmatism and Four Essays from The Meaning of Truth*. New York: New American Library.
Kekes, John. 1993. *The Morality of Pluralism*. Princeton, NJ: Princeton University Press.
Larmore, Charles. 2008. *The Autonomy of Morality*. Cambridge: Cambridge University Press.
Lynch, Michael P. 2006. *True to Life: Why Truth Matters*. Cambridge, MA: MIT Press.
Mill, John Stuart. 2006. "Utilitarianism." In *The Blackwell Guide to Mill's Utilitarianism*, edited by Henry R. West, 63–113. Oxford: Blackwell.
Nussbaum, Martha C. 2006. *Frontiers of Justice*. Cambridge, MA: Belknap Press.

Philips, Michael. 1994. *Between Universalism and Skepticism*. New York: Oxford University Press.
Quine, Willard V. O. 1953. *From a Logical Point of View*. Cambridge, MA: Harvard University Press.
Quine, Willard V. O. 1960. *Word and Object*. Cambridge, MA: MIT Press.
Rawls, John. 1992 (1972). *A Theory of Justice*. Oxford: Oxford University Press.
Rawls, John. 1993. *Political Liberalism*. New York: Columbia University Press.
Ward, Stephen J. A. 2005. *The Invention of Journalism Ethics: The Path to Objectivity and Beyond*. Montreal: McGill-Queen's University.
Ward, Stephen J. A. 2010. *Global Journalism Ethics*. Montreal: McGill-Queen's University Press.
Ward, Stephen J. A., ed. 2013. *Global Media Ethics: Problems and Perspectives*. Malden, MA: Wiley Blackwell.

Part II
The Shape of a Radical Integrated Ethics

Part II

The Shape of a Radical
Integrated Ethics

Chapter 4
Radical Media Ethics

In the Introduction, I noted that media ethics, once the somewhat sleepy domain of mainstream codes of ethics, is now a dynamic, chaotic space of contested values. I concluded that this called for a radical reform of media ethics. I then constructed a framework for this ethics.

In this chapter, we begin to apply this philosophical framework to media ethics. The goal, I will argue, is an integrated, globally minded ethics whose aims and principles can once again unify the practitioners of many types of journalism, online and offline.

I begin this chapter by describing how journalism ethics is moving from a pre-digital, parochial media ethics to a digital, global media ethics. We witness the end of a tidy, pre-digital journalism ethics for professionals and the birth of an untidy, digital journalism ethics for everyone.

Journalism ethics is dead; long live journalism ethics.

Although the digital media revolution is much discussed, the far-reaching consequences of this revolution for journalism ethics are less discussed, and not clearly understood. This chapter views the state of media ethics through the lens of this digital revolution.

Radical Media Ethics: A Global Approach, First Edition. Stephen J. A. Ward.
© 2015 John Wiley and Sons, Inc. Published 2015 by John Wiley and Sons, Inc.

To get a sense of the depth of the ethical revolution, the chapter compares pre-digital media ethics and the evolving digital media ethics. It identifies the assumptions of the pre-digital approach to ethics, and describes the "fatal blow" that digital media delivered to this traditional framework. The chapter argues for a radical media ethics and outlines some features of the emerging ethics. I argue that such changes are revolutionary and justify a radical response. The guiding idea is that we need serious and systematic responses to the situation of media ethics, and such changes should be radical – not piecemeal or conservative. The chapter concludes with an agenda for digital journalism ethics.

Origin of Pre-digital Media Ethics

Before there was media ethics, there was journalism ethics.

An explicit, craft-wide journalism ethics began to appear in the early 1900s as journalists in the United States and elsewhere established professional associations. The associations constructed codes of ethics with principles that are still familiar to us, such as the principles of objectivity, truth-telling, and editorial independence (Ward 2005). Later, as other forms of media developed, the term "media ethics" was coined to refer, collectively, to the norms of professional media practice in general. Media ethics referred to the ethics of journalism, advertising, marketing, and public relations. Journalism ethics was considered a branch of media ethics. Media ethics, in all forms, was defined as the responsible use of the freedom to publish, from journalism to advertising. Its aim was to provide the norms that define responsible media practice and to guide practitioners in making sound ethical judgments.

Professionalism

Any ethics for media communication begins with the idea of responsibility. Media ethics greatly values freedom of expression and the freedom to publish. But its defining concern is with the *responsible* use of the freedom to express and to publish. The content of media ethics are the principles, norms, and values that define what responsible publication is, or should be.

"Being responsible" in publication is neither mysterious nor threatening to freedom-loving citizens. It is part of being a good person and a good citizen. Being responsible in media work is the same as being responsible in other areas of society – it means to be aware of, and be accountable for, one's actions. Responsible journalists, therefore: consider the consequences of their actions, e.g., the impact of stories; are respectful of others; restrain their actions by moral principle; follow good methods for gathering facts and evidence; minimize the harm of publishing; acknowledge, explain, and make amends for mistakes. There are three related types of responsibility in journalism: a story-related responsibility that requires individual journalists to make sure that each of their stories is responsibly produced and published; an organization-level responsibility that applies to news outlets and corporations; and an institutional responsibility that requires all journalists, individually and collectively, to produce responsible forms of journalism that serve their publics.

In the late 19th century, a movement arose in the United States and other Western countries to define and codify what responsible publication meant for the growing ranks of professional media workers. The movement toward professionalism began as journalists started to work in the large newsrooms of the mass commercial press. Professionalism was intended to raise the social status of this group, whose members were increasingly well-educated, powerful, and numerous. But more than that. Professionalism was to be an ethic that assured the public that journalists would use responsibly their power to publish. A professional attitude would run counter to the worrisome influence on reporting of press barons, newspaper syndicates, and business.

Journalists' aspiration toward professionalism in the early 1900s is not surprising. The late 1800s and early 1900s was a time when many groups sought to be considered professionals, from doctors to lawyers. To be called a professional was a complement. Professionals were said to be distinct from tradespersons and makers of crafts, factory workers, and rank-and-file employees of corporations by virtue of their more theoretical or specialized knowledge, combined with special skills and methods. Professionals acquired this "higher" knowledge through extensive education at centers of higher education. With higher knowledge came higher social status, influence, and pay.

The ideal of professionalism favored certain values.

Professionals, it was argued, have an overriding and distinct duty to serve the public. Serving the public interest trumped serving one's own interest and serving the interests of specific groups. The trades and crafts, it was assumed, had little (or no) public interest rationale. They served the needs of clients, not society at large. They entered into private, economic contracts with clients without reference to, or impact upon, larger public interests. If their products and services were shoddy, clients could go to court to settle the matter. When you call the plumber into your home to fix a bathroom drain, talk of serving the public interest and duty to the common good is out of place. Workers in the crafts and trades in the early 1900s did not define their roles – if they defined them at all – in terms of an obligation to serve the public at large. In contrast, professional soldiers, doctors, and journalists increasingly defined their aims and duties in terms of public service.

Public duty was stressed for many reasons. From an ethical point of view, a desire to serve others was paramount. Professionals had great opportunity to cause harm or exert undue influence on their clients. There was the ever-present possibility that professionals would put themselves (and their friends) first, and the public second. In politics, professionals were exerting increasing influence on crucial areas of society, such as the impact of medical experts on health policy and bankers on financial matters. Doctors, psychologists, engineers, and accountants received sensitive, private information from people. The power imbalance between professional and client required a commitment to ethics and responsibility. For this reason, among others, the state felt justified in licensing professions. Professionals supported the idea of self-regulation, implemented through licensing, disciplinary councils, and codes of ethics.

This concept of professionalism implied a number of ethical principles. One principle was the duty to avoid or minimize harm. Another was impartiality of mind, combined with objectivity of method. Professional objectivity was the ideal of a growing information society that sought to leave behind a politically partisan, traditional society based on elitism, place of birth, and personal connections. A true professional did not allow her personal beliefs or political partiality to influence her practice, or judgment. A professional followed the facts where they led. A professional, unlike a political operative or social advocate, used impartial methods to speak truth to clients and to the public.

This was the idea of professionalism that was taken up by journalists. The signs of professionalism – associations, journals, codes – were emerging in journalism (Ward 2005, 204–213). Yet the movement had many obstacles, including skepticism that journalism was a profession. Many people thought of it as a craft or a trade. Journalists could not claim they had special theoretical knowledge and special methods acquired through years of study at university. In fact, it seemed that anyone with an ability to write tolerably well could practice journalism. As academics set up the first journalism schools and some editors talked about the profession of journalism, others in academia and in the established professions scoffed at the idea. How could a practical craft pretend to be a profession with "higher" knowledge (see Ward 2005, 209) such as in medicine or law? But journalists, when they used the term "professional," did not focus on specialized, hard-to-attain knowledge. Instead, they focused on the ethical attitudes of professionals, especially their impartial serving of the public.

This focus was not only because journalists, at least at this time, lacked special knowledge and methods. It was also because journalists sought in professionalism a response to a decline in public trust in media. In the early 1900s in the USA, there appeared an unrelenting series of articles in newspapers and magazines that criticized the reliability, sensationalism, and independence of the newspapers. This allegedly unreliable press was owned by men who had the power to choose presidents or start wars. Leaders of journalism, including publishers such as Joseph Pulitzer, argued that journalists had to adopt a professional attitude to counter "business interests" and to serve the public.

Professionalism was also a response to talk of state intervention in the media marketplace, including the threat of increased legal regulation of media practitioners (Siebert et al. 1956, 83–87). In 1927, the US Congress created a commission to bring regulatory order to the chaotic development of radio broadcasting. The commission would assign frequencies and "keep an eye on program content." Although the commission would not censure media, it would pressure broadcasters to be socially responsible in serving the needs of the public. Codes of ethics followed: codes for the movie industry in the 1930s, the radio industry in 1937, and the television industry in 1952. The movie industry's code was drawn up to forestall government regulation. Only newspapers, not needing a license, remained unregulated for the most part. Print journalists argued for self-regulation without state licensing.

Concerns about the reliability of the press were heightened by the fact that newsrooms had a virtual monopoly on what news and advertising reached the public. The power imbalance between journalists and citizens required a commitment to ethics. Journalists had a professional duty to act as responsible gate-keepers on what was published and what was not. Journalists should make sure their stories were accurate, and they should verify claims. Adhering to the professional ideal, journalists should be impartial of mind, independent in spirit, and objective in reporting. News should be separated from opinion. This self-imposed ethics, supported by accountability structures such as press councils and readers' ombudsmen, would constitute the self-regulation of journalism.

For the first time, the ethics of journalism became a self-imposed, codified ethics for journalists as a whole. National codes were constructed that applied across newsrooms, types of journalism, and regions of the country. They shared the core principles of professionalism, objectivity, and service to a democratic public. Journalism ethics became a professionally defined and publicly mandated ethics of an important social practice – so important that journalism was now discussed as an institution of democracy. Its ethics was based not on the personal and idiosyncratic values of individual journalists or even individual outlets. It was based on what the public expected, and needed, from its journalists. Times had changed. In a society dependent for information on journalism, many journalists accepted a collective responsibility and, together, endorsed principles such as truth-seeking, minimizing harm, objectivity, and accountability. Journalism, long considered romantically as the domain of the bohemian, skeptic, and iconoclast, had adopted a group ethic. In time, this professional attitude was extended to formulate the ethics of other media practitioners, such

Radical Media Ethics

as public relations. The ideas of professionalism for the public interest, social responsibility, self-regulation, and collective ethics formed the core values of media ethics.

Media ethics, in journalism and elsewhere, was developed by professionals for professionals. The principles of codes of ethics were intended to guide professionals in mass media outlets, and changes to those codes were decided by the professionals, not the public. Media ethics was not created for or by citizens. These values constituted the content and self-conception of professional media ethics throughout much of the twentieth century. This approach to media ethics is still influential today, especially among professional journalists.

The fatal blow What, then, could weaken this sturdy structure of pre-digital ethics, with its common principles, codes, and professional associations working under the watchful gaze of government and the public? What development did the most damage to pre-digital journalism ethics? As we have noted, it was a technological development that began roughly toward the end of the 20th century. It was the creation of digital media, and the many new forms of online communication and publication that it made possible, at relatively low cost.[1] The publication of information, views, and persuasive rhetoric was made increasingly accessible and attractive to non-professional writers, citizens, social groups, government, non-governmental organizations, and corporations. Networks of like-minded citizens could communicate and share information and knowledge, while critiquing professional journalists.

In retrospect, we see that the basis of the original journalism ethics was a historically contingent state of news media: the dominance, if temporary, of the mass commercial press over the public sphere's information channels. Pre-digital journalism ethics was created to guide the responsible members of mainstream news media. Once that dominance was weakened, the ethics that accompanied this form of journalism would, almost inevitably, be questioned. The fatal blow, then, was the spread of digital media and the decline of mainstream media's near-monopoly on the publication of news. I do not regard this as a "fatal" development for media ethics in general. Rather, I regard it as a fatal blow to any attempt to maintain conservatively the approach of pre-digital ethics. A new ethics for a digital media era must be constructed.

Toward a Digital Media Ethics

Two macro-trends

Any argument for reform has a view of the current state of media practice. Today, the context for media ethics is an expanding and chaotic universe of interactive global communication widely available to citizens. Since humans are social, communicating creatures, major changes to their media environment amount to more than electronic devices for disseminating information. A new media ecology shapes how humans think, feel, communicate, and live together.

Most of the turmoil is generated by two macro-trends. One trend is the emergence of a mixed news media. News media is mixed because many types of technology create many types of content. It is mixed because of the democratization of media – the fact that citizens have access to publishing technology. As a result, the kinds of media practitioners and journalists have increased dramatically beyond the ranks of professional journalists to include web writers for NGOs, scientists with blogs on the Internet, and citizen journalists.

A second trend, much discussed, is the globalization of news media, and media in general. News media are global in reach, impact, and content as they report on global issues or events, whether the issue is immigration, climate change, or international security.

Newsrooms today increasingly practice layered journalism. Layered journalism brings together different forms of journalism and different types of journalists to produce a multi-media offering of professional-styled news and analysis combined with citizen journalism and interactive chat. The newsrooms are layered vertically and horizontally. Vertically, there are many layers of roles and types of journalists. There are citizen journalists and bloggers in the newsroom, or closely associated with the newsroom. Many contributors work from countries around the world. In addition, there are different types of editors. Some editors work with the new types of journalists, while other editors will deal with unsolicited images and text sent by citizens via email, websites, and Twitter. Horizontally, the newsroom is layered in terms of the kinds of journalism it produces, from print and broadcast sections to online production centers.

Mixed, global media, organized into layered newsrooms, puts pressure on the original ethics designed for a different era. It creates a tension among media values on two levels. On one level, online journalism challenges the culture of traditional journalism, with its values of accuracy, pre-publication verification, balance, impartiality, and professional gate-keeping. Online media emphasize immediacy, transparency, and journalism with a point of view. If there are now so many sources of information, what is the rationale for careful gate-keeping for a public? Time-honored principles such as objectivity are questioned. The intersection of the amateur and the professional in journalism creates both communication possibilities and ethical debates. On breaking news stories, for example, non-professionals will circulate at a ferocious pace an unending flow of unconfirmed reports using Twitter, while others will upload images to YouTube. This puts pressure on professional newsrooms to match these reports. In turn, this puts pressure on mainstream newsrooms to *not* follow existing rules on accuracy and gate-keeping.

Meanwhile, journalists adopt new descriptions of themselves, as "sherpas" guiding readers through the information maze, as global "aggregators" of bloggers and websites, as facilitators of online dialogue. All work to the relentless demands of a 24-hour news clock.

The second level of tension is due to the emergence of a journalism that is global in reach. If journalism has global impact, what are its global responsibilities? The result is friction between local and global values, between patriotic journalism and a more global approach.

We can summarize the impact of the two trends on media ethics as a series of questions:

- *Questions of identity*: If citizens and non-professional journalists report and analyze events around the world, who is a journalist?
- *Questions about the scope of media ethics*: If everyone is potentially a publisher, does media ethics apply to everyone? If so, how does that change media ethics?
- *Questions about the content of media ethics*: What are the appropriate principles?

A Radical Integrated Ethics

- *Questions about the new journalism*: How can new forms of journalism be ethical? For example, how can nonprofit journalism maintain editorial independence from funders?
- *Questions about community engagement*: What ethical norms should guide the use of citizen content and newsroom partnerships with external groups?
- *Questions about global impact*: Should journalists see themselves as global communicators, or perhaps global agents of change?

Why go radical?

We need to create a new, more complex, and conceptually deeper ethics for responsible communication, professionally and non-professionally, mainstream and non-mainstream, online and offline.

Despite the need for change, there are people who do not think reform needs to be radical. Talk of media revolution is so ubiquitous that we sometimes become inured to the force of what we say. We nod our heads in agreement that change is everywhere, yet we fail to think through the consequences of change. I have been told repeatedly by scholars, editors, and ethicists that we do not need a new ethics to accommodate what is happening in media. It is a just a matter of "pouring new wine into old bottles." "New wine" refers to the many new forms of journalism. "Old bottles" refers to existing ethical principles.

Their view is: Just apply, with no (or little) alteration, the values of professionalism, public service, objectivity, independence, and minimizing harm to new forms of media work.

I reject this conservative strategy. My view is that we have new wine and we need new bottles. There is no going "back to basics" and reaffirming old ideas. We need to reconstruct old ideas and invent new ideas. Without radical reform, media ethics will become increasingly irrelevant to the actual media practice of both professional journalism and the growing numbers of non-professional practitioners.

If such reflections do not persuade, let me be even more explicit. Here are four types of reasons for going radical:

Theoretical and historical reasons   The history of media ethics shows that ethical revolutions follow revolutions in practice. In *Ethics and the*

Media (2011), I explained how ethical revolutions are prompted by fundamental changes in the technology, economy, and social climate of media. A media revolution prompts ethical changes because it alters the relationship of journalists and their publics. The new practices question existing media values, such as objectivity. In time, so many practices question so many norms that a consensus on media ethics is undermined. Practitioners come to see that simply patching up the holes in the old ethical system is not enough. Efforts are made to redefine the ethics from the ground up, by integrating old and new values and practices. We have a revolution in media ethics.

We can see these factors at work in revolutions in media ethics across history. For example, the creation of professional journalism ethics in the early 1900s was a response to radical change in the press. Newspapers changed from small, partisan, elite papers that focused on opinion to large newspapers interested in news. The changes eventually led to the first professional codes of ethics, whose values and aims were distinct from the journalism ethics of previous eras. A revolution in ethics followed a revolution in media.

Journalism is again being fundamentally reshaped by technology and other forces. If my theoretical model is correct, we have good reason to believe that we are in the middle of a genuine and far-reaching media revolution. "Going radical" is a plausible response to this revolution.

Breakdown in consensus Another reason for radical reform is the need to reconstruct a consensus on ethics among different forms of practice and different practitioners. Among many practitioners, there is a paper-thin agreement on abstract principles, such as truth-telling, but beyond this general level, there is little agreement. Our media revolution creates multiple and conflicting interpretations of journalism. Where consensus fails, mainstream practitioners are uncertain what norms to follow, while new media creators may see no need for ethics – if ethics is equated with traditional professional ethics. Questionable new practices can flourish in this ethical vacuum.

Practical reasons Even if journalists agree to be responsible, even if they embrace principles like truth-telling and verification, they will still not be spared the task of rethinking their norms. As noted above, it is not clear how to practically apply the values of verification, accuracy, and editorial independence to a journalism that is experimenting with new forms of media. As these situations and quandaries multiply, we need an ethics that integrates the old and the new.

Incompleteness Finally, we should pursue fundamental reform because existing media ethics is seriously incomplete. Current media ethics was created for professional journalists in newsrooms, not citizens with cell phones or bloggers with laptops. Therefore, traditional media ethics has little to say about how journalists should use content from social media. It says little about what norms are appropriate for citizen journalists. I will expand on this point below.

Features of Digital Media Ethics

Reform should be guided by awareness of the most important and contentious features of media ethics. Here are some of those features.

Integration and fragmentation

At present, two approaches (or attitudes) to journalism ethics jostle for primacy: integration and fragmentation.

"Integration" means journalists seek a coming together or agreement at the level of principle and aim which unifies their ethics as a whole. To be an integrationist is to believe that the ethics of journalism *should* be united to a substantial degree through agreement on principles. In contrast, a fragmented ethics lacks unifying principles and aims. It is characterized by deep disagreement and differences about correct aims, principles, and practices. Historically, one can think of the Protestant Reformation as a time when Christian doctrine (and ethics) fragmented into separate denominations. In journalism, fragmentation is the proliferation of different views about the purpose of journalism and its main norms. To speak metaphorically, a fragmented ethics is not a mainland where values connect to a unifying hub of principles. Instead it is an archipelago of isolated islands or value systems. The islands are the fragments of what was once a unified ethics. They lack connection and appear to espouse conflicting and irreconcilable values. To be a fragmentist is to believe that fragmentation is not only a fact about journalism ethics today but also a positive state of affairs. It is to believe that fragmentation encourages a diverse set of practices and forms of journalism. The fragmentist thinks integration in journalism ethics is not necessary and can't be realized – and that may be a good thing. Integration smacks of homogeneity, where all journalists follow the same pattern.

The metaphor of a mainland describes the state of pre-digital journalism ethics prior to the digital revolution. As noted above, journalism ethics was once integrated around the values of a pre-digital, professional ethics – seeking truth, minimizing harm, objectivity, and strict verification *before* publication.

In journalism, it may appear that only fragmentation is occurring, since the disagreements attract publicity and debate. However, if we look closer, both integration and fragmentation are occurring. We see a movement toward integration in the revision of codes of ethics. Many major news organizations, from the BBC in Britain[2] to the Society of Professional Journalists in the USA,[3] have, or are working on, substantial updates of their editorial guidelines as a response to the digital revolution. These revisions are integrative insofar as they seek to show how their principles apply to new practices. New policies are introduced but they are consistent with the overarching principles. Fragmentation also carries on. The view that social media journalism or blogging have their own separate practices and norms, and that traditional (and integrating) principles such as impartiality don't apply, has been a mantra since online journalism emerged (Friend and Singer 2007).

I follow an integrationist approach which avoids the polar opposites of treating ethics as fragmented islands of value or treating ethics as homogenized principles that ignore differences. I work against fragmentation because, as noted earlier, fragmentation can be a negative force. A breakdown in a unifying perspective divides journalists into camps, weakening their ability to join together in common cause, e.g., against threats to a free press or threats against journalists in other camps. Fragmentation suggests to the public that there is no such thing as journalism ethics; there is only each journalist's opinion. Fragmentation undermines the ideal of journalistic self-regulation,

A Radical Integrated Ethics

central to maintaining a free press. Self-regulation does *not* mean that each "self" or individual journalist regulates themselves according to their own values. Self-regulation means the regulation of journalistic conduct by a society-wide and unified group of journalists. If journalism ethics is fragmented, some people may agitate for additional forms of regulation on journalism, including new media laws.

In principle, fragmentists cannot consider what general aims and principles should be honored by all journalists for the benefit of democratic culture since they assume there are *no* general, "cross-island" principles. Worse still, the public will struggle to keep the media practitioners accountable if media outlets do not subscribe to general principles for the evaluation of media conduct. Under the flag of fragmentation, many dubious forms of journalism can be rationalized by appeal to "personal" values.

Fragmentation wrongly assumes that the source of authority for ethics is each individual journalist or each island of journalists. But ethics does not "belong" to journalists. Journalists have no special authority to announce, independently of what anyone else thinks, what rules they will follow and what restraints they will honor. To be sure, some values will be specific to certain types of journalism, such as a crowdsourcing site that values the engagement of citizens when reporting on events. However, there are also platform-neutral, general values, such as truth-telling and minimizing harm, that are not optional or subjective. Such values are society-wide expectations on its media system. At this broader level, ethics belongs to the public. Its source of authority is what the public deems essential to a well-functioning democratic public sphere and which forms of journalism (and norms) contribute most to democracy. This is the public framework for journalism ethics, within which more specific value systems, such as the values of satirical journalism, find their place. We should not return to the idea, prevalent in the days before professional journalism ethics, that journalism ethics is entirely an idiosyncratic, subjective affair.

I call my approach "unity in difference." The approach grounds journalism ethics in flexible general principles and aims that can be realized in multiple ways by different forms of journalism and different media cultures. These overlapping values unify, to some tolerable degree, the obvious differences. A "unity in difference" approach does not deny difference. Local differences are an important source of values in media work. For example, the ideas of truth-seeking, accuracy, social responsibility, impartiality, and serving the public receive different interpretations in different forms of journalism and media cultures. Yet these notions can be given a basic formulation that unites journalists of many kinds. Journalism ethics needs to respond to the digital revolution by seeking a new system of integrated principles that applies to new and old journalism, practiced by professional and citizen.

One way to think about this new integrated ethics is to *stop* thinking of journalism ethics as having one central location or source of authority, such as an elite media ethics tribunal. Nor is it realistic to think that there is, or can be, one set of principles to which all practitioners subscribe. The structure of journalism ethics is less hierarchical and unified than, say, the ethics of the Roman Catholic Church with its infallible Pope and central teachings. Instead, what responsible journalists in different regions of the world may share is a looser form of unity. They may find that they share an *overlap* of basic values such as truth-telling and acting as a watchdog on power. An important meta-ethical task is to inquire into what forms of integration are available to journalism today.

Personalized ethics

One consequence of the breakdown in consensus is a "personalization" of editorial guidelines. Personalization means that it is up to each journalist, form of journalism, or media platform to create its own ethical guidelines. Personalization, in many cases, derives from an awareness of fragmentation. If no consensus is possible, perhaps the best that can be done is to design one's own guidelines. However, personalization does not entail embracing extreme fragmentation. Some personalization projects are integrational to the extent that they ground their work in a set of abstract moral principles, such as telling the truth, keeping promises, and trying to be accurate.

Journalism ethics has always recognized differences between types of journalists, e.g., allowing columnists to ignore the rules of objectivity that were applied to news reporters. But personalization in digital media ethics goes further. It has a greater area of disagreement and a smaller area of agreement than integrative pre-digital ethics. In pre-digital ethics, the area of common values is (and was) quite large. It includes not only general principles but also a second tier of more specific norms. Codes of ethics of this type tend to be de-personalized – that is, universal (or "platform-neutral") – and they are rich in content. They are platform-neutral in prescribing rules for anyone (or any member of their association) who practices journalism. They are rich in content because they not only endorse general principles but also list, under each principle, numerous norms that express the meaning of the principle in question. Some codes include examples and case studies of how the principles work in real-world journalism.

The influential code of the Society of Professional Journalists (SPJ) in the United States exemplifies this de-personalized integrative approach.[4] After the preamble, the code places numerous norms under its four major principles: seek truth and report it, minimize harm, act independently, and be accountable. Under minimize harm the code puts such norms as showing sensitivity when covering children or victims of sexual assault.

Do-it-yourself (DIY) ethics

The SPJ's integrative approach was *not* followed when the US-based Online News Association (ONA) decided recently to create its first code of ethics.[5] The approach stressed common process, not common content. The association asked Tom Kent, standards editor for The Associated Press, to help the association develop a code. The ONA decided that, in an era of multiple forms of new journalism and a lack of ethical consensus, it would be futile to try to create an SPJ-like code with substantial agreement on integrative principles and norms. Instead the strategy was to personalize the process – to give each online journalist or online journalism outlet the "tools" to construct its own editorial guidelines.

The ONA website encourages its members to "build your own ethics" using the tools provided by Kent and his ethics committee. It says the project "is designed to help news orgs, startups, individual journalists and bloggers create their own ethics codes." It says the ONA is "curating a toolkit to help news outlets, as well as individual bloggers/journalists, create guidelines that respond to their own concepts of journalism." This process has been dubbed "DIY ethics."

On the ONA website, the toolkit starts with a small set of common principles that the ONA thinks most journalists would consider fundamental, such as tell the truth, don't plagiarize, and correct your errors. Then journalists are asked to make a choice between (a) traditional objective journalism, where "your personal opinion is kept under wraps"; and (b) transparency journalism, "meaning it's fine to write from a certain political or social point of view as long as you're upfront about it." The toolkit then provides guidance on constructing guidelines for about forty areas of practice where "honest journalists" might disagree, such as removing items from online archives, use of anonymous sources, and verification of social media sources. For each area, the toolkit provides a web page that cites various points of view and advises journalists to ask themselves certain important questions. An international group of about twenty-five contributors from news outlets, academia, and social networks assisted in writing the area pages.[6]

The ONA project is not an isolated experiment. It reflects a common attitude in online media about ethics. The DIY approach appears to be a positive, inclusive, and democratic approach, suited to a plural media world. To others it is an abandonment of journalism ethics, an ill-timed concession to relativism and subjectivism. For the latter, journalism ethics needs strong content. It needs to the stand behind principles and not retreat to a "process" that, like a smorgasbord, allows everyone to pick and choose what values they like.[7]

Open, global ethics

The digital revolution has given birth to an ethics that not only goes beyond the confines of media professions but also transcends borders. It is an "open" global media ethics in the form of online networks of citizens and professionals. The networks discuss everything from shoddy reporting in the mainstream media to the use of cell phones to monitor human rights.

This global discourse, whether angry or restrained, reflective or reactionary, misinformed or erudite, is a form of moral reasoning. It is a participatory moral reasoning in the form of debate and dialogue. Unlike many professional discussions, it is informal and unstructured, and open to voices from unexpected places. It mixes together a stew of fact, rumor, bias, interpretation, and ideology. Normative interpretations of journalism conflict. Here, discussions that tend toward integration *or* fragmentation, toward depersonalized *or* personalized ethics occur simultaneously. Digital media ethics, at this level, is contested, evolving, cross-cultural, and never settled.

For those who favor systematic thought and careful reflection, this discourse is frustrating and "goes nowhere." For those who favor inclusive, free-wheeling discourse, this form of ethics is stimulating and much needed. Whatever one's preferences, this open discourse is here to stay, given the digital revolution. This is a form of discourse that researchers and ethicists need to study, because it is the new global forum for media ethics.

In a previous article, Herman Wasserman and I (Ward and Wasserman 2010), explored the distinction between "closed" and "open" media ethics as one way to understand this shift from a pre-digital professional media ethics based on "content" (principles on paper) to a digital media ethics based on open-ended global dialogue. We noted how professional media ethics, throughout its history, has been a closed form of ethics discourse. It has been closed because it was intended to guide a restricted group of professional practitioners. Citizens and other professionals outside this group were excluded from meaningful participation in media ethics discourse. We then argued that new technologies, by democratizing media globally, were rendering media practices fluid and open, and turning a closed media ethics into an open media ethics. We also noted serious ethical issues about how to structure that discourse so it is informed and respectful. Wasserman and I (Ward and Wasserman 2014) followed this discussion with an article that explored how a global open ethics should use the method of "listening" and dialogue across cultural, economic, and political differences.

One response to this paradigm-shaking shift to open digital ethics is the emergence of a movement that seeks to construct a global media ethics (see Ward 2013). Now that journalism is global in reach and impact, media ethicists seek to create an integrative ethics that would articulate common principles for media practitioners worldwide, and for covering global issues. A favored approach is unity in difference. Theorists seek to articulate cosmopolitan aims and principles for journalism, such as serving humanity, acting as a bridge of understanding among warring groups, and promoting human rights. These aims and principles take ethical precedence over the parochial aims and principles of a previous pre-digital media ethics which placed serving a nation above serving global humanity.

The goal of global media ethics is to formulate universal, integrative principles in a manner which recognizes that such principles are interpreted differently in media cultures. Ethics seeks to bring the local and global together. Journalists are not asked to build their own guidelines on their media ethics island. Instead, journalists are asked to adopt a cosmopolitan perspective that seeks norms for journalists as a worldwide group. It is a fusion of process and content, of the local and the global.[8] Global media ethics does not refer to something singular or fully achieved. Global media ethics is a work in progress. It is an integrative project or a "movement" involving scholars and practitioners, on a much larger scale than hitherto imagined.

Reinvention of principles

The personalization of ethics has a serious conceptual problem. It adopts a few existing principles to provide a framework for its process-driven toolkit. The trouble is this: those existing principles are themselves under scrutiny. No toolkit can be conceptually sound without a clear and deep understanding of the assumptions that ground its methods. In journalism ethics, one cannot dodge the heavy lifting involved in articulating one's integrative principles by retreating to a benign or "reasonable" process. Therefore, a major task of today's journalism ethics is to create new content: to reinterpret existing principles and to invent new principles.

To understand why reinvention is needed, consider as an example our current interpretation of the central principle of editorial independence.

One implication of "everyone is a publisher" is that powerful corporations and advertisers can easily do journalism to attract customers to their websites and Twitter feeds. This is called "brand journalism." Rather than the hard sell of advertising, which lacks credibility, corporations use journalists and their story-telling to brand products, and trade on their credibility. For instance, Cisco Systems of California, which sells computer networking equipment, employs journalists to write stories on the technology sector on its website, The Network.[9] The site for Red Bull energy drink features stories on "extreme" sports.[10] In many cases, these journalists agree to never criticize their brand or highlight the competition.

However, brand journalism is often engaging. Public distrust of mainstream media means that many people don't care (or don't know?) who produces the journalism, Red Bull or News Corporation. So what's the big deal? The deal is this: Either the idea of editorial independence is being compromised, or independence is being redefined. Pick your favorite interpretation.

Similar questions arise for new forms of "agenda-driven" journalism. Take, for example, the decision by right-wing political groups in the United States to train journalists to write about politics from their point of view. Libertarian groups such as the Franklin Center for Government and Public Integrity have funded websites in dozens of states to cover legislatures. Like the corporate branders, these websites, such as www.wisconsinreporter.org, recruit professional journalists. The reporting reflects a political ideology such as lower taxes, less government, and individual liberty. These reporters claim they are nonpartisan journalists who report the facts like other journalists. They say they follow the tenets of impartial reporting as found in the code of the Society of Professional Journalists.

So, from our perch amid the media revolution, how do we evaluate politically driven journalism or corporate brand journalism? Aren't these developments new forms of journalism that diversify the public sphere? Even if the sites are partial, what is wrong with that? After all, don't we know that there is no such thing as objective journalism, and that mainstream media pursue their own agendas? Does it matter who produces the journalism? Or do we feel uncomfortable because such arguments seem to prove too much? They seem to undermine the notion of independent journalism in the public interest.

Traditional notions from media ethics are not very useful in clarifying these issues. For example, traditional news objectivity implied that all forms of opinion journalism were equal – all were subjective expressions of opinion. But today, in a world of opining, we need notions that help us distinguish between better and worse analysis. In a world of advocational journalism, we need a basis for distinguishing advocacy from propaganda. Once we leave the island of objective "straight" reporting, we find ourselves on a roiling sea of multiple forms of journalism, multiple publishers, and multiple funding models. Our once clear and simple distinctions blur and collapse, and we are not sure what to say.

The Agenda

What do these features say about the state of journalism and how journalism ethics should respond? What is the agenda for journalism ethics amid a media revolution?

Above, I indicated that we could understand the agenda as constructing a conceptually richer ethics that responds to key questions. The discussion of the features of digital media ethics deepened our understanding of that agenda. The full agenda, from my perspective, is as follows: Journalism ethics needs to be inventive in the twin domains of procedure – how it approaches ethics discourse – and content – the aims and principles that define what responsible journalism means in a digital, global world.

In terms of procedure, it should embrace the open ethics forum, allowing citizens a meaningful role in articulating and altering the content of journalism ethics. The formulation and revision of codes of journalism ethics should not be an in-house affair within professional associations of journalism. Ethics revision should include the meaningful participation not only of citizen journalists but members of the public, even if the latter do not practice journalism. At the same time, ethicists and professional journalists can provide an informed voice in code revision and in the daily global discourse about media. Moreover, journalists increasingly need to approach their ethics from a global perspective. They should support efforts to develop a global media ethics.

In terms of content, journalism ethics faces the daunting task of reinterpreting its core beliefs and norms so they apply to new practitioners and practices, without falling into a weak "anything goes" approach or an extreme Do-It-Yourself stance. The goal of journalism ethics, local and global, should be a new integrative ethics that allows for differences but overcomes the many sharp divisions within journalism. Journalism ethics should reject the idea that fragmentation is a positive state of affairs or a *fait accompli*.

In particular, we need to recognize that forms of journalism ethics that stress a narrow objectivity of "just the facts" are seriously incomplete in a media ecology that encourages interpretive journalism. Important work needs to be done to develop norms and criteria for evaluating interpretive and advocacy journalism. Rather than reject such forms of journalism as not objective or not even journalism, a new ethics should provide guidance on the features of good interpretation and ethical advocacy in journalism. This will require a redefinition of the idea of journalism objectivity to suit the new world of journalism. I have proposed, as a redefinition, the notion of "pragmatic objectivity" – a flexible method for assessing most forms of journalism (Ward 2005).

All of these changes in approach and content entail a revision of how schools and universities teach journalism. Such teaching needs to go beyond an overwhelming focus on practical writings skills for straight news reporting, supported by a traditional notion of news objectivity. Curricula need to prioritize three things. First, journalism education should teach sophisticated methods for doing journalism, ranging far beyond the "tried and true" methods of checking documents, asking officials to comment, and making sure one's report is accurate. Developments in digital software and other areas are giving citizens, and therefore journalists, new and powerful tools to investigate issues and detect hidden trends. The current attention being paid to "data journalism" – using computer technology to find deep trends in the facts – is one example. Such methods, from data visualizations to statistical analysis, will allow future journalists to do in-depth and high-impact journalism using rigorous methods. Journalism's method, once the domain of common sense and simple observation, is coming of age.

Second, an education in digital journalism and its ethics should do more than stress proficiency in technical digital skills. It should examine how journalists should use such technology to engage their publics and improve the state of the world. To do this, young journalists need greater social and cultural knowledge with a global perspective. Tomorrow's journalists will be global interpreters for a world of interconnected traditions and ideologies. They need to know much more about the global issues, from climate change to human rights, which threaten our planet and its marginalized minorities. Third, journalists need to study the methods of interpretation found in the social sciences and elsewhere. This study includes the development of clear criteria for evaluating opinion and interpretation in journalism.

Media ethics as activism

This chapter's discussion leads me to see media ethics as a domain of activism. If good journalism is to prevail, journalists and others need to drop their age-old reservations about advocacy and promote a healthy global media sphere.

For most of my life, media criticism has consisted of studies that noted the sins of mainstream journalism. The critics were, predictably, scholars and former journalists sitting on the sidelines. On my bookcase at home I have dozens of such books pointing out the "troubles" of journalism and mainstream media. It is a depressing collection.[11] These books get much publicity, and the result is that media ethics is considered an oxymoron.

Today, the critics can join the media players on the field. They can do what I call "media ethics activism." One sense of that term is summed up in the phrase: "If you don't like the media you're getting, create your own media." Media ethics goes beyond criticism. We can create new and counterbalancing media spaces committed to ethical ideals.

One such space is the development of nonprofit journalism. Across the United States, centers for nonprofit investigative journalism have sprung up, financed by foundations and individual donors. For example, Jon Sawyer left mainstream media to create the award-winning nonprofit Pulitzer Center for Crisis Reporting in Washington, DC.[12] He wanted to fill the need for independent foreign reporting. At the same time, journalism schools increasingly do the real-world journalism in the public interest that is lacking among commercial media. Other forms of nonprofit agencies, such as NGOs, are experimenting in the use of new media for social reform. For example, World Pulse, the non-profit women's media outlet, has 18,000 members. It aims "to harness the power of women to accelerate women's impact for change."[13] Not long ago, it completed its "Girls Transform the World" campaign to draw attention to the education of girls around the world. The site, started by a young female journalist in Portland, Oregon, used crowdsourcing to get girls and women to identify and share stories on barriers, while seeking solutions. The result was a compilation of 350 stories from hundreds of people in over sixty countries, which formed the basis of a communique sent to the G20 leaders.

These new media entities have potential as stand-alone initiatives. But they can have additional impact if they unite with others. There are powerful websites where global bloggers, professional reporters, and others track human rights abuses. There are global networks of non-profit journalism centers. In doing media ethics activism, we can develop global networks of citizens and journalists gathered under the umbrella of media ethics and global democratic journalism. New media, legacy media, and education units can join to shape the media universe. Negative macro-trends can only be balanced by positive macro-sized resistance.

In these ways we can preserve, at the heart of our media systems, a significant core of responsible communicators for our digital media world.

Notes

1. I am not advancing a "technological determinism" perspective. While the advance of digital technology was crucial to changes in journalism and its ethics, the existence of technology by itself does not guarantee a revolution. The media revolution was, and has been, sustained by other factors such as a literate and technologically savvy populace, and freedom of expression.
2. http://www.bbc.co.uk/editorialguidelines/ (accessed November 13, 2014).
3. http://www.spj.org/ethicscode.asp (accessed November 13, 2014).
4. Recently, I joined the committee to revise the SPJ code, a four-year process that comes eighteen years after the previous revision. At time of writing, the committee had agreed upon a final draft for consideration of SPJ members. The committee decided to retain the tradition of the code

stipulating standards for all journalists, and to not mention specific types of journalists, such as advocacy journalists, or specific types of media platforms, such as social media. The decision to maintain this approach stimulated much committee discussion.
5. The ONO website and description of the project is at: http://journalists.org/resources/build-your-own-ethics-code (accessed November 13, 2014).
6. I was one of the writers who contributed advice on how to think about different ethical questions. My area was the use of quotations.
7. For example, at one meeting of the SPJ code revision committee which I attended, a member said a DIY approach lacks the "courage" to stand behind important ethical values.
8. In Ward 2010, I provided a unifying framework for global journalism based on principles of human flourishing and global justice.
9. http://newsroom.cisco.com (accessed November 13, 2014).
10. http://www.redbull.com/us/en (accessed November 13, 2014).
11. For a sample of this genre of media criticism, see Patterson 1994, Hachten 1998, Jones 2009, and McChesney 2004.
12. The center is at http://pulitzercenter.org/ (accessed November 13, 2014).
13. The NGO's website is: http://worldpulse.com/about/worldpulse (accessed November 13, 2014).

References

Friend, Cecilia, and Jane B. Singer. 2007. *Online Journalism Ethics: Traditions and Transitions*. Armonk, NY: M. E. Sharpe.
Hachten, William A. 1998. *The Troubles of Journalism: A Critical Look at What's Right and Wrong with the Press*. Mahwah, NJ: Lawrence Erlbaum.
Jones, Alex S. 2009. *Losing the News: The Future of the News that Feeds Democracy*. Oxford: Oxford University Press.
McChesney, Robert W. 2004. *The Problem of the Media: U.S. Communication Politics in the 21st Century*. New York: Monthly Review Press.
Patterson, Thomas E. 1994. *Out of Order*. New York: Vintage Books.
Siebert, Fred, Theodore Peterson, and Wilbur Schramm. 1956. *Four Theories of the Press*. Urbana: University of Illinois.
Ward, Stephen J. A. 2005. *The Invention of Journalism Ethics: The Path to Objectivity and Beyond*. Montreal: McGill-Queen's University.
Ward, Stephen J. A. 2010. *Global Journalism Ethics*. Montreal: McGill-Queen's University Press.

Ward, Stephen J. A. 2011. *Ethics and the Media: An Introduction.* Cambridge: Cambridge University Press.
Ward, Stephen J. A., ed. 2013. *Global Media Ethics: Problems and Perspectives.* Malden, MA: Wiley Blackwell.
Ward, Stephen J. A., and Herman Wasserman. 2010. "Towards an Open Ethics: Implications of New Media Platforms for Global Ethics Discourse." Journal of Mass Media Ethics, 25(4): 275–292.
Ward, Stephen J. A., and Herman Wasserman. 2014. "Towards a Global Media Ethics of Listening." Journalism Studies, 8(2): 25–41. DOI: 10.1080/1461670X.2014.950882.

Chapter 5
Defining Journalism

A new integration of media ethics begins with a reconception of journalism that addresses the debate over who is a journalist and what is journalism. This chapter provides a schema for defining journalism for a global media world. It identifies common features that unite journalists who work in different media cultures and on different media platforms.

How Define?

Why define journalism?

One of the challenges of radical media ethics is addressing the vigorous and often unproductive debate about who should be considered a journalist and what constitutes journalism. The debate is especially unproductive when one type of journalist uses a self-serving definition to exclude others from the practice. For example, imagine that professional newspaper reporters speak derisively of citizen bloggers

---

Radical Media Ethics: A Global Approach, First Edition. Stephen J. A. Ward.
© 2015 John Wiley and Sons, Inc. Published 2015 by John Wiley and Sons, Inc.

as not really journalists, and they support their opinion by introducing a self-serving definition of journalism that praises the reporters' form of journalism. They stipulate criteria that exclude bloggers and others. Now, some limitations on the use of "journalist" must exist, and we need criteria to give the term meaning. However, exclusionary and contentious stipulations of the meaning (and extension) of "journalist" or "journalism" need well-supported, careful arguments, not declarations *ex cathedra* from one group or another. Otherwise, the definitional exercise ends in a trading of insults between the rival groups of journalists.

One response to this tiresome shouting match is to dismiss the definitional exercise *tout court* as impossible, unimportant, or "merely" a matter of semantics about the meaning of words. Or we dismiss the exercise as a power struggle masquerading as a logical attempt to define a practice. For example, some professional journalists may use narrow definitions to protect their control of the practice. They are accused of seeking to control the public use of the words "journalist" and "journalism" – to act as a language police for the profession.

There is some truth to these charges. Some debates are power struggles in disguise. Some debates deteriorate into word play. But the current debate raises deep issues that are anything but a language game or "merely" semantics. Not all definitional exercises are power struggles, and one must be careful in declaring something to be "just" semantics. Semantics is important. How we understand the meaning of terms is rarely just word play, or without consequence. Issues of meaning are bedrock issues. In deciding to use a term in a certain manner, we are embracing a certain understanding of journalism that will affect how we respond to issues in the practice.

The definitional issue facing journalism today is deeper and more substantial than games of power and language. It goes to the very conception of the practice, its future, and what ethics can serve the practice. This is because the definitional turmoil is, to a great degree, the symptom of a much greater turmoil in the normative interpretations of the practice. As we have seen, a media revolution has created multiple and clashing interpretations of journalism. Therefore, not unexpectedly, we disagree – deeply – on definitions of the practice. From an ethical perspective, why should we care about such disagreement?

Defining Journalism

Because the definitions and normative interpretations of a practice are linked. Lack of clarity in one domain rubs off on the other. If we are no longer sure what the normative point of journalism is (and what forms of journalism best serve this point), we lose track of important reasons for certain practices and methods. For example, to lose sight of the central role of journalism in informing citizens for democracy is to lose sight of the importance of journalism as a practice of verification and accuracy – features that should be part of any definition of journalism. We can underestimate or fail to fully understand why journalists have placed such stress on these practices. Vice versa, lack of clarity in definition rubs off on ethics. We can express this point as a series of questions. How can we speak intelligibly about the ethics of journalism, or seek an integration of journalism values, if we are at odds over the very meaning of "journalist" and "journalism"? In Chapters 1 and 4, I indicated that the properties "is a journalist," or "is a work of journalism" are social properties. They exist because citizens came to recognize certain activities as having a social role, from which followed certain responsibilities, duties, and rights, in much the same way that "being a judge" is a citizen-recognized property that entails responsibilities, duties, and rights. But what if the media revolution has muddied the conceptual waters to the point where there is little consensus on the meaning of "journalist" and "journalism"? What ethical duties can we ascribe to journalism if we quarrel over "journalism"? And to whom do the duties belong if we quarrel over "journalist"?

The definitional question is real, substantive, and important. But the depth of the issues means we cannot easily and quickly proceed to construct a new definition of journalism and journalist. We must work patiently, overcoming obstacles at every turn. One obstacle consists in the many misunderstandings about what a definition is, and what we can realistically expect from this exercise in conceptual clarification.

Therefore, in constructing a schema, or definition, we need to do three things: First, clarify what a definition is and *reduce* expectations (or demands) about what a definition can achieve. Second, we should pursue the concept-building with a clear purpose. I believe the purpose is not simply to achieve greater linguistic clarity about "journalist" and "journalism" as words. We should construct our schemas to promote integration, and reduce fragmentation, in journalism ethics. Third, our definitional exercises should promote journalism ethics. That is, we come to see a link between our definitions (or general conceptions) of the practice and our normative interpretations of that practice. Our definition should indicate why we *also* support certain ethical values in journalism, and vice versa.

I will construct my schema in two steps. First, I describe the best approach to the definitional task for journalism. The dispute over defining journalism is so confused that philosophizing about definition is required before we can address the issue in journalism. After exploring what sort of definition suits journalism, I propose a specific schema.

What is a definition?

Dictionaries tell us that a definition gives the meaning of a term, phrase, or symbol. This is correct but it can be deceptive. Definition, although ostensibly about language, is usually about categorizing objects into kinds. We give the meaning by identifying properties shared by the objects – properties that make the objects examples of the term. Definers seek properties that answer the question: "What is this thing?" My laptop is black in color, but the property of being black is not a defining feature of a laptop. Size and computing power are defining properties. Definitions name properties that identify the object and differentiate it from other things.

There are many types of definition. We may define an object by placing it into a system organized according to genus and species. For example, we can define "man" or "human" as a rational animal. "Animal" is the genus and "animal that is rational" is the species. We may define by giving what logicians call the "necessary and sufficient conditions" for applying the term to any instance. The necessary conditions are those properties that all instances of the term must exhibit. For example, all humans are animals. Being an animal is a necessary condition. But being an animal is not sufficient to define "humans" because birds and fish are also animals. We need additional and sufficient conditions that differentiate the object from related objects, such as rationality. Another type of definition is what I call "referential definition." We give the meaning of a term by pointing to examples.

Defining Journalism

"*That* is pornography, even if I can't define it," we might say, while watching a movie on television. Also, there are special forms of definition in logic and the sciences, e.g., a recursive definition. The varieties of things defined are as endless as our ability to conceive of objects – organisms, symbols, physical objects, and social practices. We define the responsibilities of a new employee, or I define my values. "Define" becomes an over-used term when other things are meant, such as spelling out specifics and explaining.

We define when clarity about a term's meaning and application is important to some theoretical or practical purpose. A lack of clarity can be due to ambiguity (several meanings), e.g., the meanings of "innovation," or vagueness in application, e.g., "Is this hill a mountain?" If you and I place opposing bets on who will be the most valuable player this season in the National Hockey League, we need to define "most valuable." If I study bias in journalism, I need to define "bias." Do we need to constantly define everything we say? No. Definitions are needed when there is good reason to be more precise about one's language. We stop and define where needed. Usually, we don't scratch where it doesn't itch.

How precise do our definitions need to be? It depends on the purpose or the problem in question. In mathematics, logic, and science, theories need crisp criteria of application for important terms. If the term "attention deficit disorder" is imprecise, we may apply it to instances that are not cases of the disorder. Definitions also take center stage where social policy depends on the meaning of basic concepts. Dworkin's interpretive concepts, e.g., justice, invite definition, and definitional disputes. However, in everyday life we get along nicely with referential definition or imprecisely defined terms. We apply "chair," "dog," and "hamburger" without precise definitions. We rarely disagree on examples, so lack of a precise definition causes no confusion. But things can change, quickly. We cannot assume that a clear definition of a previously accepted term, e.g., journalism, will never be needed.

The world is full of things that elude clear and simple definition, such as the meaning of happiness, black holes in space, or games. This elusiveness prompts some people to assume incorrectly that an attempt to define such terms is unnecessary or useless. To the contrary, it is precisely where key terms lack clarity, and create disagreement, that we need to make the effort to explicate their meanings. As Aristotle believed, good definitions come at the end of study.

Good definitions may not be strict definitions. Given the nature of the object in question, strict definitions may not be possible. A triangle may be clearly defined as a plane bounded by three lines, but how does one define, in strict and clear terms, something as complicated as globalization, the art deco movement, or "postmodernism"? Yet it is possible to construct reasonably clear definitions of these phenomena. We should not expect *perfectly* clear definitions when we define many terms. Precision and clarity are matters of degree. One definition is clearer, more precise, and more helpful than another.

Definitions, especially definitions of a practice, may go beyond the empirical facts. They organize our facts into groups. We do not find our definitions existing in nature. When we categorize an object, we often have a choice between definitions. Our definition is relative to the conceptual scheme that grounds our definition. For example, we can define journalism as a species of human communication, or a form of information exchange, or a socially inculcated system of skills and values. Also, our definitions incorporate normative (or non-empirical) elements such as norms and aims. The discussion of normative interpretation in Chapter 2 made it clear that, when we define happiness, justice, or a social practice, we give the definition a normative gloss. We mix facts, norms, and purposes. Often, our definition is constructed with an eye to answering certain questions or issues. For example, we may emphasize the verification of facts before publication as a defining feature of journalism because we wish to exclude stories based on rumor as examples of journalism. In many cases, the definitional question is not best understood as a factual query, e.g., How do we actually use this term? or What *are* the defining properties? The question is normative: How *should* we understand this concept, given the current disagreement on its meaning and the problems facing journalism? Definition is normative reform of our concepts.

We will return to this point. For now, I stress that much of our definitional activity is purpose-relative, normative in nature, and agreement-seeking in aim. We *construct* a definition from a list of potential definitions. We *propose* the definition as a way of understanding the term, given current issues and problems. And we propose because we seek, through collective intentionality, agreement on the definition.

Definition, in many cases, is not an abstract exercise of a disembodied mind, coolly reviewing ideas apart from the real world. Instead, definition, in many cases, is a pragmatic, conceptual response to a problem by a situated inquirer within an ongoing discipline.

This pragmatic view of definition helps us to respond to people who are surprised that journalists cannot provide a rigorous and uncontentious definition of their practice. Without such a definition, it seems that journalists do not know what they do, and journalism teachers do not know what they teach. This is too strong a conclusion to draw from the facts of the situation. It expects too much of definition. It incorrectly assumes that rigorous, perfect definitions are required, and easy to construct. Even if there were no media revolution, it should not surprise us if media practitioners struggle to provide a rigorous definition. After all, they are practical people who are not in the business of philosophical reflection and abstract definition. Moreover, as we have noted, many things in this world are complex and elude easy definition, and a complex social practice is one of those things. Many practices are carried on without the practitioners being able to give the public abstract and rigorous self-definitions. It is erroneous to say these practitioners and teachers are at a loss to say what they do. Some may be able to provide interesting, if imperfect, self-definitions. Also, it is false that there are *no* definitions of journalism on offer. The problem is the reverse: there are too many (conflicting) definitions. What eludes us is *agreement* on any one definition. So the question is not, "Why can't journalists produce a definition?" but rather, "Why is definition in this domain difficult, and what is preventing agreement?"

The illusion that a definition of journalism should be precise and easy to construct is fostered by another illusion: the belief that, in the past, journalists had a clear and precise conception of their profession. It is an example of what I call the illusion of referential definition. The illusion is produced by an over-reliance on examples to define a term, rather than examining its meaning. Referential definitions give us false confidence that we have a clear understanding.

The allegedly clear definitions of journalists and journalism in the past were, in the main, referential definitions. Journalists were able to

A Radical Integrated Ethics

point to agreed-upon examples, and ignore thorny issues of meaning. "Journalist" referred to the professional reporters, editors, TV anchors, and columnists employed by the easily recognizable newsrooms at CNN, *The New York Times*, the wire services, the British and Canadian public broadcasting systems, *The Sunday Telegraph* in London, and news magazines such as *Time* and *The Economist*. There was little deep thinking on the meaning of "journalist." If journalists in those former years had been pressed to state, precisely, the meaning of "journalist," I suspect they would have been no more able to do so than journalists today.

The illusion is supported by overlooking the existence of borderline cases of journalism in the past. For example, in the 1950s and 1960s, did "journalist" or "journalism" apply to the writers of the satirical magazine *The Onion*, Hunter S. Thompson's guerrilla journalism, reporters for Communist newspapers, or the hosts of the many new radio and TV information shows? Nevertheless, "journalist" was clear – or thought to be clear, in retrospect – because there were fewer borderline cases than today, and there was more agreement on paradigmatic examples. Few people doubted that Walter Cronkite was an example of a television journalist.

This reliance on referential definition falters if a term becomes unclear or controversial in its reference. Here again, agreement is a large factor. Professional journalists today, no doubt, could refer to clear examples of "journalist" from their own ranks. But there are many controversial examples of journalists outside the professional ranks. Application of "journalist" or "journalism" becomes problematic and we worry about its meaning.

What definition for journalism?

Given that defining journalism is important and need not be perfect, what sort of definition is most useful when we explicate "journalism"? I propose we construct a definition that captures the conceptual scheme which gives meaning to journalism. We should articulate the meaning of journalism as a flexible concept with multiple criteria that link together in the form of a web. Moreover, the definition should focus on the "core meaning" of journalism – a general meaning that allows the term to apply to many forms of journalism. To understand this sort of definition, we need to know more about flexible concepts and core meanings.

The analysis here is based on the discussion of conceptual schemes in Chapter 2. In that chapter, we discussed concepts as tools that help the mind categorize and label groups of objects. We noted that some theories think of concepts as rigid (or unchanging) and clear in all applications to new objects; other theories regard all (or most) concepts as flexible and imprecise in their application to new objects. Some theories in the "flexible" school think we recognize new objects by comparing them with a prototype (or paradigmatic example) in our minds. We then used Thagard's notion (1992) of conceptual schemes to show how the meaning of a term is given not by one or two ideas but by a web of ideas that are connected in many ways, e.g., through kind-hierarchies or by cause and effect.

If concepts are arranged in a web, then a definition should indicate the *place* of the concept in that network – the relationship of the concept to other concepts. The task is to provide a part of that network – the part that allows us to apply the term accurately. We must be selective. It cannot be a *list* of all the nodes in the web, which are too numerous and often irrelevant to the definition. We need to specify parts of the list that are more crucial in understanding the meaning of the term than other parts. We decide which features are most important from the context of the definitional attempt. Some nodes will serve only as background meaning and are not part of the definition. For example, the color blue is important to the definition of a blue jay but not to the definition of finches which come in many colors. Many background features are left out of the definition, e.g., that a blue jay is an animal or that a journalist lives on Earth.

Fluid concepts   Philosopher Michael Lynch's theory of flexible concepts is helpful in explaining the nature of concepts in Thagard's web. Lynch says there have been two dominant pictures of concepts in the 20th century: crystalline and fluid. One picture is that concepts are like crystals – "rigid, pure, and transparent, with sharp edges and definite borders" (1998, 56). This picture is favored by logician Gottlob Frege and in the early writings of Ludwig Wittgenstein.

A Radical Integrated Ethics

On the crystalline view, a concept must have an absolutely determinate application in all *possible* cases in which it could apply. Frege says a definition of a concept "must be complete; it must unambiguously determine, as regards any object, whether or not it falls under that concept ... a concept must have a sharp boundary" (Frege 1952, 159). The crystalline picture believes that to understand a concept is to know the necessary and sufficient conditions for its application. It is to provide the unchanging "essence" of the object in question. The essence of F is whatever properties make an F what it is, and separate it from everything else. A definition of "dog" should give us clear, fixed criteria that separate dogs from non-dogs. On the crystalline view, it makes no sense to talk about levels of meaning, definition by degree, or a choice of definitions relative to purpose.

The fluid picture rejects this interpretation of concepts. It believes that most concepts are flexible. They change and acquire different meanings over space and time according to individual experiences and social context. Fluid concepts, Lynch says (2005, 141), are "concepts that can be extended and enriched in new ways as circumstances demand." Lynch compares concepts to modeling clay that can be stretched and altered in shape. Fluidity means:

1. Criteria for correctly grasping and applying concepts need not be absolutely determinate for all uses. Sometimes we do not know whether a concept applies to a new object, and genuine disagreement on meaning is possible. Is a super-computer that can play chess better than humans a thinking thing?
2. Criteria can be changed or stretched to apply to new circumstances, to reflect new knowledge. Our criteria for gold changed from observable properties (shiny, yellow) to scientific properties (chemical composition) as our knowledge of metals advanced.
3. A term often has sets of criteria that may conflict. For instance, judges for an award in investigative journalism may use different evaluative criteria. Some may focus on the impact the report had on society; others will focus on how difficult it was to obtain the information; still others will look at whether the report says anything new and says it in an engaging manner. The concept of

"award-winning investigative journalism" is fluid and can have several sets of criteria. This fluidity occurs *within* webs of concepts, as Thagard describes.

For the fluid approach to concepts, we do not fail to understand a concept just because our definition fails to satisfy a demanding standard of rigidity and clarity that may not be appropriate for all domains. Frege's demand for "essences" may be appropriate for logic and mathematics, but why think it is a good model for how we use most concepts? It is more plausible to conclude that the *lack* of essences tells us that many concepts are fluid.

Core meaning   There is a type of fluid concept that helps us to define terms like journalism. It is a term that has a core meaning open to new contexts. Lynch again is helpful. He describes "open-textured" concepts as having a "shared minimal core" that can be enriched in different and even incompatible ways as circumstances demand.

Lynch compares these concepts to "sketches" (1998, 72). Imagine that we ask different artists to fill in a minimal sketch of a landscape, e.g., the beach near my home. Some ways of filling in the sketch will strike us as inappropriate, e.g., an artist fills in the sketch by painting over the sketch with one color. But other ways of filling in are interesting and accurate. While some fill-ins can be ruled out, there are a lot of good ways to fill it in.

Lynch says that our concepts of happiness and flourishing are open-textured in just this way. The idea of a happy life has a common core of characteristics – even if they are thin and sketchy. These minimal features are what anything we would count as a good life must have in common. A life without these features would be a worse life. Happiness needs a certain level of physical and psychological health, freedom from debilitating pain, some measure of pleasure and self-respect. It is a composite of such core properties. At the same time, there is a plurality of ways to go on from these minimal features – a plurality of ways to be happy, in different degrees. Like the lines of a sketch, the minimal features of a good life are open to different developments and interpretations.

Application to journalism

I propose that we understand "journalism" as acquiring meaning in the flexible web-like manner described by Thagard, Lynch, and the fluid approach to concepts.

The task of definition is to capture that part of journalism's conceptual scheme which provides its defined properties and determines how we apply the term. We should recall that this "capture" will not be a simple empirical discovery of how the term is used but also a normative choice of what properties and criteria can be proposed as most useful in clarifying the contested term.

What elements, or types of properties, are there to choose from? Once again we look to Thagard (1992) for help. Following his analysis of concepts, it would include kind- and part-hierarchies, e.g., journalism falls under the genus of public human communication, and investigative journalism is part of journalism. It would include causal links, such as how journalism has various effects on citizens. I am *not* giving a definition of journalism here. That will come later. I am only asking the reader to imagine "journalism" as a node in web of meaning, and to stop thinking of journalism as an entry in a dictionary – one or two ideas captured by a pithy sentence. On my view, defining journalism will require paragraphs, not a few sentences.

In addition to a web approach, we add the notions of flexible concepts and core meanings. The criteria that give journalism's meaning are flexible in Lynch's sense. They are open and can change. We can expect new forms of journalism to alter our definition's criteria, and we can expect our definition to be uncertain, at times, as to whether to apply "journalism" to a form of journalism or an apparent act of journalism. Finally, our definition should provide a core meaning of the term that, like a sketch, can be "filled in" or realized by many types of journalism. My schema below describes a core meaning for journalism. This flexibility and lack of precision should not be seen as a failure of definition. To the contrary, as I will argue, they are features that hold the key to building an open and evolving conception of journalism, while avoiding the unproductive, intolerant, and exclusionary definitions that have marred journalism ethics in recent years.

Before I explain my schema, let us bring together these numerous philosophical points. Given these points, what sort of definition is appropriate for journalism today? First, we should see the definitional task as seeking an imperfect but valuable construction of the meaning of journalism. We reduce our expectations about what definition can achieve, especially for definitions of social practices. We reject the idea that definitions are only acceptable if they are rigorous and precise. As imperfect, this form of definition will no doubt encounter some forms of communication that we are not sure fall under our definition. However, these imperfections are to be expected, given that we are not seeking an essence of journalism. Also, we are conscious that our definition does not arise solely from empirical facts. Definitions of journalism are meant to fit our normative interpretations of the purpose of journalism, and they involve choices and proposals. When constructing a definition, we do so with an eye as to how the definition will address current issues in the practice, such as helping to once again integrate journalism ethics.

Second, the definition should capture a web of connected criteria that are open and flexible. Because journalism is a globally diverse practice, we want our criteria to include a core of meaning that allows journalism practice to be realized in different ways.

To work in the area of definitions of journalism one needs a high degree of tolerance for doubt, imprecision, and change. This is due to the nature of the subject; it is not due to a weakness in the logical acumen of the researchers. This is the mindset we should adopt as we enter into any definitional exercise for "journalism" or "journalist."

A Schema for Journalism

In cognitive psychology, a schema is a framework that helps us to understand the world, or some part of it. Schema is short for conceptual scheme. Schemas can be large or small. We have a schema for predicting the rotation of the planets; we have a schema for understanding laptop computers; we have a schema for making sense of the symbols used in the daily weather reports of newspapers; we have a schema for understanding Morse code. Schemas are useful because of their generality, which makes them applicable to many cases.

Schemas are the conceptual equivalent of Lynch's sketches. They are conceptual schemes that can be "filled" in many ways. In mathematics, schemas are abstract structures. We fill in the values of x, y, and other symbols so that the equation in which they appear gives us a particular result. To take a simple example, I have an abstract schema for converting temperatures in Fahrenheit to Celsius. If I "plug in" some values (e.g., the temperature today at 2 p.m. in Fahrenheit), the schema gives me a specific result: the corresponding temperature in Celsius.

In this chapter, I propose that we think of a definition of journalism as a schema – a general structure which guides us in understanding the many forms of journalism. The schema helps us determine to what extent any act of communication can be regarded as journalistic. The "values" of our definition are the particular forms of journalism and acts of journalism committed daily around the world. The schema exhibits the features of good definition explained above – the scheme is a "sketch" and a flexible conceptual structure. This type of schema can serve as the basis for integrating journalism. We need a schema that is flexible and which shows how there exists a core meaning of journalism that, like a sketch, is open to multiple realization across types of journalism, types of journalists, and types of media cultures.

My schema has two distinct features. One, it defines journalism across three levels of activity – journalism as a personal activity, as a social activity, and as the activity of an institution. Two, it includes norms and ethical elements in the definition.

My definitional schema starts from the concept of journalism, not the concept of a journalist. This approach allows me to note the features of journalism wherever it occurs. Then we can discuss how and where journalism occurs, and in what format. It avoids existing disputes over who is a journalist based on whether someone is a professional or is employed by certain familiar news organizations. Acts of journalism may be done by professional reporters, columnists, bloggers, human rights activists, lawyers, public relations specialists, and so on.

I want to reiterate that I am putting forward a *proposal*: a hypothesis for understanding democratic practice. I am not trying to provide a schema that captures the meaning of every form of journalism,

Defining Journalism

including forms of journalism in totalitarian states. Rather I say this: If you wish to clarify the meaning of journalism in the democratic tradition, here is one way to think about it.

Three levels

Any schema for a social practice must consider the major forms in which people enter into the activity. The activity of journalism occurs at three levels of society – the levels of personal use, social practice, and institutional practice. Failure to distinguish these levels has caused much confusion when people debate journalism and its ethical responsibilities. Journalism at each level exhibits different characteristics, and different ethical responsibilities.

Journalism as a personal activity The history of journalism is a history of how journalism started as a personal activity and later became a social practice, a business, and an institution.

We do many things that fall under personal activity. Such activity is optional and often pleasurable for me, but not necessarily of interest to others. I am free to engage in the activity as I will. It is not a public activity, in the sense that the activity does not have an important public role; nor does the activity entail public duties or the following of prescribed practices. Activities in this category include our many interests and hobbies, from stamp collecting, reading books, and playing Scrabble to following our favorite sports team. Many of these activities involve communication. We enjoy talking to friends on the telephone; we write letters to relatives. Many activities are better called social activities, such as talking a walk with a friend, attending a cocktail party, or marching in a parade. Although these activities are social, they also do not entail special public responsibilities. Do personal and social activities touch on ethics? For many activities, it is presumed that participants will follow general rules of etiquette and the "general morality" of society, as noted in Chapter 1. In other words, they will keep promises, will not cheat, will speak truthfully, and will seek to avoid causing harm. These rules apply to anything we do. For personal activities, we usually do not need to formulate a special "ethic," replete with special duties, social roles, and political rights. Common sense and common decency are enough.[1]

One can enjoy journalism as a personal or social activity. Journalism can be a sort of "communication hobby." One may start blogging about your experiences and views from one's bedroom, or start posting one's political opinions on Facebook. One may even attract a large number of online "followers." Or one can make a simple form of journalism a pleasurable activity in one's retirement, e.g., a former newspaper editor helps his neighborhood publish a newsletter on its annual garage sale.

Historically, the first forms of modern journalism were personal or social activities, beginning as experiments in news publishing by established editors of books (Ward 2005, 89–127). The rise of a periodic news press in 17th-century Europe was a product of individuals with personal and idiosyncratic reasons for engaging in this activity. Journalism had not yet risen to the status of a social practice with widely recognized forms of conduct, skills, and duties.

Journalism as social practice By the early 18th century in Europe, America, and elsewhere, people began to refer to certain people as "journalists" in our sense. The term "journalist," originally applied to men of letters who wrote in learned journals, came to refer to the creators of the emerging daily newspapers (Ward 2005, 89n1). To work for such publications was to work in journalism. Journalism began to grow beyond its initial status as a personal activity. This was the beginning of journalism as a social activity and practice, with some identifiable functions, such as informing citizens about what was happening in the British Parliament or the progress of a civil war (Ward 2005, 128–173). However, journalism in Europe throughout most of the 1700s was not an institution, and it was barely tolerated by governments.

That journalism is a social activity is obvious. The journalist writes for others, typically a group or a public. Acts of journalism occur in society, and are permitted to occur by society. The writings of journalism are about social events, the technology that journalists use is developed by fellow members of society, and organizations that employ journalists are social entities. But journalism came to be more than a social activity. It developed, over time, into a practice. A practice is a regimented social activity, with its own skills, knowledge, aims, and responsibilities. Our most obvious examples are the professions. To practice law, for example, is not to engage in a personal activity as an occasional, unregulated hobby for pleasure. The practice does not allow you to conduct yourself in any way you please. To practice law is to follow socially prescribed rules of conduct and to fulfill socially important roles, according to certain skills and ethical norms.

The ethics of social practices are more demanding and specific than the ethics of personal activities. Practices have a real and substantial impact on citizens, and the functions carried out by social practices are important to a well-functioning society. Therefore, we have to spell out the ethics for such practices. An easygoing attitude which assumes that common decency and adherence to general morality will be enough (and rarely will be invoked) is not sufficient. Practices deal with complex situations where the interests of many parties collide. Society needs practitioners to follow specific and explicit sets of rules. This is why professional ethics exists and why practices have their codes of ethics. Similarly, this is why journalism ethics, in any robust sense, came into being in the late 1800s when journalism became a recognized, important social practice that claimed to be a profession, as described earlier. The skills and activities of journalists were no longer part of a personal crusade or a money-making hobby. Their activities were increasingly governed by codes and taught in journalism schools.

How do we begin to distinguish journalism from other social activities and practices?

Within the category of social activity, journalism belongs to the genus of public communication. Journalism is not just a form of communication. A private conversation is a form of communication but it is not journalism. Journalism is public communication in three senses. Works of journalism are public because they are accessible to citizens. They are not writings in a private journal. Works of journalism are public in the additional sense of being intended to be read by a public, and they are public in dealing with issues of interest to a public.

Yet the genus of public communication is too large to distinguish journalism from other forms of public communication. There are many acts of communication that are public but are not forms of journalism. If I use Twitter or Facebook to tell my friends I am attending a conference in New York City, I am informing people about my activities. But I do not commit an act of journalism. This point stands even if social media *can* be used to do journalism.

The factors that help to distinguish acts of journalism are timeliness, public significance, and periodic publishing. By timeliness I mean that the communication is about current events and trends in the world. A historian who writes a book about democracy in ancient Greece is not committing an act of journalism. He commits an act of scholarly communication. However, were he to write a column in a newspaper saying how the ancient Greek model should be adopted by the Japanese election system to reduce voter apathy, he engages in journalism. The "timeliness" of the column's topic, not just the fact that it appears in a newspaper, makes it an act of journalism.

Public significance means that the writings must treat a topic, development, event, or trend in a way that has implications for society and the public. A report on the effectiveness of airport security at Canadian airports has public significance. A study of the origins of Renaissance poetry may lack any discernible implication for society. However, if a scholar of Renaissance poetry goes on the BBC and calls for the inclusion of her area of expertise in Britain's high school curriculum, the poetry scholar commits an act of journalism.

Some people add "periodicy" as a criterion of journalism. Periodicy became a prominent feature of definitions of journalism in the 17th and 18th centuries, when editors in western Europe began pushing a periodic news press. I am uncertain that periodicy is a crucial property of acts of journalism. After all, one could write only one newspaper column in one's life and that column would still be an act of journalism. Periodicy seems more central to defining "journalist" since one article does not a journalist make. We are inclined to call someone a journalist when writing articles becomes a regular preoccupation.

Journalism as institutional practice Once journalism became a recognized social practice, it was not long before it was also referred to as an institution. The institutional recognition of journalism was made explicit during the American and French revolutions of the late 18th century. The constitutions that followed the revolutions gave explicit social recognition to the role of the press and the importance of free expression. As the power of the press grew in the 19th and

20th centuries, the idea that journalism was an institution of democracy became accepted (see Cook 2005).

The institutional status of journalism changed journalism ethics. It enhanced, formalized, and broadened the basis for journalism ethics. It strengthened the idea of journalism ethics as a group ethic, made the practice of journalism more significant, and anchored its ethics more securely in the fundamental needs of democracy. Good journalism, however defined, came to be spoken of as crucial to a self-governing democracy, given journalism's near-monopoly on the publication of news. The ethics of journalism was not just a system of rules for the internal regulation of a social practice. It was an ethics which made sure that journalism served members of the public as citizens and ensured the continuance of democracy. Few other professions, such as accountancy or nursing, could claim like journalism that they were a part of the fundamental political fabric of the country. To say that journalism was a political institution, a "fourth estate," was to anchor journalism ethics in something much broader and more important than anchoring journalism ethics in personal values or the mores of a particular group. It anchored journalism ethics in the institutional structure and political philosophy of an entire society.

If journalism ethics is anchored in important social practices and acts as an institution, then journalism ethics is not relative to each journalist. Journalism ethics cannot be reduced to the "personalized" ethics of individuals or groups. The anchor of journalism ethics is not subjective and personal. It is objective and public. As I argued in the section on personalized ethics, ethics does not belong to individual journalists or forms of journalism. It doesn't even belong to all journalists as a group. It belongs to the public or society at large in terms of their legitimate needs and expectations of the news media. This understanding of journalism ethics blocks the idea that bloggers, users of Twitter, or anyone who engages in journalism is free to make up their own idiosyncratic ethics – or not bother with ethics at all. It blocks the view that the general morality is sufficient for guiding journalism conduct, e.g., rules to tell the truth and to be fair. Some citizen journalists argue that a general morality is sufficient for their work, and that journalism ethics is outdated or a concern only for professional journalists. But if journalism is a social practice and an institutional practice – which I believe is

A Radical Integrated Ethics

true – we will need both the principles of general morality and the more specific norms of journalism ethics to guide journalistic conduct online and offline.

This analysis of the three levels shows how important it is to consider how ethics in journalism works across the levels, and to maintain distinctions between the levels. It also indicates that any definition of journalism must take seriously the practice and responsibilities of journalism on the level of social practice and the level of institutional practice. Any definition of ethics that ignores (or gives insufficient emphasis) to the social and institutional aspect of journalism, while emphasizing journalism as free zone of personal activity, fails to be an adequate characterization of journalism and journalism ethics.

Constructing the Schema

We arrive, then, at my first attempt to provide a schema. We begin with journalism as a social practice, not as a personal activity. Borrowing from Michael Schudson, we can say that journalism means: "The practice of periodically producing and publicly disseminating information and commentary about contemporary affairs of general public interest and importance" (2008, 12–13).

To construct this sort of empirical definition, we act like sociologists. We stand back and observe what journalists do, as an activity. One could improve on this general statement. We could pick out additional common features in journalism activity such as the use of certain information-gathering skills, writing styles, methods of investigation, and other practices. We might then define a journalist in Schudson style as someone who writes about news and events regularly for a public, and then add: She also exhibits empirical features *a*, *b*, and *c*. I am not going to carry out such "additions" because it is not central to my task of definition. The essential point is that journalism can be defined as a social activity by noting shared empirical features and functions.

An empirical understanding of journalism, generalizing from its concrete skills, interests, and practices, must be part of any definition of journalism. Yet it is not sufficient for a schematic definition of journalism. What is missing is the normative dimension of the practice.

A purely empirical definition falls short because knowing that many journalists do *this* or *that* does not answer the question: But should they do *this* and *that*? Also, what if some journalists do something new? What if journalism changes?

The social purposes, responsibilities, and norms of a practice are built into the very notion of the practice. It is difficult to define a court prosecutor, teacher, blues guitarist, or police officer without referring to purposes, values, and good practice. Therefore, I doubt that any definition of journalism can avoid adding normative criteria. So we need to combine empirical and normative features in a definition. Using the formula above, we can think of a combined definition as something like this: A journalist is someone who writes about news and events regularly for a public in a way that uses methods *a*, *b*, *c*, and follows ethical norms *d*, *e*, and *f*.

To say that norms live in the practice is to rule out what the empirical approach wants – a naturalistic definition. A naturalistic definition defines a natural object. For instance we can categorize and define types of butterflies, naturalistically, by describing their observable features, and placing them into a scheme of genus and species. We avoid reference to what butterflies *should* look like, normatively speaking. But defining practices is not the same as defining butterflies. We don't simply describe, we prescribe. Purposes and norms seep into our definitions no matter how hard we try to stick to just the facts. The dispute between new and old media journalists is *not* a conflict over facts. All parties agree on the facts. They agree that online and legacy journalists work in different ways. What they disagree on is the value and ethical probity of such styles. It is an ethical debate.

The normative dimension is inescapable when we view journalism as an institutional practice. Earlier we distinguished between social activities such as walking with a friend and institutional activities such getting married or policing – phenomena that are significant for society at large. Recognizing anything as an institution or institutional practice is inseparable from the imposition of status-functions that include such normative items as rights, responsibilities, and aims. An empirical description of social activity misses these institutional properties. We need to shift our thinking from what is practiced to what ought to be practiced.

A Radical Integrated Ethics

The institutional description of journalism is of a public service or public trust that is based, implicitly or explicitly, on a social contract. Society provides constitutional (and other) guarantees of freedom of media and communication in return for certain institutional expectations. It is expected that journalists will fulfill the most important informational or "media needs" of a democratic society. The institutional perspective considers what democracy needs from its news media system. There are six "media needs."

Media needs
- *Informational needs – wide and deep*: Citizens cannot be vigilant and informed without access to a rich informational soup of facts and reports about their world. Some of this information is "wide" (not deep) and fast-changing, e.g., the daily news in all of its forms. Some of the information is "deep" since it provides hard-to-acquire (and important) data on the state of society.
- *Explanatory needs*: Citizens need more than facts. They need context and causal explanations for properly understanding facts and events.
- *"Perspectival enrichment" needs*: Citizens need informed commentary, criticism, and multiple points of view on the information they obtain, and on the state of their society.
- *Advocational and reform needs*: Citizens should be free to go beyond commentary to use media to advocate for causes, and push for reforms, or to hear the positions of advocates and reformers.
- *Participatory needs*: Citizens should have the ability to participate in a meaningful fashion in discussions and debates, and the sharing of facts and analysis. Citizens not only consume media but use media to inquire into issues, respond to claims, and question reports.
- *Dialogic needs*: Citizens should have the opportunity to be part of reasonable and informed dialogue on common concerns, and not be subject to disrespectful attacks on their positions.

These needs are carried out by a wide spectrum of forms of journalism published in multiple formats.

Following Searle (1995), as explained in Chapter 1, the recognition of a special institutional status and function carries with it the imposition of certain rights and responsibilities. This is the institutional basis of journalism ethics. Journalism ethics outlines the institution-based principles and aims of the practice, from journalistic truth-telling and editorial independence to minimizing harm and being transparent.

Final schematic definition We can express the schema as having two intertwined elements, empirical and normative:

Empirical element: Journalism is a social activity defined by the practice of periodically producing and publicly disseminating information and commentary about contemporary affairs of general public interest and importance, and it does so by deploying a range of information-gathering and editing skills.

Normative element: Journalism is a social activity (as defined above) that is expected to carry out a normative, institutional role recognized by society, which goes beyond the activity and functions of journalism as social activity. The institutional role entails following the principles of responsible public communication. The institutional role consists in meeting the public's overall "media needs" (as listed above) and meeting those needs by following appropriate principles and norms that constitute journalism ethics.

I have provided a general schema for understanding journalism. I have not included long passages specifying the "media needs," nor have I stipulated in detail the content of journalism ethics beyond references to principles such as minimizing harm. I have not provided those details for several reasons. Such specifications would be too long and involved for this chapter. I provide these specifications in my other writings (Ward 2010). Another reason is that I don't think such specifications are appropriate for a schema of journalism. Why? Because what we need is an (intentionally) abstract schema that allows practitioners to interpret how such notions are to be applied to their specific contexts and media cultures. My schema provides a minimalist "core meaning" for journalism as institutional practice which is compatible with many actual ways of doing journalism.

Conclusion

This chapter constructed a schema for understanding journalism based on the view that such definitions are imperfect, and mix normative and empirical elements. The schema defines journalism as an open and flexible concept with a core meaning that is general enough to apply to many forms of journalism.

I use this schema as a guide in the chapters that follow.

Note

1. I am not saying that serious ethical violations in proper conduct cannot arise in the course of a personal or social activity. As I noted in Chapter 1, questions about ethics can arise anywhere. Even breaches of etiquette can be unethical. I am only noting that, for most personal activities, the general morality is enough and operates in the background.

References

Cook, Timothy W. 2005. *Governing with the News: The News Media as a Political Institution*. 2nd ed. Chicago: University of Chicago Press.
Frege, Gottlob. 1952. *Translations from the Philosophical Writings of Gottlob Frege*, edited by Peter Geach and Max Black. New York: Philosophical Library.
Lynch, Michael P. 1998. *Truth in Context: An Essay on Pluralism and Objectivity*. Cambridge, MA: MIT Press.
Lynch, Michael P. 2005. *True to Life: Why Truth Matters*, Cambridge, MA: MIT Press.
Searle, John. 1995. *The Construction of Social Reality*. New York: The Free Press.
Schudson, Michael, 2008. "Six or Seven Things News Can Do for Democracy." In *Why Democracies Need an Unlovable Press*, 3–8. Cambridge: Polity.
Thagard, Paul. 1992. *Conceptual Revolutions*. Princeton, NJ: Princeton University Press.
Ward, Stephen J. A. 2005. *The Invention of Journalism Ethics: The Path to Objectivity and Beyond*. Montreal: McGill-Queen's University.
Ward, Stephen J. A. 2010. *Global Journalism Ethics*. Montreal: McGill-Queen's University Press.

Chapter 6
Theory of Meaning for Integrated Ethics

This chapter completes my discussion of the general shape that a radical media ethics should take.

In Chapter 4, I contended that we need an integrated ethics that unites journalists around reformulated and newly invented common principles. In Chapter 5, I said that a definition of journalism should be flexible, and it should include ethical principles and aims. Further, I said the fact that journalism is a social and institutional practice means journalism ethics is based on objective, public reasons, not individual, personal values. Therefore, journalism ethics should accord a central role to broad, practice-wide principles. The principles will be the unifying points across a plurality of forms of democratic journalism. To act as unifying points, the principles will have to be ecumenical. They will have to be ethical principles that allow great latitude for differences in interpretation and application.

In this chapter, I ask how such flexible principles are possible. Radical media ethics may *require* the existence of ecumenical principles, but do such principles actually exist? Does it make sense to talk of ethical

A Radical Integrated Ethics

principles that have a determinate meaning, yet that meaning can be interpreted and applied to cases in different ways?

This chapter sets out to answer these tough philosophical questions. It seeks to explain the process by which journalists give meaning (and meanings) to principles such as serving the public, minimizing harm, being socially responsible, reporting objectively, and so on. What is the "shape" or meaning of these principles? An ethics for a global, mixed media must address this problem of unity in difference at the level of principle.

To answer these questions, we need a theory of meaning. We need a theory that explains the meanings of ecumenical ethical principles in journalism and elsewhere. To provide such a theory is to argue for the very *possibility* of such principles and, therefore, the very possibility of the type of integrative ethics that I promote.

In the past, when there was consensus on journalism ethics, codes of ethics contained principles that journalists in particular countries could endorse and still allow for some variation in interpretation. However, the breakdown in consensus and the emergence of a diverse global journalism mean that the question of the existence and nature of common principles is front and center when we do media ethics. The breakdown raises, explicitly, a question that could be safely ignored in times of consensus – what do we mean when we say that journalists agree on principles but interpret them differently? Therefore, in the history of media ethics, theories of meaning have not played a large role. This indifference to theories of meaning, and its questions, is no longer possible. An integrated media ethics cannot avoid developing its own sophisticated notion of how its principles have meaning and what form that meaning takes.

In this chapter I am not concerned with constructing a list of ecumenical principles; nor am I concerned with how such principles would be applied in various situations. I am concerned to make a philosophical argument for the plausibility and possibility of ecumenical global principles for radical media ethics. In the following chapters, I name and defend a number of actual principles.

This chapter constructs a three-level theory of meaning that explains how principles can have exhibit three forms of meaning – minimal, robust, and maximal. The three levels show that the way that ethical principles obtain meaning is much more complex than may be surmised. Moreover, the three levels of meaning show how unity in difference is possible in meaning. That is, it shows how one and the same principle can have different interpretations

Ecumenicalism at Work

Ecumenicalism

The nature of today's journalism calls for an ecumenical approach to ethics.

I borrow the term "ecumenical" from its original Christian context, which is the desire for unity among the sects of Christianity, despite their differences. Ecumenicalism does not seek to impose a unity that ignores (or is intolerant of) differences, e.g., insisting on rigid and absolute principles that allow no variation in application or interpretation. Ecumenicalism is an attempt to recognize differences within a common framework of values. It promotes cooperation and a better understanding among different religious denominations, while seeking universal Christian unity.[1] Ecumenism is not interfaith pluralism. The interfaith movement strives for respect, toleration, and cooperation among the world religions. Ecumenicalism seeks to go beyond toleration and understanding to forms of unity within Christianity, in terms of doctrine or organization. It seeks unity in difference, not just toleration of differences.

By analogy, ecumenicalism in journalism ethics is the search for unity among journalism's many "sects" or approaches. The unity sought is more than a toleration of different approaches. The unity is doctrinal – a unifying framework of beliefs and values that is realized in different ways by different forms of journalism.

There are two problems for ecumenicalism.

External disagreement: Unity is weakened where groups hold different basic beliefs. Regrettably, much of human history is a story of conflict between groups with different worldviews. Where disagreement is deep and tied to strong emotions, ecumenicalism may be impossible. For the sake of peaceful coexistence, toleration may be all that is possible.

Internal disagreement: Unity is also weakened by disagreements within groups such as disagreements over the meaning of shared principles and/or conflicts among values. We may disagree on how to balance liberty and security in our neighborhood, or journalists many disagree on the meaning of serving the public.

Whether the dispute is external or internal, the issues often are centered on questions of correct interpretation and meaning, and what sort of doctrinal unity is possible. For integrated ethics, the question of unifying meanings and interpretations involves disagreements that are both external and internal.

Ecumenicalism in media ethics needs a theory of meaning that explains how practitioners can both share and disagree on the meanings of principles and norms. How is this possible? And is there enough agreement to form a substantive new framework? An integrative conception of any principle must start from shared meanings. But what if there are no shared meanings, or the agreement is so abstract or thin that ecumenicalism is a questionable approach to media ethics? Do journalists share meanings to the degree that it allows for a common ethics, or is there only a fragmentation of meaning? Meaning pluralism is a fact of media ethics. But is there also meaning unity and, if so, to what degree? Skepticism about the project of integrative ethics results, in large part, from meaning pluralism.

If we can't make sense of the *idea* of common meanings, the project of integrative ethics is doomed to failure. We would not need to do empirical research to refute ecumenical ethics. We would know the project makes no sense from the start.

I argue that ecumenicalism is possible because ethical principles have several levels of meaning. First, there is a thin, "minimal" meaning of basic terms and principles that allows people to address the same topic. Second, there is a robust meaning that is developed for interpretations of the basic terms and principles. Third, there is maximal meaning. We give additional (or maximum) meaning to the basic terms and principles by saying what they entail for certain situations, and how the principles are applied to cases. Maximal meaning gives the principle a rich, context-relative meaning grounded in specific practices and cultures. This tri-level nature of meaning explains how shared meanings can coexist with different interpretations, and how genuine, rational disagreements are possible.

Minimal, robust, maximal

There are three levels of meaning that range from the abstract to the concrete: minimal, robust, and maximal meaning.[2] To understand the levels, let us start with (hopefully) intuitive examples.

Imagine that I am having an informal conversation with colleagues in a pub about the justice of the American penal system. As we talk about issues of race, the death penalty, and the high per capita levels of imprisonment, I call some things just and other things unjust. Then, a "Socratic moment" occurs. Someone asks me what I mean by justice. On what basis do I categorize aspects of the penal system as just or unjust?

Without much thinking, I attempt a quick and rough reply. I say justice is essentially fairness among citizens and equality under the law, and treating similar situations in similar ways. I hope this definition will fill the gap and we can return to discuss concrete examples. My reply does not pretend to be a full or adequate answer. At best, it provides a basis for further discussion.

In my terminology, I give a minimal meaning to the concept of justice. My reply is abstract. It picks out a couple of general properties – fairness and equal treatment – to give the term *some* meaning. It strikes me that these properties are so general that they are found in almost any particular act of justice. My reply abstracts from the complexities and details that surround justice in the real world. It abstracts from the different contexts in which the word is used, the many kinds of justice, and the different views of justice in different cultures. It doesn't even provide an example to help the listener understand my philosophical statement. Yet my reply should not be criticized *as* abstract. After all, the question – What is justice? – asks for an abstract, philosophical reply.

Similarly, I might discuss with friends the emergence of supercomputers that carry out some mental tasks better than humans, such as facial recognition, computing, and playing chess. Our conversation turns to the question whether such computers think and have minds. I claim they do not. A friend disagrees and asks me what I mean by "mind." I reply by quoting Lynch (1998, 67): "Minimally speaking, a mind is simply something that thinks, feels, and has conscious experience." I have proposed a minimal meaning of mind based on a functional description. A mind is whatever fulfills certain psychological functions. I abstract from the many types of things that think, compute, sense, or feel. I hope that this minimal meaning will allow us to carry on our discussion. Here I am not noting the differences in meaning between us concerning mind. Rather, I seek a common meaning – a point of unity.

Consider the case where I give a different response to the question about justice. Instead of providing an abstract definition, I elaborate, at some length, my theory of justice. Suppose I have a libertarian view of justice. I start with the aforementioned minimal definition of justice. But I say more. I say justice is about just dessert or merit – your individual right to get what comes to you from your effort and how you use your resources, talents, and property. I ridicule notions of distributive justice as anti-libertarian and not really justice at all. They are dangerous socialist strategies to impair liberty.

In this case, I provide a robust meaning for justice. It develops justice's minimal meaning. The robust meaning is a *conception* of justice. I have evoked one of the interpretive traditions around justice. My libertarian explication of justice interprets fairness and equality in a certain manner. It is robust because it puts meat on the bones of the minimal meaning. I give justice a less abstract interpretation.

However, one of my interlocutors is not satisfied by my robust reply. She asks me to say what a libertarian idea of justice means practically. By "practically," she is asking for an example or some application of my conception. I try to meet her question. I explain how a libertarian idea of justice would reform the current tax system for the United States. It would, among other things, eliminate the graduated tax system that "punishes" the smart and successful for the sake of the poor and the lazy. I provide the beginnings of a maximal meaning by defining what libertarian justice means through one or two examples. It is maximal because it attempts to fill out my minimal sketch of justice. Both the robust and maximal meanings enhance the minimal meaning of justice.

It is also possible to provide a robust conception of my minimal meaning for mind. I may say the mind is the functioning of the brain, and refer to studies in neuroscience that show how parts of the brain make certain emotions possible. Or I may reject the idea that the mind reduces to the brain. I develop a notion of mind as a special mental substance, taking concepts from Descartes and other dualists. These different criteria for defining mind stretch the minimal meaning. They are incompatible conceptions and provide different robust meanings. Yet the debate is not an illusion, or an equivocation of the meaning of mind. The dualist who believes that mind is an irreducible mental substance and the neuroscientist who thinks the mind is the brain understand each other, thanks to the mediating role of minimal meanings. They are using different concepts and yet both are employing mind concepts.

All three forms of meaning-giving – minimal, robust, and maximal – can be understood in terms of the notion of definition in Chapter 5. Each form uses varying parts of a term's conceptual scheme – its web of meaning – to satisfy demands for clarity in meaning.

Of course, it is possible that we can lose a grip on a term's minimal meaning due to confusion on the level of robust and maximal meanings. For example, we may become unclear about what basic notion of mental illness is being used when theories and treatments disagree and clash, as has happened in recent years. For example, if our catalogue of types of mental illness grows to the extent that 50 percent of the general population is said to be mentally ill, such a counter-intuitive result may force us to go back and reconsider our minimal and robust conceptions of mental illness. We ask: What is mental illness anyway?[3]

Definitions

Given these examples, we can define the three levels of meaning.

Minimal meaning is an abstract, highly general specification of the meaning of a concept, whether it is the concept of justice, responsibility, the human good, or intentional action. The concept in question is usually an important, basic concept in a conceptual scheme.

"Minimal" does not mean using few words. It means restricting oneself, in the main, to abstract concepts and meanings. To provide a minimal meaning is to define a term in a philosophical manner, via abstract properties. It is minimal in not helping itself to concrete properties and methods for specifying the meaning of the concept, e.g., by developing a detailed interpretation of the concept or by showing how the concept is applied in practice.

A Radical Integrated Ethics

Minimal meanings are implicit in our daily discourse. We talk of things being supported by reason, or say that a course of action is not rational; we speak in an abstract manner of our duties and obligations. We usually do not stop to spell out the minimal meanings of reason, rationality, or duty, except when asked or when we set out to philosophize about the concepts. The minimal meanings form a basic substratum of meaning for our conceptual schemes.

The robust meaning of a concept is a thicker meaning. It is an enhancement of the minimal meaning by providing an interpretation, conception, or theory of the concept. A robust meaning may include references to interpretive traditions, and the history of the concept. One way to elaborate, robustly, is to take a position on the ontological nature of what is under discussion. For example, we could elaborate on the minimal idea of mind by developing a theory of how the mental is reducible to physical processes or the brain. But this is only one way to make a concept more robust. Maximal meaning indicates that the meaning provider helps herself to all of the ways of giving meaning to a term. Maximal meaning is constructed from examples, cases, cultural comparisons, policy applications, and so on.

The extent to which we develop the levels of meaning depends on our purposes. In teaching an introductory class on ethics, I provide a minimal meaning for the notion of justice, since my aim is to simply note that this is a topic that belongs to ethics. I will return to the notion in a later class to provide robust and maximal meanings of the term.

The meaning of a concept can be thought of as concentric circles of more and more elaborate and detailed meanings, emanating from a minimal meaning. As we elaborate the meaning, the distinction between what we mean by the concept and our beliefs about the objects that fall under the concept blurs. Much of what we believe about minds or justice forms part of our robust and maximal meanings of the concept.

The best thinkers work on all three levels, holistically relating the levels and applying the method of reflective equilibrium to construct a coherent, overall meaning. Some writers produce a book to fully explore the meaning of a major concept. For example, we can think of Rawls's *A Theory of Justice* and Plato's *Republic* as book-length attempts to provide a complex meaning for justice, by developing its minimal, robust, and maximal meanings. Recall how the participants in *The Republic* dialogue at length about the meaning of justice. The discussion moves up and down the three levels. At the start of the book, proponents put forward minimal conceptions, from justice as "might makes right" and "justice as piety" to "justice as a social contract." Socrates uses his method of questioning to try to get the defenders of these various minimal meanings to elaborate a robust and a maximal meaning. Eventually, Socrates presents his own view about justice. He begins a long discussion where justice is minimally defined as a harmony of the society and the soul. The notion of harmony is developed in depth on the other two levels of meaning. By the end of the book we have a full theory of justice.

Today, thinkers continue to mix the three levels in developing their theories. For example, consider Nussbaum's *Political Emotions: Why Love Matters for Justice* (2013). The book examines how democracies need to develop citizens with the right political emotions, such as patriotism and love of the common good. After providing a minimal meaning for political emotions, she constructs her robust notion of democratic emotions by referring to psychological theories of emotions, historical theories of patriotism, philosophical theories of justice, facts about the "radical evil" of people, plus case studies of how different cultures have developed different notions of patriotism. By moving back and forth between the ideal and the real, the abstract and the concrete, Nussbaum creates a powerful conception of the proper emotional basis for democracy. She provides minimal, robust, and maximal forms of meanings.

Political freedom

With these definitions and examples in hand, I want to improve our understanding of the three levels by analyzing one important example at some length. The example is the important concept of political freedom.

At its thinnest, the meaning of political freedom is concerned with liberties one has by virtue of being of a citizen, e.g., liberty of association and speech. Charles Larmore (2008, 182) provides a minimal meaning for the term as "those liberties that citizens may possess compatibly with being members of a political association and with the basic purposes that any such association must set itself, such as the protection of property." This minimal meaning provides only a common topic for the discussion of robust and maximal meanings. Larmore then discusses the plurality of meanings of political freedom. Larmore notes that the history of Western liberal notions of political freedom is dominated by three or four (robust) meanings. There are two notions of negative liberty: (a) a modern idea of freedom as non-interference; and (b) an older republican notion of freedom as non-domination. There are a couple of notions of positive freedom, that is, the freedom to seek certain goals. There is (a) the freedom of having and being able to exploit opportunities; and (b) the freedom of self-actualization.

Political freedom as negative liberty means that individuals can do what they want without interference from government and other individuals. I will call this the libertarian view. Constant (1988) famously called negative liberty "the liberty of the moderns" in contrast to "the liberty of the ancients," the freedom to participate in political self-rule. Philosopher Isaiah Berlin's (1969) equally famous discussion of liberty favored negative freedom.[4]

Berlin's view of liberty agrees with non-liberal and liberal thinkers such as Hobbes and Bentham. Both Hobbes (1985 [1651]) and Bentham (1970 [1782]) viewed freedom as the absence of obstacles to actions or choices. Their views focused on actual (or existing) obstacles, not on the potential for interference in the future. Berlin (1969, 129), for example, said a benevolent despot could allow his subjects a large measure of negative freedom to pursue projects, even if he could interfere at any time. We are free to the extent we rule ourselves, shaping our individual and collective destinies in accord with our own aspirations, rather than being "driven by forces from without" (Larmore 2008, 170). In some philosophies, a stress on negative freedom is linked to rational autonomy, where we give ourselves our own rules and goals. Freedom is measured by the degree of self-mastery or control we effectively exercise over our actions and circumstances.

For Hobbes and Bentham, social structures, laws, and rules are regrettable but necessary restraints on our negative freedom. We accept such restraints only where they prevent society from slipping into a state of nature. The individual confronts the forces of society, forces that restraint her negative liberty. Hence, any attempt to restrain negative freedom should be viewed skeptically. The amount of social restraint – and the power of the restrainers (e.g., government) – should always be a matter for concern. Freedom is the silence of the law.

Republicans disagree. They have a different robust conception of negative freedom. They define political freedom as the absence of domination or "non-domination." The conception goes back to Machiavelli and political thought in ancient Rome. It has been revised in modern times by Quentin Skinner (1998) and Philip Pettit (1999).

According to this tradition, we are free to the extent that we do not find ourselves under the domination of the others. Liberty is independence from the will of others, whether in point of fact or potentially. "Potentially" means we are not free if we are governed by benevolent despots who treat us kindly, but could potentially dominate us at any time they wished. The threat of possible intervention is a substantial check on political freedom and a form of domination. Domination means domination not only by government but also by military groups and private constellations of power, such as large corporations. Freedom is a condition in which we find ourselves. We find ourselves living without the fact or the threat of serious domination by others.

Both the republican and libertarian conceptions of political freedom are negative conceptions. Both say what individuals must not do to other individuals. Both do not emphasize what people may do with their freedom, their capacities and opportunities, once they are not interfered with, or dominated. Yet the republican view differs from the libertarian view in its positive view of society, laws, and government. Republicanism thinks that social structures and laws enable and make possible political liberty. Law and liberty are not intrinsically opposed. Where laws and social structures are just, they deliver individuals from dominance by powerful groups. The citizens of a country are free only when the dominance of a few is restrained by law.

What can an ecumenicalism of meaning learn from this example?

We have a historical and important example of how the minimal and robust levels of meaning play a role in our political philosophy. These philosophers develop the minimal meaning of political freedom into robust conceptions, e.g., libertarianism or republicanism. Their interpretations are different but they are discussing the same topic provided by the minimal meaning. The meaning of political freedom exhibits a unity of meaning in difference. This unity in difference makes possible a plurality of traditions of theorizing and interpretation, such as liberal political philosophy.

The robust conceptions are made maximal by providing examples of public policy and laws. Bentham and Mill, among others, wrote at length about the social implications of their liberal utilitarianism. Mill's influential *On Liberty* draws out the concrete implications of his conception of liberty. Also, robust conceptions are made maximal when we compare how the conceptions would be understood and implemented differently in different countries. The libertarian idea of negative freedom in the United States, with its strong emphasis on minimal government and drastic cutting of social programs, will be a stronger and more right-wing version of the idea of negative freedom in Canada or other countries.

We begin to see how people can both agree and disagree about the meaning of an ethical term or principle. Different interpretations on one level of meaning do not entail that there are not, or cannot be, shared interpretations on another level of meaning.

Unity in difference can occur in at least two ways:

Unity and difference in interpretation: Interlocutors in a discussion on such issues as justice or the mind share a minimal meaning yet differ in their robust enhancements of this common meaning.

Unity and difference in application: Minimal and robust meanings tend to deal with agreement and disagreement on the level of theory. Differences in maximal meanings are about differences in the application of those ideas in the world. The idea of maximal meaning recognizes that one and the same principle can be realized differently in different social contexts. Respect for one's parents means something different in practice in Japan than it does in Canada. The norms of courage or kindness are realized differently in varying cultures.

Therefore, a theory of meaning for ecumenicalism can be based on these two notions of unity in difference: unity in minimum meaning but differences in robust elaborations; and unity in minimal and perhaps even robust conceptions, but differences in application to the world.

Meaning and Multiple Realizability

We have approached the issue of meaning from the viewpoint of conceptualization, theorizing, and use of language. We reflected on how we use certain terms, and explained them.

There is another and complementary way to see how our principles and our basic terms can have several layers of meaning. We can look at objects and practices in the world and realize that, in many cases, they are the kinds of things that can be realized in many ways: Mousetraps are realized in many ways. Recognizing the face of someone is realizable by many kinds of brain patterns or computer software. Kindness to parents is a norm realized in many ways in different cultures. The property (or properties) that make anything a mousetrap or the perception of a face is, therefore, a highly general feature. When we express this variability in realization in language, we articulate principles and concepts that have several layers of meaning. For example, the meaning of phrases such as "is a mousetrap" or "is being kind to parents" is minimal and abstract, usually described in terms of some general function. To give the term a more robust or maximal meaning, we examine how the property is realized in many ways.

In the rest of this section, I examine more closely this phenomenon of multiple realizability because it is close to the idea of multiple meanings and the idea of core meaning as stated in the previous chapter. Also, as we will see, it can be used to explain how forms of journalism can "realize" differently one and the same principle.

Realization and instantiation

Multiple realizability takes us back to our discussion in Chapter 3 of the one and the many, and the competing views of monism and pluralism. I explained monism and pluralism as disagreeing on how much emphasis to place on "the one" or "the many." When we understand anything, from cultural values to some physical phenomenon, do we focus on its many parts and components, or do we seek underlying laws and principles? Our topic here, however, is slightly different. When we think about multiple realizability, we are not separating the one and the many, as it were. Instead we are looking at the relationship of the one and the many – *how* the one manifests itself in many ways, and how the many instantiate the one.

We start with the reminder that multiple realizability is fundamental to the categorization that helps us think, as examined in Chapter 2. To categorize is to think in terms of type (kind of thing) and token (an example of that kind). It is to think of objects as realizations of types.

We have already encountered examples of multiple realizability. Lynch's idea of concepts as sketches, explained in Chapter 5, is a metaphor for multiple realizability. Similarly, the idea of a core meaning assumes the core can be realized in many ways. In Chapter 1, we examined the idea that social properties are realized in many ways and are non-reducible to physical properties. Consider Searle's "social facts." So many things we create and agree upon in society – passports, rules of the road, hockey games, money, cocktail parties, and conference panels – have a social reality that can be realized in many ways.

We encounter multiple realizability every day, in familiar objects defined by their functions. To describe a thing's function just *is* to pick out a general property that has many realizations, and for that reason cannot be reduced to a specific physical property. Mousetraps are realized in multiple ways. So are brains, given the plasticity of the brain in implementing mental functions. Functionalism in the psychology of mind argues that the mind is a confederation of mental functions, all of which can be realized in many ways. For instance, mental states, such as saving something to memory, can be realized by human neurons, silicone chips in computers, and maybe the brains of Martians.

Normative realization

What about ethics? How do multiple realizations play a role? We have noted a few examples of normative realizations of principles and meanings, such as multiple notions of political freedom and the many different ways in which cultures show respect for parents.

A good example is Nussbaum's capacity theory of human development. In *Creating Capabilities*, Nussbaum (2011) contends that theories of development, based on such measurements as Gross Domestic Product, ignore basic human needs for dignity. Her capabilities approach asks what individuals are capable of doing and what real opportunities are available to them. This approach measures development by employing a set of ten "central capacities." The capacities range from being able to live a life of normal length and bodily security, to being able to being able to use one's senses and imagination, to having control over one's environment.

Nussbaum is alert to objections to her capacities approach. She asks (2011, 101): "We live in a highly diverse world. Doesn't this way of proceeding smack of imperialism?" She rejects the charge that human rights and capacity theory are only Western ideas and that she is being dogmatic. Her theory is a result of "critical normative argument" which is set forth "to be criticized, rebutted, engaged" and open to revision (2011, 108).

She then makes use of multiple realizability. Nussbaum says she has intentionally described the items on her list in a "somewhat abstract and general way" to allow citizens, legislatures, and courts to specify how such abstract principles are to be "realized" in a constitution or any other foundational political document. Within certain parameters – the parameters of not violating human rights and not working against the development of central capacities – it is "perfectly appropriate" that different nations should realize the capacities differently, taking their histories and special circumstances into account. As an example she says a free speech right that suits Germany (e.g., bans anti-Semitic speech) would be too restrictive under the First Amendment provisions of the United States constitution. There are different and legitimate ways for countries to interpret the meaning of freedom of speech. Protections of freedom of speech can be realized in many ways, although there are some approaches that are "unacceptably repressive." Multiple realizability is not just a way to defend her theory. It is a part of the theory. The idea of common capacities is one form of the idea that general properties are realizable in various ways.

Nussbaum's approach uses all three levels of meaning to develop her theory of creating capacities. Her general ideas of human capacity and freedom are minimal meanings awaiting development. Nussbaum robustly develops an interpretation of these minimal meanings by developing her theory of central capacities. Finally, she discusses what the capacity theory means in varying contexts. In later chapters, I will use a similar approach to specify the ideal of human flourishing as an ecumenical aim for global journalists.

A Radical Integrated Ethics

Application to Media Ethics

Making the idea possible

How do these reflections provide a theory of meaning for integrated, ecumenical ethics?

Recall the discussion at the start of this chapter. I said that ecumenical ethics meant that media ethics must be based on commonly held principles that apply across different approaches to journalism. This prompted the following question: How is an integrated media ethics possible when journalists embrace different norms and principles?

My answer is: People can both agree and disagree on the meanings of various basic concepts, especially ethical concepts, because these concepts have different levels of meaning. People can agree on one level, and differ on another.

To make the idea plausible, I constructed a tri-part theory of conceptual meaning with two essential components: (1) the idea of three levels of meaning, that range from the abstract to the concrete. I distinguished between minimal, robust, and maximal meanings; (2) the idea of unity in difference at the level of interpretation and application. In addition, unity in difference was interpreted as the multiple realization of normative principles and norms.

Psychologically, my theory presumes that humans have the capacity to find unity among the many different things of the world. I understand this capacity in much the same way that Aristotle understood intuitive induction. For Aristotle, induction, as a method of knowing, moves from particular statements to general statements. Humans use induction by simple enumeration to generalize from what is true of individuals to what is presumably true of the group to which they belong. If the swans that we have seen are white, we believe all swans are white. But intuition can take more interesting forms. Aristotle believed that humans can directly intuit general principles exemplified in phenomena. Intuitive induction is a matter of insight. It is the capacity to see what is essential in the data of sense experience. Aristotle gives the example of a scientist who notices on several occasions that the bright side of the moon is turned toward the sun, and who concludes that the moon shines by reflected sunlight. In a similar way, a taxonomist "sees" the generic attributes and specific differences of a species of organism (see Losee 1972). I believe that this human capacity to see unity "in" the particulars is the mechanism by which we construct common meanings and frameworks not just in science but also in ethics. For example, our insight into common human capacities, as described by the development approach, is, to a large extent, an ability to "see" commonalties in the great diversity of human experience.[5]

So let us return to our main question: Is it possible for practitioners to share principles yet differ on interpretations and applications? The answer is yes. If philosophers and other groups work on different levels of meaning, it is plausible that media ethicists and practitioners do (or can do) the same thing. There is no reason to think that, if intuitive induction is available to all or most humans, this capacity to intuit unity in difference is not also available to the people who work in the field of media ethics.

Integrated ethics is possible if practitioners identify common minimal meanings that can be spelled out in different robust interpretations within a tradition of media ethics. Practitioners view their differences as different robust interpretations and different maximal applications of a common value or tradition. Integrated media ethics is possible if practitioners are united around overarching principles that can be realized in different ways in varying media contexts and approaches. This is how the tri-part level of theory explains differences in interpretation of principles, whether it is the principle of objectivity, independence, or freedom of the press. Let's examine how this approach works for two concepts in media ethics, social responsibility and objectivity.

Social responsibility

Consider a tri-level analysis view of the idea that media should be socially responsible. It has been argued (Christians and Nordenstreng 2004) that social responsibility is now the dominant approach to media ethics. In the United States, it refers to calls on media to follow such principles as minimizing harm, respecting privacy, and providing in-depth analysis of issues. In Europe, it often refers to the mandate of public broadcasting, as an alternative to commercial news media.

A Radical Integrated Ethics

Suppose I say the following to a couple of media ethicists, one from the United States (call her A) and one from South Africa (call her B): "Both of you discuss the importance of news media that serve the public and are socially responsible. What do you mean by such notions?"

Ethicist A responds: "News media should serve the general public and the common good, rather than specific groups, special interests, and specific goods. They are socially responsible by showing to the public at large that they are truly a free press which protects individual liberties. They are independent aggressive watchdogs, challenging government and authority. Their job is not to be loved by their audiences or to smooth over social tensions, or to not report mistakes."

Ethicist B responds: "The idea of serving the public is a difficult concept in a country like South Africa, one of the most unequal countries in the world. In South Africa, media serve different publics and public interests. However, there is still the idea that the media as a whole should serve the somewhat fragile, transitional democracy of South Africa. The approach of aggressive, investigative news media, derived from the American experience, does not fit well in South Africa. Such news media can undermine confidence in South Africa's evolving democratic institutions, or create dangerous social tensions and racism, followed by violence. News media are socially responsible when they aid South African leaders in developing their transitional democracy, and creating social solidarity in a country long divided along lines of race and economic class. A socially responsible free press is a press that is not only free to print what it considers the truth, or a press that acts as government watchdog. It is also a press that seeks to promote democracy and substantive outcomes in the body politic, such as greater equality and wealth for all citizens. In this way, social responsibility is defined relative to the democratic aims of this society."[6]

The responses by A and B are examples of how people can give different robust meanings to the concept of social responsibility. Social responsibility is interpreted robustly by A as freedom to monitor government in terms of how it uses its power and to protect the liberty of citizens from abuse of power. This is the kernel of a well-known interpretive tradition in media ethics – the American notion of an aggressive First Amendment press. It stresses the need for a watchdog on government even if revelations cause social tensions or weaken public confidence in institutions. Social responsibility is responsibility toward self-governing individuals who collectively make up the public.

Ethicist B expresses a different interpretive tradition. She defines social responsibility in a more collectivist fashion. Responsible media seek to facilitate democratic programs and equality in society as a whole. Journalists should help their institutions carry out their democratic goals. This requires the press to adopt a more conciliatory relationship with government and view itself as a partner in institution building, rather than view itself as mainly (or only) a fierce and vigilant critic for the sake of individual liberty. Responsibility is owed to the collective body of society as a whole. Ethicists A and B could provide maximal meanings for their robust interpretations. Both ethicists are thinking about what social responsibility means in their countries.

Is it possible for the two ethicists to share a minimal meaning for social responsibility? It is possible. It would be an over-reaction to conclude that the disagreement between Ethicist A and Ethicist B means there is only irreducible difference (and fragmentation) between their views. Both of our hypothetical ethicists employ the basic concepts of equality, dignity, freedom, and serving the public(s). It is reasonable to suppose that they use these terms in ways that share minimal meanings and perhaps robust meanings. Their differences at the level of robust and maximal meanings do not preclude a shared minimal meaning. This is because the notion of ethical responsibility (and social responsibility in particular) is a concept that is realizable in different contexts. Moreover, it is possible that each ethicist doesn't *deny* what the other stresses, e.g., a free press or helping democracy grow, but that they differ in the emphasis that they place on certain values, given their specific contexts.

This is how my levels-of-meaning approach would approach the principle of social responsibility. I now consider how the tri-part theory would approach another principle – the idea of news objectivity.

News objectivity

The minimal meaning of news objectivity is not difficult to state. A responsible news reporter would seek to describe events accurately and factually, and not allow their personal views or values to distort their reports or to misinform the public. The objective news reporter is willing to test the reliability of their reports in terms of facts and sources, and also to be wary of potential ideological biases in reports.

I believe that many people would agree with this abstract minimal description of objective reporting. To be sure, good reporting is *more* than being objective. Good reporting needs initiative from the reporter, strong investigative methods, and skillful writing. But the minimal idea of objectivity does not claim that objectivity is sufficient for good reporting. It claims objectivity is a necessary, but not sufficient, condition of good news reporting. Also, one can believe there is value in other forms of reporting, e.g., advocacy journalism, without rejecting the claim that there should be space in our public sphere for objective news reporting. One could even hold that some of the skills and attitudes of objective reporting should be part of non-objective journalism.

Hence, much of the disagreement over objectivity is not at the minimal level, but at the level of robust and maximal meanings. Robustly, there is disagreement on the best interpretation of objectivity and to what extent it should be followed by journalists.

Journalists in the early 1900s constructed their own robust notion of news objectivity as they sought professional status. This "traditional" or original notion of news objectivity stressed reporting just the facts in a perfectly neutral manner. The notion was then spelled out in terms of a wide range of methods for constructing and vetting news stories, such as attributing all opinion in the story. But there are many variations on the robust meaning of news objectivity, depending on what aspect of reporting is considered important. Some people interpret news objectivity to require factuality but not impartiality, e.g., investigative journalists stress the digging up of objective facts but they do not write the report from a neutral perspective. Other interpreters think objectivity should be reduced to the less controversial values of fairness and accuracy. Accuracy is accuracy of fact and fairness is accurately portraying the views of sources.

My notion of pragmatic objectivity (2005, 263–316) provides an alternate robust meaning. It rejects both neutrality and "just the facts" as defining journalistic objectivity. Objectivity is interpreted as a testing of any form of journalism by a plural and holistic set of criteria, such as coherence with existing knowledge, which go beyond citing facts. I also have sought to provide maximal meaning of pragmatic objectivity by saying how a journalist who endorses pragmatic objectivity would report on global issues, war, and other situations.

Therefore, an integrated ethics, if it decided to include objectivity among its basic principles, could begin with a minimal meaning for the principle, and allow for a variety of plausible interpretations and applications of objectivity. Fragmentation around the idea of news objectivity is not inevitable. There are common meanings.

Permissible variations

The theory of meaning allows for differences in interpretation and application. But how far can interpretations and applications go? A flexible approach has to be careful not to be *so* flexible as to be unable to rule out questionable practices and norms. What are the limits of permissible variations on basic principles by robust and maximal interpretations?

A meaning or interpretation could be rejected if it is seemingly unrelated to other existing and valuable concepts. Imagine that someone says that the principle of serving the public means pleasing audiences and sponsors. Polls of what citizens and advertisers want and enjoy should be sufficient to determine what media should cover, and how. The proposed meaning is inconsistent with the other core beliefs of journalism ethics. The core beliefs include a duty to report unpleasant stories, and to be independent from undue influence from advertisers (and audiences). An advocate for journalism-by-survey has an uphill battle to make her position plausible.

Also, imagine that someone proposes to understand the principle of social responsibility in such a way that it looks favorably on Chinese-style censorship of media and free speech. Such censorship is defended as necessary for social solidarity. This proposal would be rightly rejected as an non-permissible variation on the ethics of democratic journalism. Similarly, no robust or maximal elaboration of the meaning of a "free press" that took the media in Iran as a good example of a free press could be accepted. Our minimal meanings are rooted in a democratic tradition. Even though they are abstract, they still provide restraints on interpretation.

A Radical Integrated Ethics

We evaluate elaborations on minimal meanings using our aforementioned method of reflective equilibrium. We see how the elaboration coheres with other beliefs on various levels of our ethics. The elaboration of a Chinese idea of social responsibility conflicts with the core idea in our notion of social responsibility that the media are responsible to a democratically enabled public, *not* a dominant regime. It clashes with an authoritarian model of the press. This candidate for social responsibility also violates beliefs on the maximal level. It entails, for example, that editors of newspaper should allow their reports to be vetted by government, a practice that clashes with our notion of editorial independence.

Often, we cannot say in advance, or a priori, whether a specific interpretation is to be rejected. We have to look at the overall logic and evidence for the position held, and we must compare it with our existing understandings of the concepts in question. We do not adjudicate such positions from a position of neutrality. We adjudicate from the perspective of our existing scheme, in this case the model of democratic journalism. There may be interpretations and applications where we are not sure what to say, given the fluidity of concepts. But, as we saw, indeterminacy in some hard cases does not mean we have no general criteria for saying how flexible our scheme should be. The idea that we can seek common ground, yet allow for differences, remains a coherent approach.

Shape of an Integrated Ethics

Tri-part structure of content

My tri-part theory of meaning sees the structure of ecumenical media ethics as follows:

At the top of the structure there should be a set of principles whose minimal meanings are described in abstract ways. Their abstractness allows journalists from different traditions to agree on common principles and meanings.

At the second level will be robust interpretations of the minimal meanings such as social responsibility, truth-telling, minimizing harm, and other basic concepts. Also at this level, we discuss journalistic purposes, the relative benefits of forms of journalism, and historical traditions of journalism. The robust level of meaning is necessary because even if all discussants of media ethics agreed on a set of universal principles, such as minimal meanings of truth-telling and social responsibility, media ethics would be incomplete and not a useful guide. There would still be disagreements on how those principles are to be interpreted at the robust level, and applied at the level of maximal meaning.

At the third level, the maximal meanings are spelled out in terms of guidelines for ethically dealing with specific situations and dilemmas. These applications will lead to maxims and protocols for a wide range of media formats.

Tri-part theory of method

This idealized structure of integrative ethics is what we use to "do" ethics. But my description so far has not said how we would actually use the structure for moral reasoning in journalism. I have elaborated at length on my view of moral reasoning in journalism, using reflective equilibrium. My model explains how to reason across three levels of media ethics – how to reason about cases and situations; how to reason about our moral framework (principles and codes of ethics); and how to reason about the ultimate aims of journalism – as a method for thinking about situations, codes, and aims (Ward 2010, ch. 2). I will not repeat that theory but only indicate how these methods would use the idealized structure outlined in this chapter.

Ethics can be divided into method and content. The content of ethics is the aims, goods, values, and duties that distinguish, doctrinally, one ethics system from another. My tri-part theory of meaning explains the content of ethics – of how various types of principles and norms occur at different levels and how they are related to each other.

Ethical method refers to methods of reasoning about these principles and norms, and how to arrive at well-considered judgments. We can talk about ethical method in ethics generally, or ethical method in media ethics or some other sub-species of ethics. Ethical method shapes how we reflectively engage ethical issues. Ethics is the application of practical reason to the ethical problems of the world (see Ward 2010). Ethical thinking is one expression of the human ability to think practically: determining what to do, how to reach a goal, or how to solve a problem. An ethical method is not an approach to good journalism. An approach is a way of doing journalism such as the adversarial approach to journalism, or the approach of an objective journalist, or the approach of an investigative journalist. An ethical method is way of responsibly carrying out our approaches to journalism.

A traditional way of thinking about ethical reasoning is to see it as a vertical, top-down process that deduces specific ethical judgments from supremely general moral principles. I propose a "horizontal" scheme that reflects my commitment to holism and the method of reflective equilibrium. I divide reasoning into three levels: reasoning about cases; reasoning about frameworks of principles; reasoning about aims. Each occasion requires a distinct form or "level" of reasoning. Also, our reasoning on any one level affects our reasoning on any other level. The scheme does not purport to describe how people actually reason. It says how people should reason.

There is a close connection between my theory of meaning and theory of method. The domain of minimal meaning corresponds with the third level of method where we discuss our most general principles. On this level, we reason about meta-ethical questions, such as the nature of ethics, the meaning of basic concepts. Most importantly for this chapter, this is the level at which we reason about the ultimate aims of responsible journalism. We use some conception of those aims to reason about, and justify, our thinking on cases and frameworks.

The level of robust meaning corresponds with the second level of method, which is reasoning about specific conceptions of major terms, approaches to journalism, and frameworks. Here, for example, we find the principles of news objectivity and editorial independence. We may evaluate principles individually or evaluate frameworks of principles, such as codes of ethics. An examination of principles might be sparked by trouble with a particular principle, a clash of principles, or doubts about the adequacy of the framework as a whole. A code of journalism ethics may be too general to address practices in a specific area of journalism. For instance, general principles about reporting truthfully may fail to address deceptive practices in investigative journalism, such as when it is permissible to use hidden cameras. This failure to address a practical issue may lead to a decision to formulate a sub-code for investigative journalism.[7] In all of these cases, we ask: "What framework is appropriate for this domain or profession?" The focus is on the validity of some (or all) of the principles of the relevant framework.

The maximal level corresponds with reasoning about cases and situations in journalism. At this level, we use principles and aims to judge the probity of certain journalistic actions. We ask: "What is the right thing to do, journalistically, in situation x?" For example, we condemn a reporter for taking money to do a story because it violates the principle of editorial independence and an aim of good journalism – to tell the complete and impartial truth. Typically, these situations are difficult because values conflict, the facts are complex, and several courses of action are possible. For example, should a journalist report on a secret military mission if such a report might endanger the safety of soldiers from one's own country? How should journalists balance their feelings of patriotism and their desire to avoid causing harm with their duty to report the truth freely and independently?

Also, at this level, we reason about maxims or protocols for practice, such as procedures for asking for interviews with traumatized people. We give maximal meaning to our principles.

Reflective equilibrium seeks to adjust ideas on all three levels until they cohere, that is, provide a consistent and systematic ethical system.

Conclusion

This chapter has outlined a multi-level theory of meaning that helps us to understand how an ecumenical ethics is possible.

The goal is unity within difference. We seek agreement on basic principles but we allow differences at other levels (on approach or practice) so long as the practices do not violate basic principles. Using reflective equilibrium, our ultimate goal is that the three levels of meaning form a consistent, holistic media ethics, where what we believe at any one level can affect our commitments on other levels.

Notes

1. Different denominations have different interpretations of what sort of unity among Christian sects is possible. Some seek agreement on basic doctrines; others seek a common church structure. Others want toleration of differences to be the goal. My abstract definition of ecumenicalism is a good example of how a concept can have different but related meanings.
2. The minimal-robust distinction occurs in Lynch (1998, 66–75). I develop his distinction in several ways. For example, I add a third level, and I apply the distinction specifically to ethics.
3. This criticism was voiced in 2013 when the American Psychiatric Association released its fifth edition of the *Diagnostic and Statistical Manual*, the so-called psychiatrists' "bible" on mental illness. Some complained that the definitions were so broad that 50 percent of Western populations could now be diagnosed with a mental disorder.
4. Although Berlin favored negative freedom, he did not dismiss the value of positive freedom. In *Four Essays* (1969, xlvii), Berlin says positive liberty is a "valid universal goal." Grey (1996, 15–21) has argued that Berlin's notion of negative freedom is different from that of Hobbes or Bentham, who define it as the unimpeded pursuit of one's desire. Berlin, Grey says, defined it as "self-creation through choice-making," or the capacity for choice among options unimpeded by others.
5. In *Global Journalism Ethics* (Ward 2010, 149), I argued that constructing a comprehensive global ethics involved a form of "cumulative moral insight" that recognizes how different elements form a unifying theory.
6. For a discussion of these issues with respect to South Africa, see Wasserman (2013).
7. This example is not hypothetical. In 2003, I helped the Canadian Association of Journalism formulate a code of ethics for investigative journalism as an extension of its general code.

References

Bentham, Jeremy. 1970 (1782). *Of Laws in General*, edited by H. L. A. Hart. London: Athlone.

Berlin, Isaiah. 1969. *Four Essays on Liberty*. Oxford: Oxford University Press.

Christians, Clifford G., and Kaarle Nordenstreng. 2004. "Social Responsibility Worldwide." Journal of Mass Media Ethics, 19(1): 3–28.

Constant, Benjamin. 1988. "The Liberty of the Ancients Compared with that of the Moderns." In *Political Writings*, edited by Biancamaria Fontana, 101–130. New York: Cambridge University Press.

Grey, John, 1996. *Isaiah Berlin*. Princeton, NJ: Princeton University Press.

Hobbes, Thomas. 1985 (1651). *Leviathan*. London: Penguin.

Larmore, Charles. 2008. "The Meanings of Political Freedom." In *The Autonomy of Morality, 168–195*. New York: Cambridge University Press.

Losee, John. 1972. *A Historical Introduction to the Philosophy of Science*. London: Oxford University Press.

Lynch, Michael P. 1998. *Truth in Context: An Essay on Pluralism and Objectivity*. Cambridge, MA: MIT Press.

Nussbaum, Martha C. 2011. *Creating Capabilities: The Human Development Approach*. Cambridge, MA: Harvard University Press.

Nussbaum, Martha C. 2013. *Political Emotions: Why Love Matters for Justice*. Cambridge, MA: Harvard University Press.

Pettit, Philip. 1999. *Republicanism: A Theory of Freedom and Government*. 2nd ed. Cambridge: Cambridge University Press.

Skinner, Quentin. 1998. *Liberty before Liberalism*. Cambridge: Cambridge University Press.

Ward, Stephen J. A. 2005. *The Invention of Journalism Ethics: The Path to Objectivity and Beyond*. Montreal: McGill-Queen's University Press.

Ward, Stephen J. A. 2010. *Global Journalism Ethics*. Montreal: McGill-Queen's University Press.

Wasserman, Herman. 2013. "Media Ethics in a New Democracy: South African Perspectives on Freedom, Dignity, and Citizenship." In *Global Media Ethics: Problems and Perspectives*, edited by Stephen J. A. Ward, 126–145. Malden, MA: Wiley Blackwell.

Part III
Principles of Global Integrated Ethics

Part III
Principles of Global Integrated Ethics

Chapter 7
Political Values for Integrated Ethics

This part of the book begins the construction of the content of a radical media ethics. Previous chapters have been philosophical and methodological. They discussed how we should go about constructing a new ethics. This part of the book is substantive. It uses the methods and ideas of the previous two parts to put forward principles for a global, integrated ethics. In Chapter 6, I argued for the possibility of principles needed by an integrative approach – ethical principles that allow great latitude for differences in interpretation and application. In the rest of this book, I advance a number of such principles.

Where do we start in laying down these principles? The place to start is with the articulation of unifying political principles. By "political principles," I mean principles that state the ultimate political aims of responsible journalism, plus how and why certain types of journalism contribute substantially to such aims. How do journalists best fulfill their social and institutional roles? So far, my discussion has presumed that the ultimate political goal of journalism is the maintenance and promotion of democracy. However, this tells us little. One reason is that democracy is a general, vague term. Another reason is that the media

---

Radical Media Ethics: A Global Approach, First Edition. Stephen J. A. Ward.
© 2015 John Wiley and Sons, Inc. Published 2015 by John Wiley and Sons, Inc.

revolution has undermined a consensus on which forms of journalism are primary in a democratic country. The consensus in the pre-digital media era was that professional, objective reporting was primary because the public needed the unbiased reporting of facts upon which to form their judgments about government and institutions. However, the emergence of many new forms of journalism has challenged that consensus. The revolution has created new forms of non-objective and point-of-view journalism whose values and aims were once dominant prior to the rise of the mass commercial press and its doctrine of news objectivity. As a result, there is disagreement on the relative importance of the historically important functions of journalism – to report, to factually inform, to opine, to analyze, to interpret, and to advocate.

The key questions are:

- *In a multi-platform media world, what forms of journalism promote democracy?*
  For example, does a journalism that consists of a clash of aggressive, partisan commentators on issues promote democracy? Does coverage of Hollywood and the sex scandals of movie stars promote democracy? Does the so-called "news you can use" – items on how to shop at a supermarket to save money, or how to clean your condo windows – qualify as democratic journalism? Does sports journalism advance democracy? Does citizen "chatter" on social media constitute a form of journalism, and does it promote democracy?
- *What forms of journalism promote democracy better than other forms?*
  Is it possible to rank (roughly) various types of journalism with respect to their contribution to democracy? For instance, we can ask: Do objective journalists who report factually contribute more to the democratic public sphere than influential columnists? Is advocacy journalism equal to, or better than, objective reporting in promoting a democratic citizenship? Or is the attempt to rank misguided? Maybe, in a free society, we should tolerate all forms of journalism. In a free society, the public *needs* many (or all) forms of journalism.

I believe an integrative ethics needs to find a middle ground between the accommodating view that we value all types of journalism and the intolerant view that only one form of journalism, i.e., professional objective reporting, is democracy's friend. The accommodating view is based on the idea that each form of journalism has its strengths (and weaknesses), and each stimulates different forms of democratic discourse. However, while tolerant, this view is implausible as stated because we can easily think of forms of journalism that do not contribute to democracy and in fact may work against it, such as advocacy journalism for racist groups. The intolerant view, on the other hand, underplays the need of the public for more than straight reporting – for dialogue, questioning, and advocacy of positions.

For integrative ethics, the challenge is twofold. It needs to (1) re-establish a political unity by articulating democratic aims and values that many types of journalists, new and old, can agree upon; and (2) provide criteria and principles for judging the value of forms of journalism for democracy. If we can achieve (1) and (2), the political structure of an integrated ethics will be established.

In this chapter I put forward, as a political basis of integrative ethics, two high-level principles: the principle of dialogic journalism and the principle of "principled pluralism." The exposition of those principles begins with reflection on what we mean by democracy and a democratic public.

What Type of Democracy?

Let me begin by stating, in advance, my social and political commitments.

I believe the best form of society is an egalitarian liberal society, based on a social liberal philosophy. The best political structure for such a society is a democracy that is free, participatory, and dialogic. This is my normative interpretation of democracy "in its best light."

Social liberalism

Liberals believe society should protect a core of basic civil and political liberties, from free speech to equality before the law. Liberal society exists for the benefit of free and equal individual citizens. To the contrary, communism, fascism, and various forms of socialism make the promotion of the state, the national party, or society as a whole the primary goal, often to the detriment of individual rights and freedoms. Liberals hold that society, including its political framework and state institutions, is justified insofar as it promotes the freedoms and overall flourishing of individuals.

Liberals differ on the meaning of a society of basic liberties. Views range from right-wing libertarianism to a social liberalism. I am a moderate liberal who wants *both* sound private sector economies *and* effective social programs for the vulnerable. Social liberalism exists between libertarianism and socialism. It balances liberty, equality, and justice. It recognizes the need for well-designed social programs and a substantial role for government to reduce inequalities. The idea of social justice, including principles of distributive justice, plays an important role. To abandon the ideals of social equality and justice would be to allow the pursuit of liberty, guided only by merit and effort – plus good fortune and the ability to mobilize powerful groups – to trample on the liberties and opportunities of others.

Liberal democracies should promote a congruence of the good and the just by placing all of their laws and policies under a hard-to-change and legally fundamental constitution. A constitution is a social contract that defines the terms by which different groups can peacefully and fairly coexist, enjoying the benefits of cooperation. A constitution protects the basic liberties, while placing restrictions on the pursuit of the good. For example, constitutional democracies limit what majorities can do to minorities. Their constitutions do not allow the basic liberties of one group of citizens to be taken away by a majority vote in a legislature.

Social liberalism is not a right-wing libertarianism that seeks to minimize government intervention and social programs in the name of individual self-interest. The pursuit of the good is to be determined by an unmediated clash between competing individuals. Liberalism is not just about negative liberty (non-interference). It is about equality and justice. Nor is social liberalism a socialism that demands massive social programs or equality of outcomes – that impossible state where everyone ends up with the same wealth and welfare. This ideal would deny a proper place for merit, undermine motivation for individual effort, reduce liberty unduly, and entail gigantic social costs.

Social liberalism is egalitarian. Egalitarianism is the view that equality is a basic value of political morality. Dworkin (2000) calls it the "sovereign virtue." Egalitarianism follows Rawls's famous remark (1992 [1972], 3) that, as truth is the first virtue of theory, justice is the "first virtue" of institutions and, one might add, society at large. Egalitarianism advocates for both formal and substantial equality. Formal equality means equality of process before the law and government. As Dworkin states (2011, 2), government "must show equal concern for the fate of every person over whom it claims dominion." Substantial equality refers to equality in living standards. Liberal philosophers have different views of what equality, in substance, consists in – equality of welfare, of resources, of opportunity, and so on. Social differences in egalitarian society must be justifiable. Hierarchies and class divisions are not considered "natural." Differences in society are not based on ethnic or other group identities.

An egalitarian liberalism does more than stress negative liberty – the right to not be interfered with. It stresses positive liberty – the freedom to pursue one's dreams and life goals. But positive liberty presumes people have the means to pursue their goods. Egalitarianism, based on social liberalism, believes that society should provide opportunities and resources to those who lack such means and who suffer from the inequalities caused by birth, race, gender, and social class. Liberties without the means to enjoy them are hollow.

Conservative thinkers, such as Kekes (1997, 2003), warn that egalitarianism is based on an over-optimistic faith in humans. It blinds us to the reality of evil. By over-emphasizing equality, a state can move toward socialism and restrictions on liberty. Kekes is wrong. Egalitarianism does not entail socialism. There are versions that are quite compatible with the existence of a coercive state that punishes evil and criminal conduct. The liberal faith in the possibility of improving society need not be a Pollyannaish attitude that fails to see evil in the world.

Citizens, Publics, and Democracy

What is the political structure of a liberal egalitarian society? In modern times, democracy is the political form taken by liberal societies. We may presume that "liberal society," "democracy," "citizenship," and "the public" are clear terms and mean much the same thing. However, these terms are not synonymous, and the existence of one does not entail the existence of the other. It is important, when advocating political aims for journalism, that we are aware of the complex relationships among these terms.

What type of democracy is best? I believe it is what I call dialogic democracy. It is a constitutional liberal democracy which is egalitarian in its social structure, dialogic in its public discourse, and participatory in its decision-making and institutional life. It is a democracy that has an informed and engaged public. It is more than a country with citizens; and more than a democracy with a non-robust public. A dialogic, participatory democracy is an ideal. To be a democracy in this sense, a country must meet, to a tolerable degree, a number of demanding conditions. First, the country must have citizens. Second the citizens must live in a democracy and form a public, in some minimal sense. Third, these democratic citizens must form a public in a maximal, robust sense. I prefer to define "public" in its maximal sense.[1]

Let us examine these three levels.

Citizens

When we discuss citizenship, the public, and democracy, we are dealing with types of social association. To be more exact, we deal with types of political association. In political associations, people associate as citizens of a polity. They do not associate as consumers or members of a social club or religion. They associate politically.

Society contains many specific types of non-political associations or social unions, from families to private clubs, all operating according to their own rules and goals, democratically or non-democratically. Societies also need a political structure. In most societies, some form of political organization and coercive power invested in state officials is required to keep the peace, pass laws, and coordinate the conduct of these many social groups, whose interests may conflict. In addition, many members of society come to belong to the society's political association. In most democracies, a society's political organization is the largest and most encompassing of social unions in the nation. It is "a social union of social unions" (Rawls 1992 [1972], 527). People may belong to different sub-groups of society but, as citizens, they all belong to the country's political association.

But what defines this broad political association? Here, the views of citizenship and the practices of citizenship vary. Notions of citizenship range from minimal notions of what citizenship entails to richer notions of citizenship. What all senses of citizenship have in common is the idea that, among the people who live in a country, there is a sub-group – large or small – that in some sense "belongs" to the country, unlike non-citizens or foreigners. Historically, citizenship has been closely linked to the exclusion of others as non-citizens, and such exclusion was often based on membership in a sub-group of society, e.g., being of Christian faith. However, in modern times and with the rise of plural democracies, the idea grew that citizenship was a political association based on civil and political rights, apart from ethnic and religious identities.

In Searle's terms (1995), being a citizen is not just having a social status, such as being recognized as a professional football player. Citizens are not just people who happen to live in a country. They are not just people who are members of certain groups within the country. To be a citizen is to have an additional status, or to have an "institutional property." Belonging to a country entails (1) rights, privileges, and enhanced social status owed by the country to citizens; (2) duties, support, and roles owed to the country by citizens; (3) a mutual, and interlocking concern for the interests of each citizen and the interests of all as a whole. Examples of (1) are the right to vote and the privilege of owning a driver's license. Examples of (2) are paying taxes, obeying laws, and a willingness to fight for the protection of the country. Examples of (3) are laws that meaningfully consider the impact of new environmental regulations on regions of the country, and a demand on citizens to consider the interest of the country as a whole. Without such recognition and rights, "citizens" do not exist. It is meaningless to call people "citizens" if they lack certain political institutions, e.g., a non-corrupt election system and an independent judiciary. People who live under a tyrannical dictator are not citizens but, at best, "subjects" of the government.

What citizenship entails varies from country to country and from political system to political system. In non-democratic countries, the notion of citizenship is minimal. The list of rights is meagre and the list of duties and laws is long. In democracies, the notion of citizenship extends beyond a minimal definition to embrace additional rights and duties. Citizens in democracies are *supposed* to be accorded a long list of fundamental political rights and duties so they can participate meaningfully in the institutional life of their country. They have the right to vote, to ask for equal treatment from the institutions of justice, to run for office, and to criticize political leaders and heads of institutions.

Democratic citizens

How should we think about citizens as members of democratic political associations? I mean, how should we think about it *normatively* – what is the best way to organize such associations if we support egalitarian liberal democracy?

I propose we think about this by distinguishing between (a) the less than ideal but still important creation of democratic citizens, or "minimal" publics, and (b) the ideal creation of truly robust and meaningful "maximal" publics. Chronologically, countries must create (a) before they can aspire to (b). Most democracies in the world exist somewhere between (a) and (b) and move toward or away from (a) and (b) as they go through time. Achieving a democratic public is a matter of degree and a constant struggle. Where there are no citizens, in a democratic sense, there is no public. Where there are no democratic citizens (let alone robust publics), members of a society are a mass, a multitude, subjects of a king, or a people.

The status of democratic citizens is distinguished from the broader status of citizens *per se* by virtue of enjoying more of the things that fall under (1), (2), and (3) above. That is, they have more rights and privileges, and their interests are more likely to be heard by society. Moreover, their rights and interests are addressed in a democratic way. Democratic political society is a special way of integrating and unifying people as citizens according to core liberties, electoral rights, institutions accountable to citizens, and so on.

Democracy can be looked at in at least three ways: in terms of electoral control, political control, and political community. Electorally, a democracy, by definition, is government by the "demos" through free and fair elections. Beyond elections, government by the people means political control in terms of how decisions are made between elections and whose interests prevail. Rawls (1999, 24) defined a "well-ordered" democracy in these terms:

> The government is effectively under their [i.e., the public's] political and electoral control, and . . . it answers to and protects their fundamental interests as specified in a written or unwritten constitution and its interpretation. The regime is not an autonomous agency pursuing its own bureaucratic ambitions. Moreover, it is not directed by the interests of large corporations or private economic and corporate power veiled from public knowledge and almost entirely free from accountability.

Democracy can be seen as a form of political community or a distinct form of political association. As Dewey argued (2008 [1916], 16), democracy is a precondition for the richest kind of communal life and human flourishing. Democracy is free, equal, and respectful participation in social life. It is a way of relating to others, of carrying out projects, of designing institutions, of persuading and deciding. Within democracies, groups, schools, institutions, and political decision-making can be organized non-democratically around authoritarian, hierarchical or non-egalitarian structures. Or they can be democratic in structure and spirit – inclusive, open, and non-hierarchical. Democratic structures open up the question of how to live together to all who care to discuss; and society benefits from the input of all. For democracy, the question of how to live is open and not fully known until we engage in democratic dialogue and politics.

It is useful here to adapt Cohen's (2010, 183) distinctions, based on Rawlsian notions of democracy and justice, between (a) a democratic political regime, (b) a democratic society, and (c) a deliberative democracy.

A democratic political regime is a political arrangement with rights of participation, elections, and the surrounding rights of association and expression designed to make participation informed and effective. A democratic society is a society whose members are understood in the political culture as free and equal persons. A deliberative democracy is a political society in which the fundamental political argument appeals

Principles of Global Integrated Ethics

to reasons suited to cooperation among free and equal persons, and the authorization to exercise collective power traces to such argument. A democracy is (Cohen 2010, 1) a "political society of equals, in which the justification of institutions – as well as laws and policies addressed to consequential problems – involves public argument based on the common reason of members, who regard one another as equals."

Robust publics

The existence of democratic citizens is important because it elevates the country above dictatorship and other non-democratic species of political structure. Every day, people around the world fight to be members of minimal democratic publics. By calling publics "minimal" I do not mean to slight such struggles. I only distinguish two kinds of public, minimal and maximal.

In theory, I reserve the term "public" for citizens of a society who have the capacity and opportunity to be members of a democratic political association in ways that are participatory, dialogic, and just.[2] This is consistent with Cohen's definition of democratic society.

A true democracy with a robust public exists only where a flourishing egalitarian liberal democracy exists. Three features are primary: endorsement, participation, and the "public stance." Endorsement means that citizens are able to give explicit and free agreement to the political structure as substantially fair and democratic for all. Citizens of certain societies may go along with the political status quo for practical reasons, e.g., it maintains law and order after a period of civil war. But they would not recognize the structure as ideal or substantially democratic. Without wide consensus on the virtues of the political structure, we have citizens (or subjects) who are not part of a public. Participation means citizens enjoy active and meaningful participation in the political life of their democracy. Members of a public have substantial representation in government, and can have a significant influence on important decisions.

The public stance is the political version of the objective stance in journalism, science, and communication. A public exists only if sufficient numbers of citizens act as democratic citizens. That is, they can adopt the public stance – they engage issues from the perspective of the common good. They discourse and dialogue about the common good, about justice for all, and about the direction of their commonwealth.

A long train of thinkers and political leaders has struggled with the question of how to instill a public virtue in citizens. Virtuous citizens are supposed to rise above their parochial interests and care about the common good. Cicero, fearing the collapse of the Roman Republic, bemoaned the lack of public virtue in Romans. Self-interest and "groupism" (Haidt 2012, 189–220) weaken appeals to the common good. The public stance is both cognitive – intellectual virtues must be practiced, such as truthfulness – and emotive – citizens must care about the principles of democracy. Citizens need to have the right "political emotions" (Nussbaum, 2013). Patriotism is one attempt to motivate citizens toward the common good. But it can take on non-democratic forms.

The idea of a public as participatory citizens concerned about the common good may exist in social unions smaller than a nation. A commune, a religious group, or an organization to advance a cause could create a political structure that is egalitarian and participatory. This is democracy writ small, and such groups support democracy writ large on the national stage. However, we must be careful. It has become fashionable in academia to prefer talk of "publics" to talk of "the public" since citizens often gather into groups to address civic issues, such as protecting a green space, or to mobilize around an issue such as gay marriage. Another reason some people avoid "the public" is that, ironically, it sounds undemocratic – the imposition of the ideology of the majority on a plurality of smaller groups. It seems to deny differences. Often, when people refer to publics they don't mean anything like my notion of the public. Some of these publics are better thought of as special interest groups, not a public. I continue to insist that the ability of citizens to belong to an inclusive public and address shared concerns from the perspective of the common good is crucial to a properly functioning democracy.

Democratic public spheres

How does journalism help a public exist? It does so by influencing the flow and quality of communication in a democracy's public sphere. Publics, those creatures of democracies, are created and maintained in large part through a public sphere. Journalism is an essential part of that public sphere.

A public sphere is a space for discussion and information-sharing among citizens on political and social issues, mainly through media channels.[3] The public sphere exists between the private sphere of our lives and the sphere of the state. Its political function was stressed in the 18th-century Enlightenment public sphere. Bentham, for example, argued that "publicity" – publication of information on government – allows the public to sit in judgment on government. With online and global media, the public sphere is no longer definable as a physical space, e.g., the coffee-houses of 17th-century London. Nor is today's public sphere made possible solely by "physical" media such as printed newspapers. As Castells says (2010), we now have a global public sphere where actors in many countries use global networks of communication to discuss issues.

The public sphere, as a system of media channels, can be used for many non-democratic purposes, from selling goods to raising funds for humanitarian projects. The political purpose of the public sphere is usually described in terms of democratic citizenship. Ideally, citizens use the public sphere to participate in decision-making, to hold government (and other powerful actors) to account, to publicize how officials and institutions are performing, and to promote ideas, policies, and political parties. Citizens enter the public sphere to discuss common goods and concerns. It is a place to speak about public matters without censure from the state and at some remove from the influence of private interests.

How citizens in the public sphere communicate is crucial. Citizens are asked to adopt the public stance of someone concerned with the good of all citizens, not just their own interests. They are to dialogue and to listen to others, and to give reasons that others could accept.

The public sphere rarely reaches such ideal heights of impartial discourse. Many actors do not put first the common good. Media may foster a partisan, uncompromising, and divisive form of public discussion. Certain voices may dominate the public sphere, or use manipulative techniques of persuasion. All of these dubious practices violate the values of communication ethics and democratic communication ethics. The practices show disrespect to other people both as rational individuals and as democratic citizens.

Despite its flaws, the public sphere makes democracy possible. Castells (2010, 36) states:

> The public sphere is an essential component of sociopolitical organization because it is the space where people come together as citizens and articulate their autonomous views to influence the political institutions of society. Civil society is the organized expression of these views; and the relationship between the state and civil society is the cornerstone of democracy. Without an effective civil society capable of channeling and structuring citizen debates over diverse interests and conflicting interests, the state drifts away from its subjects.

Without a strong democratic public sphere, democracy is reduced to holding election campaigns largely shaped by "political marketing and special interest groups and characterized by choice within a narrow spectrum of political option" (Castells 2010, 36).

Dialogic democracies

There are many types of democracy, from direct, representational, egalitarian, and elitist to participatory, deliberative, and non-deliberative (e.g., confrontational).[4]

I have already argued for a liberal constitutional democracy that is egalitarian in structure. I now want to explain two other features that I think should characterize our democracies – participation and dialogue.

Participatory democracy can trace its heritage back to direct democracy in classical Athens, where citizens gathered together and voted on political questions. However, the phrase participatory democracy, as I am using it, refers more to a form of democracy defined by writers from the 1970s onward, for instance in the works of Carole Pateman and C. B. Macpherson. These writers complained that liberals – read libertarians – had not paid sufficient attention to how inequalities of class, sex, and race hinder active participation in contemporary democracy. Today, in countries like the United States, representative democracy is dominant but many states supplement it with forms of direct democracy, such as referenda. The growth of the Internet has encouraged grassroots citizen activism.

Participatory democracy rejects elite democracy. The latter believes the issues of modern society are too complex for the busy, muddling, and easily manipulated masses. Government by experts and elites should shape government policy, and the media should report on their views to the masses. Participatory democracy can include elements of elitism, e.g., consulting expert knowledge, but the emphasis is on participation by citizens.

As noble as participatory democracy may sound, it is still not sufficient. The participation should, in large part, take the form of a dialogue. This is my version of deliberative democracy. Deliberative democracy thinks that what is missing from the participatory model of democracy is the notion of deliberation. Deliberation is more than simply participating in public communication and discourse; it is a special and important way of participating. Philosopher Michael Walzer (1999, 58) defined deliberation as a particular way of thinking: "quiet, reflective, open to a wide range of evidence, respectful of different views. It is a rational process of weighing the available data, considering alternative possibilities, arguing about relevance and worthiness, and then choosing the best policy or person."

I endorse dialogue as the ideal, rather than deliberation as defined by Walzer, since dialogue is a less demanding form of conversation appropriate for the hurly burly of the public sphere. I call a democracy that governs itself to a substantial degree through reasonable dialogue a dialogic democracy. The aim is dialogue, informed analysis, and a fair sharing of views, not quiet deliberation, which happens too infrequently in society and in the media. The goal is reasonable discourse. Dialogue is not about reaching unanimous, watered-down consensus, liking your interlocutor, or avoiding tough topics. As I shall explain in Chapter 8, dialogue, as a form of "listening," can be a method for discussions across great differences in culture and economic status, especially when global issues are debated.

What are some of the distinguishing features of dialogue? For dialogic democracy, a public dialogue is a cooperative inquiry into a topic from different standpoints, where we partially transcend our situations to listen and strike a critical distance (if temporarily) from our beliefs. The aim is not simply to express my view; it is not to portray those who disagree with me as unpatriotic enemies who must be crushed. This is not a winner-takes-all affair. Dialogue is not a monologue. It is about listening, learning. It expects robust disagreement, but it also seeks areas of compromise and new solutions. Democracy is about how we speak to each other. It needs the democratic virtues of tolerance and reciprocity.

The value of dialogue in the public sphere is manifold. It promotes what Rawls (1993, 4) called a "reasonable pluralism" – a reasonable discourse among groups with different values and philosophies of life. This discourse enlarges the factual base for choices, encourages compromise and mutual understanding, and assists the critical evaluation of policies and actions. It leads to the "perspectival enrichment" of citizens.

In recent years, especially in the United States, there have been many calls for politicians, journalists, and advocacy groups to overcome the fragmentation of politics by avoiding non-dialogic communication. Makau and Marty (2013) argue that substantial harm to the US body politic – and the country's ability to respond to urgent issues – is caused by a communication philosophy based on a simplistic individualism that creates an intolerant, non-listening "argument culture." They propose a number of techniques and methods to strengthen dialogue and deliberation in politics.

Canadian philosopher Mark Kingwell has summarized nicely why civility and dialogue are important for democracy. It is not just about being "nice" to others. When taken to extremes, incivility is "a creeping nihilism here, a disregard for the very idea of reason" (2012, 13). He continues:

> Parliamentary democracy is nothing more or less than a conversation among citizens, both directly and by way of their elected leaders. Here, and only here, can our interests and desires be made into law. . . . We all have a direct personal stake in seeing it thrive, because every time a good citizen checks out, the tactical forces of incivility lower democracy's value one more notch. (2012, 13)

Therefore, I conclude that one of the political principles of an integrative ethics should be a firm commitment to dialogic democracy. An integrated ethics portrays responsible journalism as promoting an egalitarian liberal democracy that is participatory and dialogic.

Principles of Global Integrated Ethics

The chief political aim of journalism is the promotion of Cohen's three types of political association – a democratic political regime, a democratic society, and a society that is dialogic and deliberative. Working through the public sphere, its aim is to help create, maintain, and enhance a robust and maximal public in a democratic system.

Dialogic Journalism

The ideas of dialogic democracy and a robust democratic public sharpen our notion of democracy as the political aim of responsible journalism. However, how does it help us evaluate what forms of journalism are most valuable to democracy, beyond an appeal to journalism that promoted reasoned dialogue? Also, how does a preference for dialogic journalism fit our other political values, such as a free press in an open society? By opting to support certain types of journalism, are we doubting the value of a free press and the diversity of forms of communication?

In the following sections, I answer questions about evaluating forms of journalism by developing the idea of dialogic journalism in terms of the "media needs" of the public. Later, I reply to the question about a diverse free press by putting forward the idea of principled pluralism.

What does the public need?

We can make our analysis of valued forms of democratic journalism more specific by asking about the communication needs of publics. In Chapter 5, I introduced the idea of a society's six "media needs" as a way of defining journalism's institutional role. The media needs also help us to determine what types of journalism are democratically valuable.

To repeat, the six media needs are (1) informational needs – wide and deep; (2) explanatory needs; (3) "perspectival enrichment" needs; (4) advocational and reform needs; (5) participatory needs; (6) dialogic needs.

What forms of journalism best meet these media needs?

The "wide" informational needs depend on accurate, unbiased reportage on events and what is happening in the world. Solid reporting provides a platform for everything else we want to do in the public sphere, from commenting and criticizing to taking action. Providing "deep" information is an area where investigative journalism plays an important democratic role.

The explanatory needs require a journalism of good and insightful interpretation. Explanatory journalism includes the analysis of a decision (e.g., a leader's decision to resign) and events (e.g., a nuclear arms treaty). The motivation of the actors, the process that led to the event, and the consequences of their actions are all part of the story. Explanatory journalism also includes "backgrounders," "reporter notebooks", "interpretive journalism," and explanatory articles in science magazines. The interpretive approach was pioneered in the early 1900s by the emerging news magazines, such as *Time* magazine (Ward 2005, 235–237). *Time*'s interpretive approach, from the start, was developed as an alternative to the traditional news reporting then prevailing. Henry Luce, co-founder of *Time*, believed citizens wanted (and needed) the meaning of facts and events.

Perspectival enrichment needs are satisfied by opinion journalism, from editorials and columns to sharply worded posts by bloggers. This journalism provides a plurality of points of view, and the language is less cautious and analytical. Often, the writing is clearly political and ideological. Explanatory journalism seeks to explain, opinion journalism seeks to persuade.

Participatory needs focus not on journalists providing information and views to citizens but the ability of citizens to participate in the commenting, interpreting, and providing of information across the public sphere. They also are at the heart of a new development called "participatory journalism" (Singer et al. 2011) where newsrooms use citizens to identify stories, provide accounts and images, and evaluate the usefulness of stories. The participation goes beyond citizens writing comments on articles. It includes citizens setting up their own blogs, and groups of citizens creating their own websites to do journalism.

The dialogic needs require a public sphere where how people communicate is important. Citizens need communication and conversation in the form of reasoned dialogue. Dialogic journalism structures the discussion of issues in news stories, broadcast programs, and online at websites in such a way as to increase the possibility of dialogue. It provides a format for tolerant sharing of views, while precluding intolerant, non-dialogic forms of communication.[5]

Therefore, these are the forms of journalism that a dialogic approach to journalism would consider of greatest value to democracy.

A free and democratic press

How does a dialogic approach to journalism differ from other perspectives on democratic communication? Let's start with the idea of a free press and then ask: Is freedom enough for a democratic press?[6]

A free press is a press that enjoys a substantial negative freedom. It is relatively unfettered by government and law in its newsgathering and publications. A democratic press is a free press that, in principle and in fact, advocates for and substantially advances democracy – in our sense, an egalitarian, informed, participatory and dialogic democracy. On my view, journalists have a positive duty to promote dialogic public discussions.

It is in this area – the promotion of dialogue – that we find libertarianism wanting as a theory of the press. Libertarianism may promote participation, but it does not promote dialogue, let alone deliberation. From a strict libertarian perspective, journalists and citizens who publish news and viewpoints often do not, and have no duty to, aim at reasoned dialogue. There is no duty to include a diversity of perspectives in their publications. Their primary aim is to express their own views in whatever fashion they prefer.

The limitations of libertarian theory cannot be "fixed" by adopting a participatory view of democracy, updated by the Internet. However, libertarians of the Net have a valid point. The Internet and new forms of communication do provide better public access to the public sphere, better means for the expression of views, and new opportunities for citizens to participate in debate. The political value of the "new media" is the many voices now online. Praise for the democratization of media via the Internet rests on a participatory model of democracy. It is said that the new media have created a "democratic media" movement, where citizens are no longer passive consumers of news but actively help to shape the news and public discussion. Journalist Dan Gillmor's influential book *We the Media* (2004) argues, in the subtitle, that the new media allow "Grassroots Journalism by the People, for the People." Of course, there are good and bad uses of the new media. Cell phones and Twitter can help citizens report election abuses in developing countries, or they can be used to spread malicious gossip. Writers like Gillmor emphasize the positive potential of new media.

This enthusiasm for new media takes a wrong turn when it adopts a libertarian viewpoint that ethical standards which restrain the freedom to publish are not relevant to the wired world and not central to democracy. Is a high level of citizen participation in the media all that is needed for democratic media? Dialogic theory answers no. Participatory media are not sufficient to create democratic media. What is missing from the participatory model of democracy is dialogic communication. *How* we participate is crucial.

The problem with modern democracy is not only that too many citizens are not able to participate in their society in equal measure with other citizens. The problem is that the mode of participation is often non-deliberative. News media are thought to be part of this growing non- deliberative public sphere, resorting to "hot talk" radio shows, eight-second soundbites, and a blurring of news and entertainment. The trend, then, is away from dialogue, which is the key to wiser and more inclusive decisions.

The celebration of a diversity of voices online has little to say about whose voices these are and how such voices have to interact in order to address issues democratically. It says nothing about the type of information available for discussion, the obstacles put up by governments to free speech, or the selfish (or intolerant) attitudes that can thwart attempts at fruitful online discussion. Conversation, offline or online, may lead nowhere – or somewhere. It may promote informed rational opinion or emotional shouting. Moreover, the issues that confront countries in a globalized world, from climate change to healthcare reform, are so complex that dialogue and study are needed, not just random exchanges of views. Organized, reasoned debate, not ideological ranting or simplistic analysis, is desperately needed in public communication. To make things worse, many powerful agents have a stake in how public discussion turns out. Millions of dollars are spent on attempting to influence and manipulate public opinion. Our society may be a communicative society of the highest order. It has more accessible forms of communication for sharing information than were present at any other time in history. Yet it may still fail to be a dialogic democracy. To assume that interactivity is by itself sufficient for democracy is as naïve as thinking, in the late 1800s, that a mass commercial press was the answer to the woes of democracy.

Dialogic democracy should be the ultimate goal of a free press. News media have positive duties to create dialogic spaces in the public sphere. They should offer programs on current issues that encourage reasoned exchanges among people of differing views. Without a public culture of dialogue and deliberation, without institutional practices and media coverage that encourage citizens to come together to discuss, democracy declines into the irrational rule of the insufficiently informed, whose desires and views are the result of manipulation by powerful elites who distort and dominate channels of communication. Only under conditions of dialogic democracy can we speak about the free and reasonable agreement among citizens, and of rational public opinion.

Principled pluralism

The discussion leads to the concept of principled pluralism.

The principle states: *A democracy should regard most highly those forms of journalism that create, maintain, and promote dialogic democracy. Forms of journalism should be judged by the extent to which they meet the crucial media needs of a robust democratic public.*

This is my reply to the worry that my approach is intolerant of a diversity of forms of journalism. My notion of principled pluralism supports a plurality of forms of journalism. But I do not adopt the "accommodating" view that all forms are equally valuable to the public sphere.

Combining the principles of dialogic journalism and principled pluralism, what standards have we found to evaluate forms of journalism?

The most general standard is *having significant democratic value*, defined as meeting the important media needs of a dialogic democracy. This standard recognizes the following as valid forms: reporting and investigative journalism, explanatory journalism, participatory journalism, and dialogic journalism.

Principled pluralism excludes unethical applications of these major forms of journalism, such as inaccurate reporting, uninformed explanatory journalism, and a disrespectful opinion journalism that maligns other views.

Principled pluralism allows us to be critical of democratic countries where one or more of these forms of journalism are restricted by press laws and to critique authoritarian countries where such forms of journalism are severely restrained, e.g., critical political media in China, investigative journalism in Iran, or independent reporting in North Korea.

The dialogic approach distinguishes between valuable opinion journalism and non-valuable opinion journalism, when we consider the needs of democracy. This is important at a time of increasingly partisan and intolerant journalism. Dialogic theory believes the most valuable form of opinion journalism is a *moderate* opinion journalism that brings forward a diversity of positions for reasonable public scrutiny. Dialogic theory agrees with Mill's argument for freedom of expression – that no one, even if they speak harshly, should be censured since there may be a grain of truth in what he or she says. But the issue here is not of censorship or freedom of expression. The issue is how best to use the freedom of expression in democracy. On this issue, dialogic theory has reasons to value dialogue and moderate opinion journalism. In fact, it can argue that, in plural societies, intolerant opinion journalism works against democracy.

The categories of dialogic journalism are consistent with how previous theories have divided up the roles of journalism. For example, as discussed in Chapter 2, *Normative Theories of the Media* (Christians et al. 2009) identified the roles as monitorial, facilitative, radical, and collaborative. These roles, and their relative importance, are explained by dialogic theory in terms of meeting media needs. Dialogic theory also fits the shape of journalism history. Since the periodic press arose in the 17th century, journalists have seen themselves as reporters, interpreters, opiners, or reformers – or some combination of the four. The scheme of dialogic journalism is consistent with this historical fact.

Principles of Global Integrated Ethics

Conclusion

This chapter has proposed that the principles of dialogic journalism and principled pluralism be embraced as two basic political principles for an integrated media ethics. Other principles will need to be developed in time. But we can start with these principles as we construct our integrative ethics.

Principled pluralism allows us to acknowledge a wide range of forms of journalism as democratically valuable, in ways that are platform-neutral. What technology you use to do journalism, from printing newspapers to postings blogs, is not relevant to defining dialogic journalism. What matters is *how* you use those platforms to communicate in the public sphere. The principle of dialogic journalism provides standards by which to evaluate which forms of journalism are most valuable to democracy.

In conclusion, I propose a principled pluralism that advocates dialogic journalism as a common, unifying concept for the political structure of an integrative journalism ethics.

In the next chapter, I develop cosmopolitan, humanitarian principles for a global media ethics.

Notes

1. For my detailed examination of the idea of public and citizenship, see Ward 2010, ch. 5.
2. The public is related to but not identical with what is public. The latter refers to physical objects (e.g., roads), information, and institutions that are in the service of a public, or are open and accessible to a public.
3. The literature on the public sphere is voluminous, especially since Habermas's groundbreaking work (1989) on the origin of the European public sphere. Here I summarize my perspective.
4. See Held 2006 for an overview of the many forms of democracy over many centuries.
5. These categories of journalism are not pigeonholes. A story or a form of journalism may fulfill several of these needs. For example, reporting can providing explanations. Investigative journalism can promote a point of view. Advocacy journalism can contain accurate reporting.
6. For an extended discussion of a free and democratic press, see Ward 2011, ch. 3.

References

Castells, Manuel. 2010. "The New Public Sphere." In *International Communication: A Reader*, edited by Daya Kishan Thussu, 36–47. New York: Routledge.

Christians, Clifford G., Theodore L. Glasser, Denis McQuail, Kaarle Nordenstreng, and Robert A. White. 2009. *Normative Theories of the Media: Journalism in Democratic Societies*. Urbana: University of Illinois Press.

Cohen Joshua. 2010. *The Arc of the Moral Universe and Other Essays*. Cambridge, MA: Harvard University Press.

Dewey, John. 2008 (1916). *Democracy and Education*. Radford, VA: Wilder Publications.

Dworkin, Ronald. 2000. *Sovereign Virtue: The Theory and Practice of Equality*. Cambridge, MA: Harvard University Press.

Dworkin, Ronald. 2011. *Justice for Hedgehogs*. Cambridge, MA: Harvard University Press.

Gillmor, Dan. 2004. *We the Media: Grassroots Journalism for the People, by the People*. Sebastopol, CA: O'Reilly Media.

Habermas, Jürgen. 1989. *The Structural Transformation of the Public Sphere*. Trans. Thomas Burger with the assistance of Frederick Lawrence. Cambridge: Polity Press.

Haidt, Jonathan. 2012. *The Righteous Mind*. New York: Pantheon Books.

Held, David. 2006. *Models of Democracy*. 3rd ed. Cambridge: Polity.

Kekes, John. 1997. *Against Liberalism*, 88–119. Ithaca, NY: Cornell University Press.

Kekes, John. 2003. *The Illusions of Egalitarianism*. Ithaca, NY: Cornell University Press.

Kingwell, Mark. 2012. *Unruly Voices: Essays on Democracy, Civility and the Human Imagination*. Ottawa: Biblioasis.

Makau, Josina M., and Debian L. Marty. 2013. *Dialogue and Deliberation*. Long Grove, IL: Waveland Press.

Nussbaum, Martha C. 2013. *Political Emotions: Why Love Matters for Justice*. Cambridge, MA: Harvard University Press.

Rawls, John. 1992 (1972). *A Theory of Justice*. Oxford: Oxford University Press.

Rawls, John. 1993. *Political Liberalism*. New York: Columbia University Press.

Rawls, John. 1999. *The Law of Peoples*. Cambridge, MA: Harvard University Press.

Searle, John. 1995. *The Construction of Social Reality*. New York: The Free Press.

Singer, Jane B., David Domingo, Ari Heinonen, and Alfred Hermida. 2011. *Participatory Journalism*. Malden, MA: Wiley-Blackwell.

Walzer, Michael. 1999. "Deliberation and What Else." In *Essays on Democracy and Disagreement*, edited by Stephen Macedo, 30–45. Oxford: Oxford University Press.

Ward, Stephen J. A. 2005. *The Invention of Journalism Ethics: The Path to Objectivity and Beyond*. Montreal: McGill-Queen's University Press.

Ward, Stephen, J. A. 2010. *Global Journalism Ethics*. Montreal: McGill-Queen's University Press.

Ward Stephen J. A. 2011. *Ethics and the Media: An Introduction*. Cambridge: Cambridge University Press.

Chapter 8
Aims for Global Integrated Ethics

In this chapter, I formulate a second set of principles for an integrated media ethics. They are principles for a *global* integrated ethics. I look at the aims that journalists have if they are to practice responsibly a journalism with global reach and impact. These aims are cosmopolitan and humanistic. They extend beyond the nation-based political principles of Chapter 7.

I propose that the ultimate aims of journalism should be global human flourishing and global democratic structures.

Aims

Ultimate aims

An ultimate aim is an overarching goal that integrates our actions and values. An ultimate aim can be ethical, unethical, or not directly connected to ethics. To dedicate my life to the study and cure of cancer is an ultimate aim. It is a scientific aim, a personal aim, and an ethical aim all at the same time. To dedicate myself to achieving political power at whatever cost or by whatever method is an unethical ultimate aim. To aim at writing the greatest novel ever written is, as it stands, an aesthetic ultimate aim not directly connected to ethics.

Ultimate aims are ethical in a weak and a strong sense. The weak sense says the pursuit of the aim, and the manner by which it is to be pursued, raise no serious ethical issues, e.g., I pursue writing a great novel in an ethically "innocent" or neutral manner. In the strong sense, ultimate aims either aim at realized ethical states of affairs or goals, e.g., the alleviation of childhood starvation or the protection of human rights in war zones, or pursue something that is ethically laudable, e.g., doing science to cure cancer. In this chapter, I will refer to ethical ultimate aims in this strong sense.

Ethical ultimate aims are often ideals that express what we are attempting to honor or bring into existence. Or the aim is some conception of the good life, or the virtuous life. The aim is a target at which the ethical impulse, described in Chapter 1, aims. We theorize about ultimate aims and the good life because we are uncertain about our many aims and goods. What goods are worth pursuing and which goods have priority? Should we seek happiness or virtue? Are some goods more basic and important? Philosophers have proposed many ultimate aims for life, such as an ascetic life of self-denial, a hedonistic life of pleasure, the creation of utopian societies, the perfection of human nature, or the pursuit of happiness.

Philosophers have depicted the ultimate good as either a single, highest good, such as intellectual knowledge, or as a composite of goods. They also distinguish between instrumental and intrinsic goods. Money is instrumentally good as a means to other goods. Happiness in intrinsically good, valued for itself and not some other thing.

Aristotle (1976), for instance, developed an ethics of eudaimonia or well-being. Eudaimonia is the ultimate good for life. It is the flourishing of the distinctive capacities of the rational soul as exhibited in the virtues. Humans naturally seek such flourishing just as all living things seek their ideal form. Eudaimonia is a composite good, a convergence of virtues and excellences. Flourishing is developing and actively exercising different kinds of virtue through a lifetime shaped by nature, habit, and education, and supported by favorable conditions over a lifetime. For

Aristotle, every good is located in a hierarchy that constitutes the human good. The lowest rung consists of goods necessary for existence, such as food and shelter. Above this rung are intrinsically desirable goods such as honor, and on the next rung are ethical goods such as the virtues of justice and temperance. The hierarchy is capped by the highest form of life – philosophical contemplation.

Ethical aims in journalism

As with ethics in general, there are many aims in journalism, good, bad, and indifferent. Some people do journalism to be famous, to make money, or to change the world. The aims can be expressed as a single good, e.g., to promote democracy. Or the aim may be a composite of goods, e.g., to inform, to entertain, and to advance democracy.

We have seen that normative interpretations of practice are constructed around ethical aims. We state the purpose or "point" of the practice. These aims are ultimate in being intrinsically valued, and most other goods are valued as means to these ends. We ask what the ultimate aims are for responsible practice. What is the target at which journalists should aim?

What aims are embraced has an important influence on how we judge approaches to journalism, types of stories, and types of journalistic conduct. If journalism's primary role is thought to be supporting the existing social and political order, as is the case in many non-democratic countries, then officials (and many citizens) will frown on a critical press that embarrasses authority, questions policies, and generates debate. However, if journalism's role is thought to be that of helping citizens govern themselves and holding authorities to account, citizens will support an independent press that challenges and embarrasses.

In Chapter 7, I argued that the ultimate political aim of journalism was the advancement of an egalitarian democracy of a dialogic character. I expressed this political aim as a composite of related goods – the six "media needs" that a democratic press should fulfill. In addition, many of the principles found in codes of journalism ethics were reconceived as means to the general "media needs" of publics in democracies. For instance, the principles of truth-telling, editorial independence, accuracy, objectivity, and accountability are valued, at least in part, as methods and means to a democratic journalism for informed and self-governing citizens. The idea that an ultimate aim of journalism is to promote egalitarian liberal democracy justified (and gave birth to) the framework of principles that guides many Western news outlets: the principles of journalistic independence, the watchdog role of the press, and the right to criticize public officials. The idea that journalism ought to impartially provide facts to citizens so they can be self-governing gave birth to the doctrine of news objectivity. Take away the aims of liberal democracy, and the framework can be questioned.

However, it is important to note that not all principles seem to be directly and firmly rooted in the political aims of responsible integrated journalism. For example, the norms of minimizing harm appear to be based on more general values such as avoiding harm to anyone, respecting the dignity of others, and so on. Moreover, the political aims in Chapter 7 were nationalistic in character. The principle directed journalists to promote dialogic democracy among their own citizens. I mention these apparent exceptions and limitations for a reason – to underline that political aims and principles are only a part of a full integrated ethics. Other goals and aims will have to be considered. But what *other* ultimate aims are needed?

It is now time for me to state what I think the ultimate aim is, or should be. I propose that the aim is global human flourishing, a comprehensive and composite good that includes but goes beyond my previous nation-based principles of egalitarian liberalism, dialogic democracy, and principled pluralism. I "go global." I develop our notions from a global perspective. The rest of this chapter explains and defends this proposal.

Human Flourishing as the Ultimate Aim

I propose that the ethics of a global, integrated media should be based on the supremely general principle that all humans are equally valuable moral agents of a single humanity, and all deserve a full and flourishing life.[1] Through this idea we affirm humanity, or express our love of humanity. Human flourishing is the all-encompassing human good. As such, it is the ultimate aim for ethics in general and media ethics in particular. To accept this principle is to also accept what follows from it. It is to accept what I call the "claim of humanity" upon us. Other people, as humans, make moral claims upon us.

The implication of these affirmations is clear: any ethics, including any media ethics, will be guided by a cosmopolitan desire to create, maintain, or advance the good life for all humans. The conceptual task is to provide the minimal meaning of the claim of humanity and then to develop robust and maximal conceptions for the claim, i.e., what principles and applications flow from it. A conception of human flourishing must be more than a hazy love for the brotherhood of mankind. We must show how particular principles and duties follow from a commitment to human flourishing.

The first step is to spell out the idea of the human good. The human good is not one single type of good, but a composite of goods that together define a morally good and dignified form of life. To identify such goods, we need to think about what all humans have in common. What are the common needs to be met and capacities to be developed that (a) establish the basis for a decent human life, and, after that, (b) lead, hopefully, to a flourishing life?

These goods are called "primary goods" because they allow us to pursue other goods. All of us can think of some primary goods – physical security, shelter, food and drink, education, health, sufficient wealth and freedom to pursue one's plans.

In *Global Journalism Ethics* (2010), I presented a theory of the human flourishing as consisting of four types of primary goods. I argued that a global journalism should promote the goods on all four levels. Here is a summary of the main ideas.

Flourishing means the exercise of one's intellectual, emotional, and other capacities to a high degree in a supportive social context. Ideally, flourishing is the fullest expression of human development under favorable conditions. In reality, humans flourish in varying degrees. Few people flourish fully. Life often goes badly; many live in desperate conditions where flourishing is a remote ideal. Nevertheless, the ideal of flourishing is important for evaluating social and political systems.

The concept of flourishing in ethics is not the concept of individuals maximizing their self-interests and goods, in any manner. We can pursue our goods (and flourish) unethically, at the expense of the good (and the flourishing) of others. Any capacity, virtue, emotion, or talent – from the capacity for rational thought to the virtue of loyalty – can be misused or employed for dubious purposes. We do not want people to develop their capacities for cruelty, hatred, and war-mongering. These capacities should not be part of an ethical notion of flourishing. We need to develop capacities in ways that support our sense of the ethically good life. When we ethically flourish, we enjoy such goods as trust, friendship, and right relations with others.

Four levels

Ethical flourishing is the development of four levels of primary goods common to all humans – individual, social, political, and ethical goods. To achieve the goods of each level is to achieve a corresponding form of human dignity: individual, social, political, and ethical dignity.

By individual goods, I mean the goods that come from the development of each individual's capacities. This level includes the physical goods that allow physical dignity. All persons need food, shelter, and security to live a normal length of life in health. This level also contains the rational and moral goods that allow physical capacity to flower into distinct human traits. A person enjoys the rational and moral goods when she develops her capacities to observe and think as a critical individual, and to carry out a rational plan of life. Such a person is able to form emotional attachments, and to use her imagination to produce (or enjoy) creative and intellectual works. Also, the person is able to be a moral agent. She is able to empathize with others and to form a sense of justice. She is able to deliberate about the good of others. She has the dignity of an individual person.

The social goods arise when we use our rational and moral capacities to participate in society. Human reality is "social" not just because, instrumentally, humans need society to develop language and culture. Humans come to value participating in common projects as a good-in-itself. Among the social goods are the freedom to enter into and benefit from economic association, the goods of love and friendship; the need for mutual recognition and respect. In this manner, we achieve social dignity.

By political goods, I mean the goods that accrue to us as citizens living in a just political association. The latter is a participatory, dialogic democracy. These goods include the basic liberties, such as freedom of speech, combined with the opportunity and resources to exercise these freedoms. Citizens are able to participate in political life, to hold office, and to influence decisions. The primary means to these public goods are constitutional protections, the rule of law and barriers against undue coercion, and means for the peaceful resolution of disputes. A citizen who enjoys these goods has political dignity, through self-government

By ethical goods, I mean the goods that come from living among persons and institutions of ethical character. We can rely on them to act ethically. We do not only need to live in a society of rational people – that is, people motivated to pursue their own interests. A society motivated only by purely self-interested rational agents would be a terrifying "private" (or extremely individualistic) society. To flourish, we need to live among people who are disposed to be what Rawls (1993, 48) calls morally "reasonable." Reasonable citizens are motivated to consider the interests of others and the greater public good. We need to create societies where people appreciate living in right relations, not simply follow the law for fear of reprisals.

Congruence

These are the four levels of the human good. How should the levels be related?

The goods of each level should be integrated and developed simultaneously. I do not pick out one good (or one level) as sufficient to define the human good, such as pleasure, or utility. The human good is a composite of basic goods, none of which are reducible or eliminable. The satisfaction of one type of good allows another to exist. To be sure, we need to secure the physical goods before we can move on to other goods, but that doesn't make the other levels less important. In many countries, unstable political structures – that is, the lack of political goods — interfere with attempts to provide physical and social goods to citizens.

Moreover, the proper relationship between the levels is governed by the fundamental moral principle that we pursue these goods within the bounds of justice. What we owe to others, and our duty to act justly, is prior and should not be overridden by our desire to enlarge our goods. The pursuit of the good needs to be restrained by justice because of the ever-present danger that people will act selfishly, violating the cosmopolitan principle that all people are of equal moral value, and, therefore, should enjoy the right to flourish as much as any other person.

A contrary view – that justice is a means to the pursuit of individual or social goods – has a long history in ethical and political thought. Classical utilitarian conceptions of society stress the maximization of goods to promote utility overall. Justice has instrumental value, not intrinsic value. The rules of justice and law are valued insofar as they contribute to overall utility. The implication is that if the rules of justice, in whole or in part, do not contribute to overall utility, then they can be abridged or violated. Pursuing the good – in this case, maximizing utility – is primary. The same view grounds many of the conceptions of political freedom surveyed in Chapter 6. There, certain conceptions of negative liberty regarded social restraints of any kind, including presumably the restraints of justice, as regrettable but necessary means to peace. On my view, justice *is* a great good – an intrinsic good that should not be abridged or violated by the individual's pursuit of their goods.

To promote flourishing is to promote what Rawls called a "congruence" (1992 [1972], 567) between liberty (and the individual pursuit of goods) and justice and equality. Liberty or the pursuit of goods is not necessarily at odds with the principles of justice. They conflict where the pursuit is reckless, without proportion, or at the expense of the pursuit of goods by others. Far from being at odds, principles of justice should recognize, and allow for, the pursuit of many goods. For example, Rawls's first principle of justice establishes a core of basic liberties as bedrock goods in any decent democracy. We should see the good and the just as components of the greatest good – the flourishing of humanity. No such flourishing is possible unless we establish congruence between these components.

The aim of ethics, then, is affirming humanity by aiming at ethical flourishing, understood as the promotion of the four levels for dignity, and a congruence of the good and the just. The aim is global. It is not the promotion of flourishing only in Canada or China. The goal is flourishing across all borders. The individual, social, political, and ethical dignity that we seek for citizens in our society, we seek for humanity at large.

In terms of political structure, the best chance for a reasonable congruence of the good and the right is in a liberal, egalitarian democracy. In this historically contingent entity called democracy, humans have created a political structure whose principles come closer to capturing the idea of human flourishing than any other structure. Ideally, democracy means core liberties and the freedom to develop the capacities of citizens. It means equality of opportunity and rights, justice, and equality under the law. Therefore, we can include the promotion of democracy as part of the ethics of humanity in two ways: strengthening individual democracies and promoting international agencies that support democratic governance of global problems.

In the final analysis, the ethics of humanity provides two ultimate aims for journalism in a global age: to promote global human flourishing and, as a sub-component, to promote global democracy. These two aims help us to redefine our normative interpretation of journalism from a domestic serving of citizens to a global serving of humanity. This global normative interpretation integrates the various forms of journalism under one unifying theme: human flourishing. This is global journalism seen in its best light.

Applying Human Flourishing

My fourfold theory of the human good can be used to turn media ethics into a global media ethics, by redefining the allegiances, aims, and principles of journalism. These fundamental changes will entail changes to practice. If journalists were to adopt ethical flourishing as a primary concept, it would begin a chain of reinterpretations of primary concepts and revisions of codes of ethics.

I indicate the scope of these changes in what follows in three ways: I consider changes in the self-conception of journalists; I indicate how journalists can promote the four levels of human flourishing; and I show how adopting a global ethics based on flourishing would call for changes in journalistic concepts and practices.

Principles of Global Integrated Ethics

Self-consciousness

If journalists adopted the cosmopolitanism approach, they would alter their self-identity and alter their notion of who they serve. They would embrace three imperatives:

- *Act as global agents*: Journalists should see themselves as agents of a global public sphere. The goal of their collective actions is a well-informed, diverse, and tolerant global "info-sphere" that challenges the distortions of tyrants, the abuse of human rights, and the manipulation of information by special interests.
- *Serve the citizens of the world*: The global journalist's primary loyalty is to the information needs of world citizens. Journalists should refuse to define themselves as attached primarily to factions, regions, or even countries. Serving the public means serving more than one's local readership or audience, or even the public of one's country.
- *Promote non-parochial understandings*: The global journalist frames issues broadly and uses a diversity of sources and perspectives to promote a nuanced understanding of issues from an international perspective. Journalism should work against a narrow ethnocentrism or patriotism.

These imperatives, by themselves, are worthy of exploration. Yet even without a detailed exposition of the directives, we sense their revolutionary import. Human flourishing as ultimate aim changes journalists' self-conception from that of a citizen of one country to that of a global citizen serving humanity. It makes the serving of humanity the primary allegiance of journalists. Journalists owe credible journalism to all potential readers of a global public sphere. Loyalty to humanity trumps other loyalties, where they conflict.

This cosmopolitan definition of who is a journalist flies in the face of the dominant form of journalist's self-conception. Journalists have defined themselves non-globally and parochially, as serving local, regional, and national audiences. This loyalty to one's co-nationals is primary and trumps talk of serving foreigners or citizens in other countries.

Promoting the four levels

This change in identity is further specified by adding the aim of promoting the four levels of primary goods. Journalists, as global citizens, seek individual, social, political, and ethical dignity for humanity at large. One important implication of adopting the four levels is that the political goal of journalism changes. To be sure, the political goods tell journalists to use their powers of investigation and communication for the development of a just and participatory political association at home. But the political goods, globalized, expand the aim from the promotion of a just liberal democracy at home to an attempt to establish well-ordered global society, a global community marked both by the development of democracy abroad and the development of global democratic institutions.

Global ethical flourishing may be attractive as a philosophical idea. But, practically speaking, how can global journalism promote something as abstract as levels of primary goods? We need to specify how media can promote each level.

Individual goods Journalists can promote the individual goods by monitoring basic levels of physical and rational dignity in their own country and around the world. Journalism can promote individual goods in at least three ways:

1. Provide information on (and an analysis of) world events and trends. Journalism should be occupied with providing timely, accurate, and contextual information on political, social, and economic developments, from reports on new legislation and political instability to news of global trends in business and environment. This information is the basis for the deliberation of autonomous citizens in any nation.
2. Monitor basic levels of physical, individual, and social dignity. Physical dignity: journalism has a duty to help citizens be aware of the ability of their society and other societies to provide for citizens a decent level of physical goods such as food, shelter, health, wealth, a reasonable length of life, and physical security through effective laws (and regulatory agencies) to protect the vulnerable. Journalism

has a duty to provide the same scrutiny of the ability of citizens in the development of their rational and moral capacities. This duty requires journalistic inquiry into the educational system's effectiveness in developing rational and imaginative citizens, the capacity of the social fabric to develop citizens' emotional capacity through supportive communities, and the capacity of the public sphere to develop citizens' rational capacities through opportunities for philosophical, scientific, and cultural engagement.

Journalism has a duty to bring forward for debate the fairness of existing physical, social, and educational opportunities within countries and also globally. By using a variety of metrics and by making cross-cultural comparisons, journalism can contribute to progress in these areas.

3. Investigate inequality. Journalism has a duty to conduct in-depth investigative stories on people and groups who have been denied physical, rational, and moral dignity, and to support global institutions that seek redress of these inequalities. Global journalism should reveal whether gender, ethnicity, and other differences account for inequalities. By exploring below the surface of society and our global economic systems, journalism promotes citizens' awareness of how egalitarian their society is, and the impact of policies on human development and dignity.

Social goods Journalism can promote the social goods by taking up its duty to report on, analyze, and critique the ways in which citizens interact and create associations so as to enjoy the goods of social cooperation. Journalism should promote social goods in at least five ways:

1. Report critically on economic associations. Journalism has a duty to report on and analyze how societies allow citizens to participate in and benefit from its various forms of economic association, including fair economic competition. It needs to monitor society's use of economic power and its effect on egalitarian democracy and the principles of justice.
2. Assess the quality of social life. Journalism should report on the types of social life, social and technological trends, and social

possibilities available for citizens. It should inquire into whether such trends nurture caring relationships, meaningful collective activity, and flourishing communities.
3. Assist social bridging. In a pluralistic world, journalism has a duty to act as a bridge between diverse classes, ethnic groups, religions, and cultures within and among countries. Journalism has a twofold task to make visible, for consideration and critique, both the commonalities and the differences among citizens, and to encourage tolerant but frank cross-cultural discussion of issues.
4. Assist media literacy and the evaluation of media. Journalism has a duty to inquire into the impact of journalism, media, and communication technology on the global public sphere and on their society; and into how new communication technology and new forms of journalism can be used to advance ethical flourishing and the social goods.
5. Use global comparisons. Journalism has a duty to evaluate the level of human and social goods among countries and to investigative different approaches to major social problems. In this way, journalism is a force for progressive ideas and "experiments in living."

Political goods Journalism can promote the political and ethical goods by helping to nurture morally reasonable citizens willing to discuss essential issues objectively and fairly, and to nurture a society where the pursuit of the rational side of life is restrained within firm and effective principles of justice. Journalism can promote the political goods in at least four ways:

1. Critique the basic structure. Journalism of the public good has a duty to inquire into and to encourage deliberation upon fundamental justice from a global perspective. Journalism should report on the basic institutional structures of societies and how well the principles of justice and international law are embodied by institutions, political processes, and legal systems.
2. Monitor the basic liberties. Journalism has a duty to promote and defend basic liberties around the world and to ask to what extent citizens are able to enjoy the full value of basic liberties, such as freedom of speech, freedom of association, freedom from

discrimination, and other constitutional protections. Are citizens able to exercise these freedoms for the purpose of self-development and to enjoy the goods on the other three levels?
3. Encourage participation. Journalism needs to monitor (and help to make possible) citizen participation in public life and citizens' ability to have a meaningful influence on debate about government decisions. Journalists should engage in various forms of "civic" journalism that enhance public involvement in basic social issues and discourage public cynicism about civic engagement.
4. Report on diversity and representation. Journalism has a duty to insist on, and to help make possible, a diverse public forum within and across borders, with adequate representation of non-dominant groups. Journalism must be self-conscious about how groups can use language to manipulate, stereotype, and persuade citizens unethically. Through the media, powerful groups can dominate the public sphere.

Ethical goods Journalism contributes to the ethical goods by helping to produce citizens who value ethical flourishing (including the public good). Journalism can promote the ethical goods as follows:

1. Take the public good perspective. When covering major public issues or major public events, such as elections, media should focus on how the public good is served or not served by proposals, promises, and actions. They should examine critically any claims by public officials, large private corporations, and any other agency to be acting for the public good.
2. Highlight those who enhance the public good. Cover individuals and groups who enhance society through courageous and public-minded actions.
3. Support the exercise of public reason through dialogic media. As discussed in previous chapters, how citizens speak to each other is almost as important as what they say. At the core of the global media system should be deliberative spaces where reasonable citizens can robustly but respectfully exchange views and evaluate proposals.

In summary, journalism has a twofold task in developing these levels. One is to promote the free and creative self-realization of liberal citizens in the spirit of Mill. Journalism should promote liberal, autonomous persons fulfilling their capacities. Journalism should oppose social structures that would unduly limit creative plans of life. At the same time, journalism has a commitment to liberal ideas of equality and justice. It should support not only creative, energetic individuals, but also a reasonable citizenry and reasonable discussion in pursuit of just social arrangements.

Journalism, from an ethical perspective, is not only about freedoms and rights; that is, helping people to seek their goods. Nor is it just about supporting communal solidarity, justice, or "harmonious" structures. It is about constantly seeking to combine the rational and reasonable, the pursuit of the goods and the just structures that allow and restrain such a pursuit. Journalism is neither about free speech nor any particular freedom or basic right; it is concerned with a family of rights and values, which include equality and justice. Journalism ethics is neither libertarian nor communitarian; it is both. It seeks to support the good in the right and the right in the good. It should help societies deal with the precarious and difficult task of finding ways to balance these ethical ideals. In this view, justice is a sort of freedom, or it is a condition of freedom. This dual task defines the contemporary meaning of "a free and responsible press."

Changing concepts and practices

These aims require a sea change in media ethics' basic concepts and ways of practice.

To get a sense of the change needed, consider the idea of journalism's social contract. In a global public sphere, if global journalism has a social contract, it is not with a particular public or society; instead, it seems to be something much more diffuse – a multi-society contract. The cosmopolitan journalist is a transnational public communicator who seeks the trust and credence of a global audience. Also, the ideal of objectivity in news coverage takes on an international sense. Traditionally, news objectivity asks journalists to avoid bias toward groups within one's own country. Global objectivity would discourage allowing bias toward one's country as a whole to distort reports on international issues. The ideas of accuracy and balance become enlarged to include reports with international sources and cross-cultural perspectives. Global media ethics asks journalists to be more conscious of how they frame major stories, how they set the international news agenda, and how they can spark violence in tense societies.

Adopting a global media ethics also requires a major change in serving the public. What happens when the journalist's commitment to informing their country conflicts with informing the world as global citizens? Global media ethics holds that transnational principles of human rights and social justice take precedence over personal interests and national interests when they conflict. This emphasis on what is ethically prior provides some direction to journalists caught in the ethical maze of international events. When my country embarks on an unjust war against another country, I, as a journalist (or citizen), should say so. If I am a Canadian journalist and I learn that Canada is engaged in trading practices that condemn citizens of an African country to continuing abject poverty, I should not hesitate to report the injustice. It is not a violation of any reasonable form of patriotism or citizenship to hold one's country to higher standards.

A globally minded media would alter how journalists approach covering international events such as a conference on climate change or talks on a new global trade agreement. A parochial journalism ethics would not object to journalists serving the public of their nations by reporting a climate change conference mainly from the perspective of their co-patriots. With regard to the climate conference, parochial journalists would tend to ask: What is in it for my country? What strategies will serve the national interests of my fellow citizens? As for global trade, parochial journalists would focus on how changes to a global trade agreement could open up markets for their own country's farmers or oil producers.

A global attitude would oppose such narrow, nationalistic reporting. It would require that journalists approach such events from the perspective of the global public good. What is the global problem concerning climate change and how should all countries cooperate to reach a fair and effective agreement? Globally minded journalists from the West would report the legitimate complaints that developing nations have against the environmental policy of their own country. They would question a global trade proposal made by their country if it advanced its own national interests while impoverishing developing nations. Global media ethics directs journalists to make issues of global justice a major part of their reporting and analysis.

A global ethics attitude limits parochial attachments in journalism by drawing a ring of broader ethical principles around them. When there is no conflict with global principles, journalists can report in ways that support local and national communities. They can practice their craft parochially.

Finally, a global media ethics rethinks the role of patriotism. In a global world, patriotism should play a decreasing role in ethical reasoning about media issues. At best, nation-based forms of patriotism remain ethically permissible if they do not conflict with the demands of a global ethical flourishing. Global media ethics requires that journalists commit themselves only to a moderate patriotism, subjecting the easily inflamed emotion of love of country to rational and ethical restraint (see Ward 2010, ch. 6). A moderate patriotism means that one has a special affection for one's country and that one is willing to help it flourish and pursue its goals. But this special affection, based either on a love of the culture or respect for its laws, does not make one's country superior to other countries. A loyalty to one's country does not justify an aggressive national posture on the world stage whereby one's country pursues its goals at the expense of other countries. Where patriotism is extreme, and it asks journalists to ignore global justice and violations of human rights, such patriotic claims are to be denied.

Moderate patriotism, therefore, rejects all forms of extreme nationalism and patriotism based on race or superiority of culture. It rejects xenophobic portrayals of other cultures. A globally minded media should not participate in demonizing other groups, especially in times of tension. The duty of journalism in times of looming conflict or war is not to follow a patriotism of blind allegiance or muted criticism of the actions of one's country. In such times, journalists serve their countries – that is, are patriotic – by continuing to provide independent news and analysis. It is not a violation of any reasonable form of patriotism or citizenship to hold one's country to higher standards.

Global media ethics does not entail that news organizations should ignore local issues or regional audiences. It does not mean that every story requires a cosmopolitan attitude. However, there are situations, such as military intervention in a foreign country, climate change, and the establishment of a fair world trading system, where we need to assess actions from a perspective of global justice and reasonableness. What is at issue is a gradual widening of basic editorial attitudes and standards – a widening of journalists' vision of their responsibilities. It asks them to consider their society's actions, policies, and values from a broader perspective.

Conclusion

This chapter concludes my description of the structure of a global, integrated ethics.

Previous chapters have contributed the ideas of ecumenicalism, a tri-part theory of meaning, and the concepts of principled pluralism and dialogic journalism. This chapter rounded out the structure with the ideal of global human flourishing. In the next chapter we ask why, and how, journalists might come to endorse this form of ethics. What sort of consensus is needed and how might a consensus be obtained?

Note

1. For extended treatments of the human good and human flourishing see chapter 7 of Ward 2013 and chapters 3 and 5 of Ward 2010.

References

Aristotle. *Ethics*. 1976. Trans. J. A. K. Thomson. London: Penguin.
Rawls, John. 1992 (1972). *A Theory of Justice*. Oxford: Oxford University Press.
Rawls, John. 1993. *Political Liberalism*. New York: Columbia University Press.
Ward, Stephen J. A. 2010. *Global Journalism Ethics*. Montreal: McGill-Queen's University Press.
Ward, Stephen J. A., ed. 2013. *Global Media Ethics: Problems and Perspectives*. Malden, MA: Wiley Blackwell.

Chapter 9
Realizing Global Integrated Ethics

Let's presume that we agree with the book's description of radical integrated ethics.

There still remain important practical questions: What is the likelihood that sufficient numbers of media practitioners would agree to this new normative interpretation of what they do, and implement it in their work? Could this ethics be realized?

"Being realized" in media ethics means that its moral content is endorsed, adopted, and put into practice by practitioners, and its ideas form a dominant theory of media ethics.

It would be disappointing if, after spinning out a theory of global integrated ethics, the response from ethicists and practitioners was, to paraphrase Kant's famous article (2006): "This may be true in theory, but it does not hold in practice." A theory of integrated ethics, therefore, cannot ignore the question as to what extent its ideas might be adopted by responsible journalists.

To discuss this question we shift from what ought to be to what is. We discuss real-world obstacles to global media ethics. In general, predicting the success of ideas is fraught with uncertainty. So we should not

---

Radical Media Ethics: A Global Approach, First Edition. Stephen J. A. Ward.
© 2015 John Wiley and Sons, Inc. Published 2015 by John Wiley and Sons, Inc.

expect precise answers. Yet we can indicate how practitioners might be persuaded to agree to the tenets of global, integrated ethics.

I approach the issue, analytically, by getting clear on what sort of questions we are trying to answer when we consider the future of global integrated ethics. I investigate the type of agreement among practitioners that a radical integrated ethics presumes. I suggest practical steps that could make integrated, global media ethics a dominant interpretation.

I am not asking these questions from a skeptical view of journalists. Someone might believe that most journalists care little about ethical norms. From this viewpoint, why would practitioners endorse integrated ethics when they care so little for any form of ethics? I ask a different question: Why would responsible media practitioners – people who *do* care about ethics – embrace a global, integrated approach?

My answer is that the global, integrated scheme in this book is a (hopefully) persuasive response to the key ethical issues of contemporary media practice. It is a normative *proposal* to practitioners. It proposes that journalists should embrace this form of integrated ethics, if they wish to develop a new and more relevant ethics for news media today.

There are two ways these questions could be asked. We could ask about the possibility of realizing a global, integrated ethics in *some* shape or form. Or, we could ask about the possibility of realizing *my* conception of global, integrated ethics. Probability theory tells us that a more general conception has a greater likelihood of being realized than a more specific conception. In what follows, I talk mainly about the likelihood of a global integrated ethics in general.

Supporters of global integrated ethics should recognize that their project may fail. Perhaps a global integrated ethics will remain on the fringes of media ethics as an under-developed proposal. Perhaps the integrative aspects of ethics – an ethics for multiple forms of journalism – will develop more quickly than its global aspects. In this chapter I focus on the global aspect.

It is easy to think of obstacles: journalists' patriotism may reject global ethics; the economy of media production may favor non-global reporting; the media world may be too complex to find unifying threads; practitioners may not see value in seeking integration in ethics.

What Type of Endorsement?

Scope

The possibility of failure means we need realistic expectations. The first realistic expectation has to do with the scope of endorsement by practitioners. It would be unrealistic to think that the project, to be realized, needs the consent of every news organization and journalist on the planet. A universal consensus is out of the question. No such consensus has ever existed in the world of journalism, and never will. Yet this does not mean the project cannot be realized. Being realized, after all, is a matter of degree.

I propose this realistic goal: In terms of practice, the project of a global, integrated ethics can realistically hope that its content will be endorsed by a significant and influential number of journalists over the next decade, especially by news media that are leaders in coverage of global issues. In terms of theory, the project of globally integrated ethics can realistically hope that it will become a dominant conception of media ethics within the next decade in terms of ethics books, discussions, and theoretical elaboration. We should add a further qualification: The project should be measured primarily in terms of its growth in democratic countries. It is unrealistic to expect a global ethics for a free press to grow in undemocratic nations, although the ideal may inspire media reform.

The project can only be realized through the simultaneous development of content and an increasing number of endorsements. Under content, the goal is the articulation and defense of a set of ultimate aims and principles (plus more specific norms and standards) for global integrated media. This ethical content is meant to be a new addition to media ethics. Under endorsement, the goal is an ever-increasing endorsement of global media ethics by professional and citizen journalists, plus news organizations and journalism associations.

The endorsement should come from practitioners who work in all forms of media, online or offline, traditional or new media. The proposal would be extended to five primary groups: (1) individual journalists; (2) well-known news organizations such as CNN or Reuters news service; (3) writers employed by journalistic organizations of all kinds and all media formats, e.g., writers for a journalistic website, or NGO sites for human rights; (4) journalism and communication associations, usually of an academic or professional nature, e.g., the Canadian Association of Journalists, or members of the Ethics Division of the Association for Education in Journalism and Mass Communication; (5) transnational associations of journalists, such as the International Federation of Journalists.

In the end, the project hopes that a *significant number* of democratic journalists and news organizations endorse all or parts of a global ethics, or develop their own global standards. It is difficult to be more precise in terms of numbers. Does "significant number" mean 30 percent of all news organizations, or 60 percent? How does one measure "significance" in this matter? An endorsement from the BBC would be more significant than an endorsement by a small-town newspaper. In terms of impact on the study of ethics, do we count the number of books and journal articles on global integrated ethics in any given year? Fortunately, having a reasonable belief that the project can be realized does not depend on having precise quantitative benchmarks and precise quantitative methods for determining benchmarks. It is enough that we can indicate, generally, the types of criteria that would be used to evaluate the growth of a global media ethics.

A Code for Global Integrated Ethics

In the appendix, I provide a code for a global integrated ethics. I regard this code as a first draft of a perfected code to be constructed in the future.

By "code" I do not mean a legal instrument, like the Code of Hammurabi. I mean an instrument of ethics. It is an ethical document that codifies or brings together in a convenient manner the principles of an ethical system. There are many codes of journalism ethics. They vary from ethical documents that inspire good conduct and guide decisions to codes that have a legal dimension since the code is used by lawfully appointed councils to review press misconduct.

My code is an aspirational ethical document.

I have arranged my views on a future ethics into a code for several reasons. The code gives readers a succinct view of the ethics I propose.

It provides an outline of the main principles apart from long discussions of each principle. A code is a useful teaching tool in academia and a quick reference for newsroom discussions. By comparing my code with previous codes, students of media ethics identify interesting similarities and differences. Also, I constructed the code because there are few codes for global media ethics, let alone codes that combine globalization and integration into a set of principles. I hope the code stimulates discussion and furthers the project of global media ethics.

A lengthy discussion on the code is not necessary because its principles are discussed at length in this book. Therefore, I only note similarities and differences between my code and other codes.

Like most media codes, my code starts with a preamble on media today and the need for a code. Like many codes, it provides mainly general principles, avoiding details and examples. The length of my code – several pages – places it between extremely brief codes and extremely long codes. The code for the Society of Professional Journalists can be printed on one page. The code for the German press is dozens of pages long.

I see my succinct code as part of a full set of editorial guidelines for media work. A code is the most general part of editorial guidelines. It states the essential goals and principles. Editorial guidelines should have two other parts: A second section on more specific norms and standards that follow from the principles, such as accuracy, verification, transparency, and so on; and a third section on how the guidelines apply to specific situations such as covering suicides, hostage-takings, and terrorist attacks. My hope is that, someday, a full three-part global integrated media ethics will exist.

The differences between my code and other codes strike me as more important than the similarities. First, my code is directed at all media practitioners. The code is not intended to be a code for a "closed" ethics – a code for professional journalists only.

Second, from the start, it is evident that the content of my code is distinct. My code is based on global (or universal) principles, and I use these principles to define the new responsibilities of media today. Most previous codes do not employ this global approach but, as noted, start from parochial values. Parochial codes do mention broad political and social values in their preamble, values such as democracy and justice. But those concepts are defined nationally and are not used beyond the preamble to shape the code's content. In contrast, my code does use the global principles stated at the opening to shape the rest of the code's content.

Third, my code emphasizes substance over procedure or method. My code is substantive because it grounds media ethics on the promotion of global moral goods and aims, such as human flourishing. The code goes beyond saying *how* journalists should do their reports. Many codes are procedural in stressing how media should report, e.g., double-checking presumed facts, verifying the claims of whistle blowers, and avoiding conflicts of interest. Such procedural rules are important and should be part of any media ethics. However, methods only make sense as means to the substantive social aims of responsible, public media. It is not the case that my code lacks procedural content. But the heart and soul of my code is a substantive vision of human flourishing.

Steps to Realization

We now approach the most practical question of all.

We have said the goal of the project of global media ethics was the endorsement of a significant number of leading journalists and news organizations. This endorsement would help to make global, integrated media ethics dominant in theory and practice.

So the final question about realization is: how might we start the process of realizing global, integrated media ethics? We can think of the process as involving three steps:

Stage 1: Injecting ideas into public discourse

Stage 1 – the stage we currently occupy – is an initial stage where the project needs to introduce global ideas and attitudes to public discourse about media, while showing the inadequacies of non-global ethics for today's media. The goal is a gradual widening of the ethical attitudes of increasing numbers of journalists and people who write about (and teach) news media. To achieve this evolution in attitudes, globalists, media ethics institutes, and educators need to put the topic of global ethics on the agenda of conferences. Global media ethics needs to be discussed on television and radio programs. It needs to be the subject of a growing number of articles and books. Global media ethics needs to have a place in the curriculum of communication and journalism schools. Meanwhile, journalism organizations, media ethicists, human rights workers, and others should continue to hold media practices up to global standards. Coalitions of journalists and citizens can work together to maintain constant pressure on media organizations to view their work from a global perspective. In this manner, we will be sowing the seeds of a global ethics attitude. This is the first practical step in making the project a significant part of media culture and media ethics.

As for endorsement during this period, the most important endorsements would be from global news organizations such as CNN, newspapers with an international focus, Al Jazeera, worldwide public broadcasters such as the BBC, the major international wire services, and major global websites and bloggers. Initially, local, regional, and even national news media will be less interested in global media ethics than global organizations. Global news organizations need to lead the way.

Stage 2: Codifying the principles

Stage 1 is experimentation with the many approaches to global media ethics. Stage 1 should lead to Stage 2, where there emerges an increasing overlapping consensus among theorists and journalists on the content of a global media ethics. It is plausible (and realistic) to expect that intense discussions on what global ethics means will converge on a significant set of common ideals, aims, and principles.

This convergence will result in widely discussed editorial guidelines for global media ethics, perhaps first formulated by international news organizations and media associations. Hopefully, these guidelines and codes will become templates for other guidelines and codes. At some point, the guidelines may be consolidated into a smaller number of widely accepted codes of global media ethics. The guidelines and codes would receive elaboration and critique from ethicists, scholars, and researchers. At this stage, non-global and global media ethics will coexist in an uneasy tension. Global media ethics will be a new and ascendant ethical approach.

Stage 3: Completion of the ethics revolution

In the long run, we can speculate about a third stage where global media ethics becomes the dominant approach to media ethics. Ethical content will be clearly formulated and receive substantial endorsement. At this stage, the current ethical revolution will be over and a new media ethics will hold the field.

Conclusion

This book has been an act of intellectual construction in three giant steps.

In Part I, I argued that a radical approach to ethics and media ethics was the best response to revolutionary changes to our world and our media. In Part II, I described the structure of an integrated ethics, and I defined journalism. In Part III, I provided two sets of principles for the new radical ethics – political and cosmopolitan principles. I described how an integrated ethics could become a global ethics, and I argued that the global ideal of human flourishing should be its ultimate aim. In the appendix, I present a code of principles for global, integrated media ethics.

I hope that other scholars and media practitioners can improve on the framework of this book. I hope they will join me in showing how the values of a global integrated ethics can be applied to practice. If we do all of this, we will be truly radical.

References

Kant, Immanuel. 2006. "On the Common Saying: This May Be True in Theory, But It Does Not Hold in Practice." In *Toward Perpetual Peace and Other Writings on Politics, Peace, and History*, edited by Pauline Kleingeld, translated by David L. Colclasure, 44–66. New Haven, CT: Yale University Press.

Appendix

Ward Code for Global Integrated Ethics

Preamble: Global Responsibilities

Media ethics is the responsible use of the freedom to publish in any format, no matter who creates the content or who owns the means of publication.

News media are global in reach and impact. Global power entails global responsibilities.

Responsible freedom to publish is no longer a parochial responsibility owed to city, region, or nation. It is a global responsibility owed to a global public. The moral aim of media is no longer the parochial promotion of city, province or nation. It is the promotion of humanity.

Creators, sharers, and consumers of media are part of a global public sphere linked by a web of ever-new communication channels. Networks offer information, analysis, and advocacy under conditions of social inequality, cultural difference, and imbalance in power. Formidable powers of communication can promote or damage prospects for peace, justice, and the good.

Radical Media Ethics: A Global Approach, First Edition. Stephen J. A. Ward.
© 2015 John Wiley and Sons, Inc. Published 2015 by John Wiley and Sons, Inc.

Appendix

The future of humanity on this blue planet depends in no small part on the emergence of a globally minded media dedicated to principles of human flourishing and global justice.

There is a need to construct an ethics for global media and global news media.

Moral Roots

Definition

Global media ethics articulates and critiques the responsibilities of a news media that is global in content, reach, and impact. It is the project of developing aims, principles, and norms of practice specifically formulated for a global, media-linked world.

Claim of Humanity

Advancing humanity through media requires agreement on common principles. The moral basis of global media ethics is the belief that all individuals are equally valuable moral agents of a single humanity. All deserve a flourishing, dignified life within the bounds of justice. This is the claim of humanity on all of us as fellow humans.

Unity in Difference

Working within their traditions, media practitioners should seek common ground in principles of human rights, human flourishing, and global justice. Global media ethics seeks unity among media approaches through overarching principles of the human good.

Promote Human Flourishing

Global ethics, and global media ethics, promotes human flourishing. Flourishing is the significant development of one's intellectual, emotional, and other capacities in a supportive social context. We should promote four levels of flourishing: individual, social, political, and ethical.

Individual goods: These are goods that make possible the development of each individual's capacities, such as food, health care, security, and education.

Social goods: These are goods that arise when individuals participate in society, such as freedom of association, economic benefits, love and friendship, mutual recognition and respect.

Political goods: Political goods accrue to citizens living in just political associations, such as basic liberties, rule of law, just institutions, and meaningful participation in democracy.

Ethical goods: These are goods that arise from sharing community and society with citizens of ethical character who promote the common good.

To flourish on each of the four levels is to achieve a corresponding form of human dignity: individual, social, and political dignity.

Promotion of the four levels is the ultimate aim of all media practitioners, as journalists, citizen creators of content, networks of information sharing, or conveners of public discussion.

Global Democratic Journalism

The best political association for realizing these goods is egalitarian democracy. Global media ethics seeks the development of strong egalitarian democracies around the world, and the creation of global democratic institutions for governance of transnational issues such as the violation of human rights.

Fundamental Concepts and Principles

Self-consciousness

The self-consciousness of globally minded journalists and other media workers is defined by the following moral imperatives:

Act as global agents: Journalists see themselves as agents of a global public sphere. The goal of their collective actions is a well-informed, diverse, and tolerant global info-sphere that challenges the distortions of tyrants, the abuse of human rights, and the manipulation of information by special interests.

Appendix

Serve the citizens of the world: The global journalist's primary loyalty is to the informational needs of world citizens, even as they promote social reform or specific causes.

Promote non-parochial understandings: The global journalist frames issues broadly and uses a diversity of sources to promote a nuanced understanding of issues from an international perspective. Global journalists work against a narrow ethnocentrism or patriotism.

Principles of Integration

The Global as Primary

Global media ethics regards parochial values, such as love of one's kin or country, as legitimate but not primary values. Parochial values can be integrated into ethics so long as practitioners recognize the greater ethical weight of global values. Loyalty to humanity trumps other loyalties, where they conflict. Parochial values, such as promoting the welfare of one's country, do not justify one-sided reporting on a nation's actions, or uncritical support for war.

The Global and the Local

Global media ethics recognizes that global principles are realized in different ways in different media cultures. The local and the global interact and define each other. Global principles are not imposed on all media cultures in the same way. Principles such as promoting human flourishing, democracy, a free press, and social responsibility can be interpreted differently by different cultures.

Multiple Approaches

Global flourishing and democracy are best accomplished by public spheres characterized by diverse approaches to journalism and communication. Approaches include objective reporting, investigative and explanatory journalism, opinion journalism, and advocacy. Each has distinct purposes and norms. Global media ethics constructs overarching purposes and principles that allow a pluralism of approaches and purposes.

The guiding standard for integrating approaches is *principled pluralism*. Not all ways of doing journalism are acceptable. Approaches must have significant democratic value. They must fulfill important informational needs of the public, such as the need for accurate news, insightful explanation, important investigations, reasoned opinion, and diverse public dialogue.

Norms of Practice

Doing, Participating, Accounting

At the foundation of global media ethics are general principles of promoting humanity. In addition, this ethics requires practitioners to follow more specific and familiar norms such as accuracy, truth-telling, verification of fact, and minimizing harm.

All norms should fall under three categories: right doing, allowing citizen participation, and being accountable to the public.

Norms of right doing direct journalists to report according to methods that enhance accuracy and truth, editorial independence, and the diversity of voices. Norms of citizen participation direct journalists to allow citizens meaningful participation in public discussion of issues and public discussion of media performance. Participatory norms also guide how citizens participate in constructing news stories by contributing images, eyewitness accounts, and text. Norms of accountability include transparency on how stories were constructed and explaining controversial editorial decisions.

Dialogue Across Borders

Global media ethics emphasizes the role of media as a means of dialogue among different ethnic groups, cultures, and religions. The fair representation of groups and traditions is vital, as is the creation of respectful exchanges among groups. A dialogic journalism structures the discussion of issues in news stories, broadcast programs, and at websites in such a way that participants search for common ground and for solutions to problems. It provides a format for

Appendix

tolerant sharing of views, while precluding intolerant, non-dialogic forms of communication.

Media Ethics for Everyone

Global media ethics must construct its principles with everyone in view. Principles and norms should apply not only to professional journalists but also to citizens creating media. Moreover, media ethics needs to deals with issues beyond journalism, such as cyberbullying, digital media and privacy, online pornography, and the use of mobile devices to spread rumors.

Index

absolutism vs. arbitrariness 83–5
action 13
activism
  ethics as 87
  media ethics as 115–16
administrative democracy 64
advocacy journalism 113, 114, 162, 194 n. 5
advocational and reform needs 140, 188
agenda for journalism ethics 113–14
agenda-driven journalism 112
aims
  ethical, in journalism 199–200
  human flourishing, applying 205–14
  human flourishing, as ultimate aim 200–5
  political 199
  ultimate 197–9
Al Jazeera 221
amateur vs. professional journalism 101
Anglin, Jeremy M. 36
animal welfare 6, 7
applied ethics 7
arbitrariness vs. absolutism 83–5
Arendt, Hannah 31 n. 4
Aristotle
  on definitions 124
  on eudaimonia 198=9
  on intuitive induction 158
Associated Press 108
Augustine, St 13
Authoritarian theory of press 63

Index

basic beliefs 40–1
BBC 105, 136, 218, 221
Beitz, Charles 86
beliefs
  basic 40–1
  grounding of 80
  webs of 39, 41
Bentham, Jeremy 60, 152
  on liberal utilitarianism 154
  on publicity 184
Berlin, Isaiah 152
  Four Essays 168 n. 4
Bible
  interpretation 51
  Psalm 8 10
  Ten Commandments 7
Borden, Sandra 61
brain, cruelty and 81
brand journalism 111–12
Buddhist ethics 7

Camus, Alfred: *Myth of Sisyphus, The* 16
capacities 202
capacity theory of human development 156–7
  central capabilities 157
  objections to 157
Case, Jennifer 39
Castells, Manuel: on global public sphere 184, 185
categorization 36
Christians, Clifford G. 159, 193
  Normative Theories of the Media 64, 65, 66
Cicero 183
Cisco Systems 112
citizen journalism 100
citizens 178–80
  communication in 184

democratic 180–2
  participation 64
citizenship 178–80
  democratic 180–2
civic democracy 64
civic journalism 210
classical utilitarianism 204
closed vs open media ethics 110
CNN 126, 217, 221
code
  for globally integrated ethics 218–20, 223–8
  of journalism ethics 113
  of the Society of Professional Journalists (SPJ) 108, 112, 219
Cohen, Joshua
  on democratic society 181, 182
  on political association 188
Cold War 3
collaborative role of journalism 65
collaborative role of normative theories 193
collective intentionality 16–17, 19–20, 24
common morality 32 n. 10
communication hobby, journalism as 134
communism 176
concepts 35–9, 127
  crystalline 127, 128
  fluid 127, 128, 129
  as frames 37
  human flourishing and changing 211–14
  language and 38
  propositions and 38
  prototypes of 37
  viewpoint or perspective and 39
conceptual schemes 35–41, 127
  models of 39-

230

Index

Constant, Benjamin 152
constitution 176
contestation 50
conventionalism 55
Cook, Timothy 137
core concept 36–7
core meaning 156
cosmopolitan approach 206
courtesy, conept of 76
creation, ethics as 24
critical normative reason 8
Cronkite, Walter 126
crystalline concepts 127, 128

Darwin, Charles 40
data journalism 114
Davidson, Richardson 43
definition 126–7
  applied to journalism 130–1
  appropriateness for
    journalism 131
  definition of 122–6
definition of journalism
  construction of definition 124
  construction of schema 121–2
  definition of definition 122–6
  precision of definitions 123–4
  proposal of definition 124–5
  reason for 119–22
  recursive definition 123
  referential definition 122–3, 125
  types of definition 122
deliberation, definition 186
deliberative democracy 181–2. 186
democracy 205
  democratic citizens 180–2
  electoral 180–1
  forms of journalism and 174–5
  models of 64, 65
  as political community 180, 181

  as political control 180, 181
  roles of journalism in 65
  types of 175–7
democratic citizens 180–2
democratic emotions 151
democratic political regime 181
democratic press 190
democratic public spheres 183–8
  citizen communication in 184
  dialogic democracies 185–8
democratic society 181
denial 15
Dennett, Daniel 31 n. 2
  on intention 43, 48
deontological theories 7, 59
Descartes 10, 82, 149
descriptivism 7
Dewey, John 85
  on democracy 181
dialogic journalism 188–93, 194
  advocational and reform need 188
  dialogic need 188, 189–90,
    191, 192
  explanatory need 188, 189
  free and democratic press 190–2
  as goal of free press 192
  informational need 188–9
  media needs 188–9
  participatory need 188, 189, 191
  perspectival enrichment 188, 189
  public need 188–90
dialogic need 140, 188, 189–90,
  191, 192
digital journalism, ethics, training
  in 114–15
digital media ethics 100–13
  do-it-yourself (DIY)
    ethics 108–9, 114
  features of 104–13
  global responsibilities 101

Index

digital media ethics (*cont'd*)
  globalization of news
    media 100–1
  integration and
    fragmentation 104–7
  mixed news media 100
  need for consensus 103
  need for radical change 102–4
  open, global ethics 109–11
  personalized ethics 107–8
  professional vs amateur
    journalism 101
  reinvention of principles 111–13
dignity 207–8
direct democracy 64
do-it-yourself (DIY)
    ethics 108–9, 114
domination 153
dualism 149
  mind-body 10
duty 8
Dworkin, Richard 45, 71
  on egalitarianism 177
  on interpretation 46, 52–4, 123
  on justice 77, 78, 79
  on law as integrity 56
  on morality 82
  on purpose of law 55

economic associations, reporting
    on 208
ecumenicalism in journalism 145
  definition 145, 168 n. 1
  external disagreement 145
  internal disagreement 146
  levels of meaning 146–9, 149–51
  news objectivity 161–3
  permissible variations 163–4
  problems for 145–6
  social responsibility 159–61

  theory of meaning for 158–64
  tri-part theory of meaning 164–7
  tri-part theory of method 165–7
egalitarian pluralism 71–5
egalitarianism 177
Elgin, Catherine Z. 84
emergence and contestation 85–7
empirical interpretation 49
empiricism 36
enabling conditions 11–24
environmental ethics 6, 7
epistemic distinction 28
ethical goods 199, 202, 203, 209, 210
ethical impulse 12, 198
ethical interpretation
  definition 33–4
  need for 34
  skepticism and 35
ethical method 165–6
ethical reasoning 166
  about aims 166
  about cases 166
  about frameworks of
    principles 166
ethics
  definition 4–5, 7
  as proposal 27
  as reflective engagement 6
etiquette 22, 23
evolution, theory of 9, 13
existential sources 11–14
explanatory journalism 193
explanatory needs 140, 188, 189
explicit interpretation 51
extreme relativism 71

facilitative role of journalism 65
facilitative role of normative
    theories 193
fascism 176

232

fluid concepts 127, 128
  core meaning of 129
fluidity, definition 128–9
Fodor, Jerry 36, 78
formal equality 177
Four Theories of the Press (Siebert et al). 62–3, 64, 65, 66
  criticisms of 63–4
fragmentation 15, 104–5
Frankfurt, Harry 13–14
Franklin Center for Government and Public Integrity 112
free and democratic press 190–2
freedom from discrimination 209–10
freedom of association 209
freedom of speech 157, 209
free press 190
Frege, Gottlob, on concepts 127–8, 129
fuzzy (non-rigid) concepts 37

gay rights 7
Gert, Bernard 32 n. 10
Gillmor, Dan: *We the Media* 190–1
global ethics 109–11
global media ethics 211–14
globalization 86
  of news media 100–1
globally integrated ethics
  code for 218–20, 223–8
  endorsement of 217–18
  goals of 217
  groups endorsing 217–18
  steps to realization 220–2
Grey, John 168 n. 4
grounding of ethical beliefs 80
guerrilla journalism 126

Habermas, Jürgen on public sphere 194 n. 3

Haidt, Jonathan 183
harm minimization 95, 96–7, 98, 102, 105, 106, 108, 141, 144, 159, 200
Heidegger, Martin 13
Henrik Von Wright, Georg 42
Hobbes, Thomas 152
holism vs individualism 75
holistic interpretation 75–9
human-based realism 29
human flourishing
  applying 205–14
  congruence of levels 203–5
  four levels of 202–3
  as ultimate aim 200–5
human good 201, 203–4
human rights 86
Hume, David 80

impartiality 3
imperfectionist approach 85
independence of ethics 80–2
individual dignity 207
individual goods 202, 204, 207–8
inequality, investigation of 208
informational needs 140, 188–9
instantiation 155–6
institutions 18–19
integration 15
integrationism 104
intentional meaning in language 38
intentionality 24
interpretation
  as act of categorization 44
  creative 47–8
  definition 41, 44–7
  disproving 76–7
  group 48–9
  holistic 45
  individual 47–8
  individual actions 48

233

Index

interpretation (*cont'd*)
  linguistic 47
  practices 48–9
  slack between fact and 79–80
  societies 48
  types of 47–51
interpreting 41–2
interpretive concepts 77
interpretive journalism 114, 189
intuitionism 7
investigative journalism 193, 194 n. 5

James, William 85
Johnston, David, on interpretations of justice 59–60
journalism as institutional practice 136–8
journalism as personal activity 133–4
journalism as social practice 134–6
journalism ethics
  agenda for 113–14
  'being responsible' 95
  codes of 113
  common values in 107–8
  curriculum for 114
  fatal blow to 99–100
  group ethic of 98
  professionalism 94–9
  types of responsibiity in 95
  unity in difference approach 106–7
journalist
  amateur vs professional 101
  as global agents 206
  definition of 126
  promotion of non-parochial understandings 206
  self-imposed codes of ethics 98
  serving citizens of the world 206

justice
  instrumental value of 204
  libertarian view of 77–8
  principles of 30, 204
  theory of 148, 150–1
  utilitarianism of 77–8

Kahneman, Daniel 67 n. 3
Kant, Imanuel 36, 80
  on global integrated ethics 215
  model of conceptual schemes 39
Kekes, John
  on egalitarianism 177
  on monism 74
Kent, Tom 108
Kierkegaard, Søren 15
Kingwell, Mark 187

Larmore, Charles 11, 88, 88. n. 1
  on political freedom 151–2
law
  normative domain 23
  overlap with ethics 22–3
layered journalism 100
legal pragmatism 56
Lepore, Ernest 78
levels in journalism 133–8
liberalism vs. libertarianism 62
Libertarian theory of press 63
libertarianism 77, 176
  on political freedom 153, 154
  participation and 190
  vs. liberalism 62
linguistic meaning 38
Lippmann, Walter 61
Locke, John, on concepts 36
Losee, John 159
Luce, Henry 189
Lynch, Michael P. 39, 83, 130, 132

on concepts of happiness and
 flourishing 129
on fluid concepts 128, 129
on meaning of mind 147–8
on minimal-robust
 distinction 168 n. 2
on theory of flexible concepts 127,
 130, 156

Machiavelli 153
MacIntyre, Alasdair, on normative
 analysis and practice 56
Macpherson, C.B. 185
Makau, Josina N. 187
Marty, Debian L. 187
Marxist attitude on art 57
maximal meaning 146–9, 150, 154,
 158, 167
meaning
 definitions 149–51
 in language 38
 levels of 146–9
meaning of mind 147–8
meaning pluralism 146
media literacy 209
media needs 140, 141, 188–92
 dialogic 140, 188, 189–90,
  191, 192
 explanatory 140, 188, 189
 informational 140, 188–9
 participatory 140, 188, 189, 191
 perspectival enrichment 140,
  188, 189
mentality 16
meta-ethics (philosophical
 ethics) 4, 6–7, 34, 59
metaphysics 14–16
Mill, J.S.
 on freedom of expression 193
 on happiness 80

On Liberty 154
 on utilitarianism of 73
mind, meaning of 147–9
mind-body dualism 10
minimal meaning 146–9, 150, 154,
 158, 166
Minsky, Marvin 37
mixed news media 100
monism 72, 73–4, 155
 vs pluralism 73
monitorial role of journalism 65
monitorial role of normative
 theories 193
morality, general, of society 133
movie industry, codes of ethics 98
multiple realizability 155–7
Murrow, Edward R. 61

normative realization 156–7
nationalism 14
natural selection 40
naturalism 8–10, 31 n. 1
negative freedom 152–3, 168 n. 4
negative liberty 204
Neisser, Ulric 36
Nelson, Katherine 37
Nerone, John 63
Neurath, Otto 82
new media, political value
 of 190–1
newsrooms, layered journalism
 in 100–1
Nietzsche, Friedrich 31 n. 7, 58 58
nihilism in ethics 58, 71
non-deliberative public
 sphere 191
non-profit journalism 115
non-reducible properties 25
Nordenstreng, Kaarle 159
normative domains 21–4

Index

normative interpretation 34, 49, 51–9, 124
  applied to journalism 61–2
  degree of consensus 52
  elements 51–2
  in ethics 59–61
  examples 52–3
  explicitness of shared understandings 52
  interpreting creative works 56–7
  practice of courtesy 52–4
  practice of ethics 58–9
  practice of law 54–5
  purpose of practice 51
  shared practice 51
  shared understandings 51–2
normative traditions 64
norms 49–51
Nussbaum, Martha C. 79, 183
  on capacity theory of human development 156–7
  Creating Capabilities 156
  Political Emotions: Why Love Matters for Justice 151

objectivity 28–9
  as holistic concept 76
  professionalism and 96–7
observer-relative features 26
Onion, The 126
Online News Association (ONA) code of ethics 108–9
ontological naturalism 24
ontology 8–10
  of practice 8, 30
  of language and assertion 8, 30
  reference 8 30
open vs. closed media ethics 110

opinion journalism 112–13
  valuable vs non-valuable 193
ought-gap 81
ownership 19

parliamentary democracy 187
participation, encouragement of 210
participatory democracy 185–6
participatory journalism 193
participatory needs 140, 188, 189, 191
Pateman, Carole 185
patriotism 14, 183, 213
periodicy, journalism and 136
personal and social activities 133
personalization of ethics 107–8
personalized ethics 107–8
perspectival enrichment needs 140, 188, 189
Peterson, Theodore 62–3, 64, 65, 66
Pettit, Philip 153
Philips, Michael 73
physical dignity 207
Piaget, Jean 37
Plato 16
  on eros 31 n. 5
  Republic, The 60, 150–1
pluralism 58, 71–5, 155, 192–3, 194
  monism vs. 73
  non-pluralism 72
  simple 72
pluralist democracy 64
political aims 199
political community democracy as 180, 181
political control, democracy as 180, 181
political freedom 151–4
  negative 152–3
  as negative liberty 152
  positive 152

Index

political goods 203, 209–10
political principles, definition 173
popular music, interpretative traditions in 57–8
positive freedom 168 n. 4
Posner, Michael 36
pragmatic objectivity 114, 162–3
pre-digital media ethics, origin of *see* journalism ethics
Press Council of India. 50
press, theories of 62, 63–5
primary goods 201
  promoting levels of 207–11
principled pluralism 175, 192–3, 194
privacy, respect for 82, 159
probability theory 216
professional vs. amateur journalism 101
professionalism
  journalism ethics and 94–9
  objectivity and 96–7
  public duty and 96
prototype (schema) theory 36
public communication, journalism as 135–6
public duty, professionalism and 96
public need 188–90
public significance of journalism 136
Pulitzer Center for Crisis Reporting in Washington, DC 115
Pulitzer, Joseph 97
purpose of ethics 59
pursuit of goods 204

quality of social life, assessment of 208–9
Quine, Willard V.O. 79–80, 82
  on basic beliefs 40
  on linguistic structures 39
  model of conceptual schemes 39, 40, 41
  webs of belief 39, 41

radical, definition 3
radical role of normative theories 193
realization 155–6
radio broadcasting codes of ethics 97–8
Raphael 48
rational justification 56
Rawls, John 177, 178
  on congruence 204
  on justification 78, 79
  on moral reasonableness 203
  on principles of justice 204
  on reasonable pluralism 187
  on reflective equilibrium 78, 79
  Theory of Justice, A 150
realism 7
  human-based 29–30
reciprocity, principle of 81
referential meaning in language 38
reflective equilibrium 75, 76, 78–9, 82, 84, 150, 164–7
relativism 7, 83, 109
republicanism on political freedom 153
respect
  for ethical thinking 69–71
  for privacy 82
responsible publishing 3
right 8
robust meaning 146–9, 150, 154, 158, 166
robust publics 182–3
  endorsement 182
  participation 182
  public stance 182–3

237

Index

Roman Catholic Church 107
Roman Republic, lack of public virtue in 183
rule of law conception 55
Rumelhart, David 37

satirical journalism 106
Sawyer, Jon 115
schema for journalism 131–3
　constructing 138–41
　definition 131–2
　final schematic definition 141
　in cognitive science 131
　in mathematics 132
　levels in journalism 133–8
　media needs 140, 141
　normative dimension 139
Schopenhauer, Arthur 31 n. 7, 31 n. 8
Schramm, William 62–3, 64, 65, 66
Schudson, Michael 138
Searle, John 10–11, 141
　on citizens 179
　on collective intentionality 17, 31 n. 8
　on objective –subjective distinction 28
　on observer-relative features 26. 29
　on status functions 20
　social facts 156
self-consciousness of journalists 206
Siebert, Fred 62–3, 64, 65, 66, 97
Singer, Jane B. 189
Skinner, Quentin 153
social and ethical properties 24–5
social bridging 209
social contract theory 25
social dignity 207
social goods 202–3, 204, 208–9
social liberalism 175–7
social reality, distinctive 17–21

Social Responsibility theory of press 63
social roles 19
social structure, formal 18, 20
socialism 16
Society of Professional Journalists (SPJ) 50, 105
　code of 62
society, definition 17–18
Socrates 37, 151
Socratic moment 147
Soviet Communist theories of press 63
status functions 20–1
subjective ontology 28–9
subjectivism 109
subjectivity, statement 28
substantial equality 177
System 1 and 2 thinking 67 n. 3

teleological theories 59
television industry, codes of ethics 98
Ten Commandments 73
Thagard, Paul: on webs of conceptual schemes 37, 127, 129, 130, 131
Thompson, Hunter S. 61, 126
Time magazine, interpretive approach and 189
timeliness, journalism and 136
tri-part theory of meaning 164–7
tri-part theory of method 165–7

ultimate aims 197–9
　applying human flourishing as 205–14
　human flourishing as 200–5
understanding 41–2
　intentional 42–3
　non-intentional 41–2, 43

unity
    in difference 110–11, 154, 159, 167
    in journalism 145–6
universal value 27–8
utilitarian ethics 7
utilitarian theories 59
utilitarianism 60–1
utility maximization 204
utility principle 30

values, default 37
valuing, acts of 27
Vanier, Jean: *Becoming Human* 16
virtue, theories of 7

Walzer, Michael: on deliberation 186
Ward code for globally integrated
    ethics 218–20, 223–8
Ward, Stephen J. A.
    Ethics and the Media 102–3
    Global Journalism Ethics 201, 168 n. 5
Wasserman, Herman 110
Wittgenstein, Ludwig 45, 66 n. 2,
    77, 127
    on basic beliefs 40–1
    model of conceptual
        schemes 39–40, 41
    Philosophical Investigations 39–40
World Pulse 115–16